T0330796

ROUTLEDGE LIBRARY EDITIONS:
ADAM SMITH

HUMAN DOCUMENTS OF ADAM SMITH'S TIME

HUMAN DOCUMENTS OF ADAM SMITH'S TIME

E. ROYSTON PIKE

Volume 5

Routledge
Taylor & Francis Group

LONDON AND NEW YORK

First published in 1974

This edition first published in 2010
by Routledge
2 Park Square, Milton Park, Abingdon, Oxon, OX14 4RN

Simultaneously published in the USA and Canada
by Routledge
711 Third Avenue, New York, NY 10017 USA

*Routledge is an imprint of the Taylor & Francis Group, an
informa business*

© 1974 George Allen & Unwin Ltd

British Library Cataloguing in Publication Data
A catalogue record for this book is available from the
British Library

ISBN 10: 0-415-56194-9 (Set)
ISBN 10: 0-415-56203-1 (Volume 5)
ISBN 10: 0-203-09272-4 (ebook)

ISBN 13: 978-0-415-56194-5 (Set)
ISBN 13: 978-0-415-56203-4 (Volume 5)
ISBN 13: 978-0-203-09272-9 (ebook)

Publisher's Note
The publisher has gone to great lengths to ensure the quality of
this reprint but points out that some imperfections in the original
copies may be apparent. The publisher has made every effort to
trace copyright holders and welcomes correspondence from those
they have been unable to contact.

The Author of the Wealth of Nations

1. Adam Smith, drawn by John Kay of Edinburgh in 1790.

National Galleries of Scotland

HUMAN DOCUMENTS
OF
ADAM SMITH'S TIME

BY

E. ROYSTON PIKE

London
GEORGE ALLEN & UNWIN LTD
RUSKIN HOUSE   MUSEUM STREET

© George Allen & Unwin Ltd., 1974

ISBN 0 04 942118 2 hardback
0 04 942119 0 paperback

Printed in Great Britain
in 10 point Plantin type
by Cox & Wyman Ltd,
London, Fakenham and Reading

ACKNOWLEDGEMENTS

Grateful acknowledgements are made to the London Library (from whose altogether exceptional resources most of the textual material has been drawn), Manchester Public Libraries, the British Museum, the Library of the Corporation of London, and Surrey County Library (Esher District). As regards illustrations: Manchester Public Libraries, the National Galleries of Scotland, John R. Freeman & Co. (Hogarth prints), and T. & R. Annan & Sons Ltd. of Glasgow.

CONTENTS

THE HOGARTH PICTURE GALLERY

ILLUSTRATIONS IN TEXT

CHAPTER I

ADAM SMITH:
THE MAN AND HIS BOOK

On 9 March 1776, there was published in London a book in two quarto-sized volumes, each of over five hundred pages, bearing the title: *An Inquiry into the Nature and Causes of THE WEALTH OF NATIONS*, and described on the title-page as being by 'Adam Smith, LL.D. and F.R.S. Formerly Professor of Moral Philosophy in the University of Glasgow'. The publisher was William Strahan, and the price of the two volumes was £1 16s.

There was no great rush to buy it, and the reviewers were in no hurry to give it notice in the press. But the author had no reason to complain of its reception among those whose opinion he held in most high regard. To quote but one example, we find Edward Gibbon describing it within three weeks of its publication as 'an excellent work . . . an extensive science in a single book, and the most profound ideas expressed in the most perspicuous language'.

The 'extensive science', it need hardly be said, is economics, or political economy as it was generally called in Adam Smith's time (and indeed much later); and it says a good deal for Gibbon's acumen that he was able to recognise that Adam Smith had succeeded in elevating into a science what had been hitherto the subject of unrelated speculation and disordered observation. Posterity has agreed with his evaluation, so that there is nothing extravagant in hailing Adam Smith as the founder of the science of economics.

Nearly two hundred years have passed since *The Wealth of Nations* was published, and in all that time it has never gone out of print. Nor is it ever likely to do so. For it is one of those books that have changed men's minds, their ways of thinking, and it may be expected to continue to go on doing so as long as men are perplexed by the problems of wealth and poverty, the satisfaction of the basic necessities of human existence.

It was in the Britain of the eighteenth century that these problems emerged from the study and the counting-house to become the matter of public discussion and decision. For that development Adam Smith was mainly responsible, and thus there is surely no need for apology or explanation in applying his name to this collection of 'documents' intended to illustrate the everyday life of 'the great body of the people' (his phrase), living in the country and the century to which he himself belonged.

Before examining the 'documents', however, it is only fitting that we should know something of Adam Smith, the man himself and the circumstances of his life, and of the book which he wrote and left as an abiding legacy to Mankind.

The Man

Adam Smith was a Scotsman, or Scotchman as he would probably have preferred to say it, and this is one of the most important things about him. For he possessed in abundant measure the peculiarly Scottish quality of *canniness*; and only a canny man, one who was knowing and shrewd and carefully calculating, could have written *The Wealth of Nations*.

He was born (on 5 June 1723) at Kirkcaldy, a small place in Fifeshire, on the east coast of Scotland, looking across the Firth of Forth to Edinburgh. Thus he was a Lowlander; and the only part of Scotland that he knew really well was the Lowlands that stretch south-west from Kirkcaldy through Edinburgh to Glasgow. So far as has been ascertained, he never crossed the 'Highland line'. He seems never to have felt any such urge as that which sent the elderly Dr Johnson (as typically English as Adam Smith was Scottish) to explore the unmapped and largely unknown region of the Scottish Highlands in the company of that eager young Scot, James Boswell.

It has been remarked that there were very few 'Macs' among his acquaintance. In religion, he was a Presbyterian, adhering like most of his countrymen to the Established Church of Scotland; while as for politics, he may be numbered among the Whigs, and as such was a firm supporter of the Hanoverian dynasty. The romantic accompaniments of the Jacobite legend left him completely cold.

Adam Smith's father, also Adam Smith, was a native of Aberdeenshire, but early in life removed to Edinburgh where he practised as a Writer to the Signet (more or less equivalent to the English solicitor). Clearly a man of parts and enterprise, he entered the government service, and was private secretary to the Earl of Loudoun when he was Secretary of State for Scotland. Then in 1713 or 1714 he received the appointment of comptroller of the customs at Kirkcaldy, in which he continued until his death early in 1723. This was some months before the birth of his son. As a posthumous child, then, Adam Smith was brought up by his mother – Margaret Douglas, daughter of a laird or small landowner in the neighbourhood – who was a woman of fine character, lived to a great age, and was the last as she had been the first, and perhaps the only, woman in his life.

Round about 1730, when he was seven, Adam Smith was sent to the Burgh school at Kirkcaldy which comprised two rooms, in one of which the master taught and in the other the usher or second master. The master in Adam Smith's time was David Millar, who had the reputation of being an excellent teacher. The curriculum was very much on the lines of grammar schools in England, which means that the basis of instruction was the Latin grammar. This is clear enough from the report of a committee of inquiry that was set up by the Burgh council in 1732. Five of the six classes seem to have spent most of their time translating Latin passages into English, and then back again into Latin, coupled with 'storing their minds' with 'vocables', i.e. Latin words. The sixth class, in which were the juniors, were taught to read (mostly from the Bible), write, and 'accompt', that is, to do simple sums.

In 1737, when he was fourteen, Adam Smith was entered at the College, or University, of Glasgow, as a student. He spent three years there, receiving a sound classical education as it was understood in those days. He won no special distinction as a scholar, and seems never to have joined any of the students' societies or clubs; but all the same, the impress of the place was on him to the end of his days. The teachers as a class were first rate, and one in particular influenced him greatly – Francis Hutcheson, who held the chair of moral philosophy. Hutcheson (1694–1746) was one of the founders of the typically Scottish 'common sense' school of philosophy. He was inclined to take a remarkably optimistic view of human nature and the human situation, and he has a place in the dictionaries of quotations with his saying, 'That action is best, which procures the greatest happiness for the greatest numbers.' He was a firm advocate of Liberty in every sphere, even in matters of religion – which so scandalised the clergy of the city that they tried to get him censured for heresy. Half a century later Adam Smith made public acknowledgement of his debt to 'the never-to-be forgotten Hutcheson'.

After three years at Glasgow Smith was awarded an Exhibition at Balliol College, Oxford. He was at Oxford from 1740 to 1746, and his experience was far from happy. He learnt practically nothing from the teachers: as he remarked in *The Wealth of Nations* years afterwards, 'the greater part of the public professors at Oxford have, for these many years, given up even the pretence of teaching'. Furthermore, as a

2. Glasgow College, on the occasion of an art exhibition held in 1762 in honour of the birthday of King George III.

Scotsman he was something of a social outcast, and he was always dreadfully poor. His exhibition was worth only £40 a year, and by the time he had paid £30 for his food and £5 for tutors' fees, he had only £5 left for books and all other expenses. In all the time he was at Oxford he never went home once – for the very good reason that he could not afford to. Fortunately, the college had an excellent library, and here he largely educated himself by reading, not only the Greek and Latin classics but the prose and poetry of the great masters of French and Italian literature. After he had taken his B.A. he became entitled to a reader's ticket at the Bodleian Library, and this, too, he made the fullest use of.

Returning home to Kirkcaldy in 1746 he was for some time at a loose end, until he was invited to give some public lectures in Edinburgh on English literature. These were highly popular, and, his gift for popular exposition having been thus demonstrated, he was elected in 1751 to the professorship of logic at his old university at Glasgow. The year following he was transferred to the chair of moral philosophy which suited him much better, as the holder was in a position to lecture on practically any subject that appealed to him. Thus opened a period of some twelve years, which he long afterwards declared to have been 'by far the most useful, and therefore by far the happiest and most honourable period' of his life.

At the college his lectures were warmly appreciated by the students, and the authorities were quick to discover that he was possessed of a sound business sense that made him a most useful member of the faculty in all matters of administration. In the city, too, he made many friends, for he was no academic recluse but one who loved to mix with his fellow men of whatever class and situation. Notwithstanding these many outside interests he remained still the scholar, and the publication in 1759 of his *Theory of Moral Sentiments* won him something of a European reputation. Three years later the university conferred upon him the honorary doctorate of laws.

But he was not destined to remain an academic. Among the appreciative readers of Smith's *Theory* was the prominent politician Charles Townshend, who had married the widowed mother of the young Duke of Buccleuch and was at the time seeking a suitable person to accompany the youth on the customary 'grand tour' of the continent. Townshend considered there could be no better choice than the author of so excellent a book, and forthwith he approached Adam Smith. The terms he offered were generous, and Smith felt obliged to accept, although characteristically he insisted on returning to his students that part of the term's fees which he considered he had not rightly earned.

From the spring of 1764 until the late autumn of 1766 Smith and his young charge were in France, at first at Toulouse and latterly in Paris, where Smith was able to meet many of the most eminent persons of the time. Probably the man he was most at home with was Dr François Quesnay, one of the royal physicians and the acknowledged master of (as they came to be described in *The Wealth of Nations*) 'a pretty considerable sect, distinguished in the French republic of letters by the name of the Economists'. (Another name for them is the Physiocrats). These economic thinkers constituted the opposition to the Mercantilists, whose principles had been those officially approved and adopted in France since the days of Louis XIV a hundred years before. Whereas the Mercantilists held that a wealthy country was one abounding in money and strongly favoured the state encouragement of the manufacturing interests, the *Economistes* took the contrary view, that 'the labour which is employed on land is the only productive labour', and they therefore championed the interests of the agriculturists. Adam Smith, while thinking that some of the Economists' notion were 'too narrow and confined', yet allowed that Quesnay's system was perhaps 'the nearest approximation to the truth that has yet been published upon the subject of political economy'. For Quesnay himself Adam Smith retained a deep admiration; and although he was never his disciple he carried away from their conversations much that was of value to him when he set about the presentation of his own conclusions.

For some months after returning to England, Adam Smith was in London, spending much of his time in the reading-room of the British Museum. In the spring of 1767 he went back to Kirkcaldy and settled in the old home still presided over by his now aged mother, with a cousin, Miss Jean Douglas, who did the housekeeping. Here he dictated every morning to a secretary, to such good purpose that most of his book was in manuscript by 1772. But there was still a great deal of revision to do, much of which was completed in London. Then at length, the book was published in the spring of 1776.

For a couple of years Adam Smith remained in London, where he was a member of the Johnsonian club and circle; but in 1778 he was appointed by Lord North, the prime minister, on the recommendation of Smith's former pupil the Duke of Buccleuch, one of the Commissioners of Customs in Scotland. This required his settlement in Edinburgh, and, since the salary attached to his new post was the substantial one of £500 a year, plus £100 a year in respect of the commissionership of stamp duties which went with it, he was able to afford a large house in a good residential district (Panmure House, in the Canongate), to which he lost no time in bringing his mother and Miss Douglas.

For some years his life in Edinburgh was happy and successful. He had money enough to indulge his favourite weakness, the collection of a fine library, and to welcome his friends to a very hospitable table. It was also suspected that much of his income was expended in secret charities and good works. In Edinburgh he became something of a 'character', as he walked every morning to his office in the Custom House, often talking to himself and indulging in quaint mannerisms, and back again in the afternoon. In 1787 his old University at Glasgow honoured him, and themselves, by electing him Lord Rector, an honour which he acknowledged in the most sincerely grateful terms.

But his last phase was sad. His mother died in 1784 when in her ninetieth year, and four years later Miss Douglas died too. Smith was left a lonely and rapidly ageing man, but he managed to see the fifth edition of *The Wealth of Nations* through the press in 1789.

A few days before his death he remarked to a friend that he regretted that 'he had done so little'. Then he gave orders that some volumes of unfinished manuscripts should be thrust into the fire.

Adam Smith died on 17 July 1790, and he was buried in the graveyard of the Canongate church in Edinburgh.

The Book

Writing in the meridian of the Victorian age, when the principles of Adam Smith, and in particular the principle of free trade, had won signal triumphs, the English historian Henry Thomas Buckle declared that 'looking at its ultimate results, Adam Smith's *Wealth of Nations* is probably the most important book that has ever been written'.

As though this were not sufficient, a page or two further on we have this passage:

'Well may it be said of Adam Smith, and said too without fear of contradiction, that this solitary Scotchman has, by the publication of one single work, contributed more towards the happiness of man, than has been effected by the united abilities of all the statesmen and legislators of whom history has preserved an authentic account.'

Extravagant? Why, yes, of course; and yet, not outrageously so. For *The Wealth of Nations*, now nearly two hundred years old and with the argument that constitutes its core a matter of history, still has the capacity to challenge the attention and hold the interest of thinking men and women, wherever they may be, of whatever race, culture, creed and circumstance.

If this be true, then the book must be something more than an economic textbook, even when that textbook is the foundation-document of a great and flourishing science. This is indeed the case.

In the first place, it is a prime source of information on the country and people of the times in which it was written.

Those times saw the beginnings of the most revolutionary changes in agriculture and industry, but it is still the genuine Olde England which is reflected in Adam Smith's pages. Down the deeply rutted roads rumble the great broad-wheeled waggons, and hugging the coast scurry fleets of wherries bearing coals from Newcastle to keep the Londoners warm. It is a world in which half the children born die before the age of manhood, even a common workman may maintain a menial servant, and ninety-nine houses out of a hundred are not insured against fire. It is a world in which (as Oliver Goldsmith had stated in a famous line a few years before) £40 a year is reckoned very good pay for a curate, while plenty of London shoemakers may earn as much. It is a world in which, while a linen shirt is not strictly speaking a necessary of life, leather shoes most certainly are – at least in England: in Scotland women of the lower orders (but not the men) may walk about barefooted without any discredit. Soap and candles are also necessaries of life, and yet they are taxed, and pretty heavily at that.

At the centre of this world is London. In no city in Europe is house-rent so dear, and in no other capital are lodgings so cheap. It is a city in which common labourers earn eighteen pence a day, tailors are often out of jobs, and carpenters are so apt to overwork that they ruin their health and constitution in a few years. It is a city in which the private bankers pay no interest on their deposits, so high is their credit – in which the merchants have not become such magnificent lords as those of Cadiz and Lisbon, but are not 'such attentive and parsimonious burghers' as those of Amsterdam.

Then there are the neat expressions, the pithy little sentences, which ought to be in the dictionaries of quotations but so seldom are; such as,

The 'delightful art' of gardeners.
Coals are a less agreeable fuel than wood.
A man is of all sorts of luggage the most difficult to be transported.
The lottery of the law.
Money makes money. When you have got a little, it is often easy to get more. The great difficulty is to get that little.
By nature a philosopher is not in genius and disposition half so different from a street porter, as a mastiff is from a greyhound.
The desire of food is limited in every man by the narrow capacity of the human stomach.
All families are equally ancient.
Nobody ever saw a dog make a fair and deliberate exchange of one bone for another with another dog.
A nation of shopkeepers. (*See* Chapter 3.)
That unprosperous race of men commonly called men of letters.
Science is the great antidote to the poison of enthusiasm and super-stition.

Many other examples of Adam Smith's gift for precise expression, his snappy and sometimes quaint observations, will be found in the introductions to the chapters that follow, but here in conclusion some-thing should be said of his very practical philosophy.

Basically, this was *religious*. This may sound strange, but it should be remembered that Smith was a moralist before he was an economist and his system of morality was coloured by – perhaps we may say, was derived from – the religious optimism of his old teacher, Professor Hutcheson. No one has ever said harsher things about the trading class, the merchants and manufacturers, the businessmen in general; and yet he was firmly persuaded that in their grabbing and grasping, their constant striving after personal profit, their unresting efforts to get on in the world, they were (all unwittingly) doing what they *had* to do. As he explains in a famous passage, an individual who directs his industry in such a manner as its produce may be of the greatest value, is intending only his own gain, but, 'in this, as in many other cases, he is led by an invisible hand to promote an end which was no part of his intention'. 'Invisible hand' is Adam Smith's synonym for God.

But what is that end which the 'invisible hand' has in view? We are left in no doubt of Adam Smith's answer: it is the promotion of the wealth and welfare of *all* the people. And that, in Adam Smith's scheme of things, is what political economy is all about.

CHAPTER 2

'LOW LIFE' IN LONDON

London in Adam Smith's time was what it had been since King Alfred's, in every respect the metropolis: the greatest concentration of population of political power, trade, industry and finance, the mirror of fashion and the principal seat of every amusement. For most of the intervening centuries its history had been one of almost uninterrupted growth so that by the middle of the eighteenth century the built-up areas extended from Whitechapel to Hyde Park, from 'the Fields' about the British Museum to the districts across the river that had been made accessible by the opening of Westminster Bridge in 1750 and were to be made even more so by the opening of Blackfriars bridge in 1769. Vital statistics of the period are hard to come by and, those that exist, are far from reliable; but it is generally stated that the population of London in 1760, when George III came to the throne, was in the neighbourhood of 750,000.

Three-quarters of a million of human beings, on whose existence history has, as a rule, persisted in turning an incorrigibly blind eye. If we were to take our notions from the memoir-writers, diarists, political scribes and social gossips, we might well suppose that the London of those days was peopled almost entirely by the gay and clever, the beautiful, the highly placed and those who were well-to-do if not downright rich. And how utterly wrong we should be!

For, no doubt about it, the reality was very different. Then as always the vast majority of Londoners were not especially cheerful, and indeed they had little to make them so; their looks were very ordinary, their intelligence was limited, and they had no education to speak of; and for the most part, their lives were short and laborious, an almost continuous struggle to keep themselves from falling into the abyss of destitution.

Two authors represent the Londoners of those times with a sharp fidelity that is not open to question. One of them was William Hogarth; and if it be objected that Hogarth was an *artist*, then it may be rejoined that he preferred to regard himself as an *author*, one whose pictures should be *read*. Hogarth's name is known to everybody; but no one knows the name of our second authority, since he wrote from behind a veil of anonymity.

As will be abundantly apparent, both were concerned almost entirely with 'low life'. But as the term is to be understood here, it is not confined to what is sordid, mean, socially disreputable, but includes every aspect of the everyday existence of the 'lower orders', the workers, the wage-earners, 'the great body of the people', to make use of Adam Smith's phrase.

(a) HOGARTH'S 'FOUR TIMES OF THE DAY'

Of Westmorland yeoman stock, William Hogarth (1697–1764) was born in London, where his father was a schoolmaster and author of sorts. Very early he showed a marked talent for drawing, and in about 1712 he was apprenticed to a silver-plate engraver, who taught him to engrave shop-bills and armorial bearings on silver cups and the like. In 1720 he set up as an engraver on his own account, with a shop off Leicester Fields, a district exceptionally rich in characters of 'low life' – beaux and belles on the loose, pickpockets and bruisers, highwaymen, military men, coach-drivers and chairmen, shopkeepers and trades-men, pimps and prostitutes, men about town and ladies of quality and of no quality at all – whom he was to reproduce with pencil and brush and engraver's tool with the most startling fidelity.

Before long he was executing clever little satires on contemporary follies, masquerade tickets, and book illustrations. In 1729 he made a runaway marriage with the daughter of the successful painter Sir James Thornhill, but his prospects were not at all promising until he produced, in 1730–1, the series of paintings entitled 'The Harlot's Progress'. These were very well received in their engraved form, and Hogarth proceeded to develop his gifts as a painter of domestic chron-icles with 'A Rake's Progress' (1733–5, now in the Soane Museum, London); 'Marriage à la Mode' (1743–5, Tate Gallery, London); and 'Industry and Idleness' (1747). A large number of pictures, paintings and engravings, added to his reputation.

'To the student of history', wrote Thackeray in his *English Humour-ists of the Eighteenth Century* (1853), 'Hogarth's admirable works must be invaluable, since they give us the most complete and truthful picture of the manners, and even the thoughts, of the time.'

Twenty-three of these 'admirable works' are reproduced in the plates contained in this volume, beginning with the 'Four Times of the Day', which date from 1738 (Plates 1 to 4). In most cases the reproductions are supported by an 'illustrative text' taken from *Hogarth Illustrated*

(1791), by John Ireland (died 1808), a watchmaker with a shop in Maiden Lane who spent his years in a close study of Hogarth's life and works.

I

Morning

Covent Garden is the scene. The principal figure, a withered representative of Miss Bridget Alworthy [in Fielding's *Tom Jones*], with a shivering footboy carrying her prayer-book, never fails in her attendance at morning service. She is a symbol of the season. She looks with scowling eye, and all the conscious pride of severe and stubborn virginity, on the poor girls who are suffering the embraces of two drunken beaux that have just staggered out of Tom King's Coffeehouse. One of them, from the basket on her arm, I conjecture to be an orange-girl: she shows no displeasure at the boisterous salute of her Hibernian lover. That the hero in a laced hat is from the banks of the Shannon is apparent in his countenance. The female whose face is partly concealed and whose neck has a more easy turn than we always see in the works of this artist, is not formed of the most inflexible materials.

An old woman, seated upon a basket; the girl, warming her hands by a few withered sticks that are blazing on the ground; and a wretched mendicant, wrapped in a tattered and partly-coloured blanket, entreating charity from the rosy-fingered vestal who is going to church, complete the group. Behind them, at the door of Tom King's Coffeehouse, are a party engaged in a fray likely to create business for both surgeon and magistrate; we discover swords and cudgels in the combatants' hands.

On the opposite side of the print are two little schoolboys. Near the woman who has a basket on her head, Dr Rock is expatiating to an admiring audience on the never-failing virtues of his wonder-working medicines. One hand holds a bottle of his miraculous panacea, and the other supports a board on which is the king's arms, to indicate that his practice is sanctioned by royal letters patent. Two porringers and a spoon, placed on the bottom of an inverted basket, intimate that the woman seated near is a vendor of rice-milk, which was at that time brought into the market every morning. A fatigued porter leans on a rail, and a blind beggar is going towards the church. Snow on the ground and icicles hanging from the penthouse exhibit a very chilling prospect; but to dissipate the cold, there is happily a shop where spirituous liquors are sold at a very little distance. A large pewter measure is placed upon a post before the door, and three of a smaller size hang over the window of the house. Extreme cold is very well expressed in the slipshod footboy and the girl who is warming her hands.

2

Noon

The scene is laid at the door of a French chapel in Hog Lane, a part of the town at that time almost wholly peopled by French refugees. Among the figures who are coming out of church, an affected, flighty Frenchwoman, with her fluttering fop of a husband, claim our first attention. The whole congregation, whether male or female, old or young, carry the air of their country in countenance, dress, and deportment.

The old fellow in a black periwig has a most vinegar-like aspect, and looks with great contempt at the frippery gentlewoman immediately before him. The woman with a demure countenance seems very piously considering how she can contrive to pick the embroidered beau's pocket. Two old sibyls joining their lips in a chaste salute is nauseous enough, but, being a national custom, must be forgiven.

Under a sign of the Baptist's Head is written, 'Good eating', and on each side of the inscription is a mutton chop. In opposition to this head without a body, unaccountably displayed as a sign at an eating-house, there is a body without a head hanging out as the sign of a distiller's. This, by common consent, has been quaintly denominated 'the good woman'. At a window above, one of the *softer sex* proves her indisputable right to the title by her temperate conduct to her husband, with whom having had a little disagreement, she throws their Sunday's dinner into the street.

A girl bringing a pie from the bakehouse is stopped in her career by the rude embraces of a blackamoor, who eagerly rubs his sable visage against her blooming cheek. A boy, placing a baked pudding upon a post with rather too violent an action, the dish breaks, the fragments fall to the ground; and while he is loudly lamenting his misfortune and with tears anticipating his punishment, the smoking remnants are eagerly snatched up by a poor girl.

By the dial of St Giles' church in the distance, we see that it is only half-past eleven. At this early hour, in those good times, there was as much good eating as there is now at six o'clock in the evening. From twenty pewter measures which are hung up before the houses of different distillers, it seems that good drinking was considered as equally worthy of their serious attention. The dead cat and the choked kennels mark the little attention shown to the streets by the scavengers of St Giles.

3

Evening

It is not easy to imagine fatigue better delineated than in the appearance of this amiable pair. In a few of the earliest impressions, Mr Hogarth printed the hands of the man in blue, to show that he was a dyer, and the face and neck of the woman in red, to intimate her extreme heat. The lady's aspect lets us at once into her character; we are certain that she was born to command. As to her husband, 'God made him, and he must pass for a man': what his wife has made him, is indicated by the cow's horns, which are so placed as to become his own. The hope of the family, with a cockade in his hat and riding upon papa's cane, seems much dissatisfied with female sway. A face with more of the shrew in embryo than that of the girl, it is scarcely possible to conceive.

Nothing can be better imagined than the group in the alehouse. They have taken a refreshing walk into the country, and being determined to have a cooling pipe, seat themselves in a chair-lumbered closet with a low ceiling; where every man pulling off his wig, and throwing a pocket-handkerchief over his head, inhales the fumes of hot punch, the smoke of half a dozen pipes, and the dust from the road. The old gentleman in a black bag-wig, and the two women near him, sensibly enough, take their seats in the open air.

From a woman milking a cow, we conjecture the hour to be about five in the afternoon. The cow and dog appear as much inconvenienced by heat as any of the party. On the side of the New River, where the scene is laid, lies one of the wooden pipes employed in the water-works. Opposite Sadler's Wells there is shown the sign of Sir Hugh Myddleton's head.

4

Night

By the oaken boughs on the sign of the Rummer Tavern [*rummer*, a large drinking-glass], it seems that this rejoicing night is 29 May, the anniversary of our second Charles's restoration; this might be one reason for the artist choosing a scene contiguous to the beautiful equestrian statue of Charles I at Charing Cross.

The wounded freemason in the foreground, who, in zeal of brotherly love, has drunk his bumpers to the craft till he is unable to find his way home and is under the guidance of a watchman, has been generally considered as intended for Sir Thomas de Veil [a celebrated magistrate at Bow Street police court]. The woman showering her favours from the window upon his head may have its source in that respect which the inmates of such houses as the Rummer Tavern had for a justice of the peace. The watchman who supports his worship, seems, from the patch on his forehead, to have been in a recent affray.

The Salisbury flying-coach oversetting and broken, by passing through the bonfire, is said to be an intended burlesque upon a right honourable peer who was accustomed to drive his own carriage over hedges, ditches, and rivers; and had been sometimes known to drive three or four of his maidservants into a deep water, and there leave them in the coach to shift for themselves. The butcher and little fellow who are assisting the terrified passengers, are possibly free and accepted Masons. To crown the joys of the populace, a man with a pipe in his mouth is filling a capacious hogshead with British Burgundy.

The joint operation of shaving and bleeding performed by a drunken 'prentice on a greasy oilman, does not seem a very natural exhibition on a rejoicing night. There is humour in the barber's sign and inscription: 'Shaving, bleeding, and teeth drawn with a touch. *Ecce signum!*' The poor wretches under the barber's bench display a prospect of penury and wretchedness. In the distance is a cart laden with furniture, which some unfortunate tenant is removing out of the reach of his landlord's execution; and a house on fire, an accident very likely to happen on such a night as this.

JOHN IRELAND, *Hogarth Illustrated* (1791), vol. I, pp. 125–51.

(b) 'LOW LIFE – HOW THE OTHER HALF LIVE'

In May 1752 there was published in London a small book the title of which is disproportionately long. It runs as follows: *LOW LIFE; or, One half of the World knows not how the Other Half Live, being a critical account of what is transacted by People of almost all Religions, Nations, Circumstances, and Sizes of Understanding, in the Twenty-four hours between Saturday-Night and Monday-Morning. In a true Description of a Sunday, as it is usually spent within the Bills of Mortality. Calculated for the Tenth of June, with an Address to the ingenious and ingenuous Mr Hogarth* . . . (N.B. The 'Bills of Mortality—referred to an area of 109 parishes in and immediately around London.)

As already mentioned, the book is anonymous. A second edition was published in November 1754 and a third (which contains a frontispiece, 'St Monday') in 1764. Between the publication of the second and the third editions the change in the calendar was effected whereby eleven days were 'lost'; and because of this the third edition is 'calculated for the 21st of June'. The book ends with the statement that the bell-ringers were crowding about the doors of the churches, 'to have speedy admittance into the belfries, to usher in the twenty-second day of June, New Style, being the anniversary of his present Majesty's accession [George II, in 1727] to the Throne of these Kingdoms'.

The book is prefaced with an 'Address to Mr Hogarth', which runs,

'Sir, In the following sheets (which humbly claim the honour of your Patronage) You will find a true Delineation of the various Methods which the People in and about this Metropolis have ingeniously contrived to murder not only Common Time but that Portion of it, which is more immediately consecrated to the Glory of their great Creator. In this, you will see, they have not wanted such Success as the extraordinary Attempt deserves; For they have left no Hour unemployed, either in the different scenes of Debauchery, Luxury, or Yawning Stupidity, if the latter can merit even the Title of Life . . . Permit me to

3. St Monday: the frontispiece of the 1764 edition of 'Low Life'. A party of tradesmen are shown idling and drinking, each characterized by an emblem of his trade – shoemaker, tailor, bricklayer, plasterer, painter, etc., while the butcher's wife interrupts a game of cards and the landlady chalks up double scores.

observe that this work has in a great measure owed its rise to several hints which I have taken from your admirable Pencil . . . I say, owes its existence partly to your Works. And who will not believe me, when I direct them to those Pieces of Yours, called Morning, Noon, Evening, and Night?'

Low Life has never been without its appreciative readers. Thackeray had a copy, and doubtless referred to it when he was writing his *English Humourists*. He lent it to Charles Dickens, so that it may have left traces in *Bleak House* and *Little Dorrit*. A little later the eminent Victorian journalist George Augustus Sala acknowledged that *Low Life* had given him the idea for his *Twice Round the Clock* (1859), and he described it as 'one of the minutest, the most graphic, the most pathetic pictures of London life a century ago that has ever been written'.

I

Saturday Night to Monday Morning

Hour 1. From twelve o'clock on Saturday night to one o'clock on Sunday morning

Hackney coachmen full of employment about Charing Cross, Covent Garden, and the Inns of Court, carrying to their habitations such people who are either too drunk or too lazy to walk. Poor tradesmen's wives hanging about their husbands at little ale-houses to secure some money to support their family, before it is all lost at whist, cribbage, etc. Victuallers carrying the scores of tradesmen, such as coachmakers, carpenters, smiths, plasterers, plumbers, and others in the building branch of business, to the pay-tables, in order to clear their last week's reckoning, and if possible to get a trifle paid off from an old score. The markets begin to swarm with the wives of poor journeymen shoemakers, smiths, tinkers, tailors, etc., who come to buy great bargains with very little money.

Fiddlers, harpers and other itinerant musicians, in great esteem at the public-houses in back alleys, courts, yards, etc., in playing hornpipes and jigs to nimble-footed, noisy, drunken fools. Poor people who have been in bed some time and are thoroughly warm, groping about for their tinder-boxes, that they may strike a light in order to go a bug-hunting.

Common whores telling their lamentable cases to watchmen on their stands and treating them with Geneva [gin] and tobacco, for the liberty of walking about their respective beats. Terrible vengeance pronounced by termagant wives against drunken husbands, who have not found their way as yet home to their families.

More drunken than sober people walking about the streets. It is now midday with people who keep gaming-tables, night-houses, Geneva shops, and other places of resort which are contrary to Act of Parliament. People of real merit retired to their sweet and wholesome rest several hours. The unhappy lunatics in Bethlehem-hospital [Bedlam] at Moorfields, rattling their chains and making a terrible outcry, occasioned by the heat of the weather having too great an effect over their rambling brains.

Hour II. From one till two o'clock on Sunday morning
Tailors whose work is in a hurry, leaving off labour in order to take two
or three hours sleep, that they may be able to make a fresh attack on
business. Several petty officers, as constables and head-boroughs, by
order of the Justices, and members of the Society for the Reformation
of Manners, in full search after bawdy-houses and whores. Drapers',
mercers', lacemen's, and booksellers' apprentices, creeping from the
women servants' bed-chambers to their own.

Bunters with bits of candle between their fingers, and baskets on their
heads, rummaging the dirty dung-hills at the corners of lanes, courts,
yards, alleys, etc., for rags and bones, to purchase the ensuing day's
dinner with. Apprentices who intend to run away from their masters,
are packing up their clothes, that they may make off by the help of
the trap-door on the top of the house, while all the family are fast
asleep.

Young fellows who are shut out of their lodgings, walking about the
streets, to pass away the time till daylight. Poor men who have lived
retired all the past week, for fear of being carried to gaol for debt,
returning God thanks for the liberty of eating their sabbath-day's
dinner with their families in their own apartments. Thieves and
whores lurking about the avenues of dark gateways, courts and alleys,
in hopes of meeting drunken tradesmen that they may hurry them up
and rob them. Poor men whose business has called them to work till
this time, just got home, where they too often find their children
crying, the fires out, their wives on the ground, drunk and asleep, and
no provision or clean linen for the ensuing day. Some husbands, who
after an hour's conversation in bed, and finding no evasions will do, are
willing to end all disputes with their loving wives, by performing family
duty.

Young fellows of shallow understanding and very small fortunes,
who have undergone a great fatigue of several hours, drinking, smoking,
and singing at places of mirth and jollity, are beginning to break up and
retire to their respective habitations.

Hour III. From two till three o'clock on Sunday morning
Most private shops where Geneva is publicly sold in defiance of the
Acts of Parliament, filled with whores, thieves, and beggars, who have
got drunk and are talking of Scripture. Young fellows who have been
out all night on the *ran-dan* stealing staves and lanthorns from such
watchmen as they find sleeping at their stands. Sextons of parish
churches privately digging up and carrying to the houses of surgeons,
the bodies of such persons who were buried the preceding night, that
died young and after a short illness, to be anatomised; at which time

they take the opportunity of ripping the velvet and cloth off large coffins, pulling out the brass nails, and tearing away the plates and handles, to sell for Geneva, snuff, and tobacco.

Hackney coachmen searching the seats and boots of their coaches in hopes of finding things of value accidentally left there in the hurry of the night. Noblemen and gentlemen going home from bawdy-houses and gaming-tables with heavy hearts and empty pockets. Sailors on board inward-bound merchant ships in the River, bringing out their rum and brandy, and contriving how to make the Customs House Officers on board drunk; that they may get on shore such goods as they have neither money nor inclination to pay for. Vagabonds who have been sleeping under hay-ricks in the neighbouring villages and fields awake, begin to rub their eyes, shake their feathers, and get out of their nests.

Hour IV. From three till four o'clock on Sunday morning
Pigeon fanciers preparing to take long rambles out of London in order to give their pigeons a flight, that they may show which are the quickest fliers. The men and boys who live at the cow-keepers about the villages adjacent to London, hallowing about the fields to get their kine into cowhouses to be milked. Bawds, whores, bullies, fools, and drunkards, fighting under the Piazzas in Covent Garden surrounded by a number of daring pickpockets and frightened constables.

Poor honest women who are waiting in their apartments for the coming home of their drunken husbands from night-cellars or bawdy-houses, are mending stockings and shirts, ironing linen, washing infants' apparel, or performing some other act of good housewifery to pass the time till they return. Young maidens who have been awake two-thirds of the night, kicking and sprawling as they lie in bed, and praying for strong-backed husbands, no matter of what nation, religion, or occupation.

Such persons as intend to act the characters of highwaymen the ensuing day, and have received intelligence the preceding night what road some particular gentlemen are to travel (who are known to be cowards and worth robbing) from the runners and sweepers of inns, are setting out on their expeditions, to reconnoitre the ground and find out a proper place for the attack. Poor people carrying their dead children nailed up in small deal boxes into the fields to bury them privately, and save the extravagant charge of parish dues. Most people, such as petty gentlemen, creditable shopkeepers, and regular-lived mechanics, who enjoy a moderate fortune, a settled temper of mind, and a good state of health, fast asleep.

Turncocks belonging to the several water-works round this metropolis going their rounds and turning the waters on or off for the use of the inhabitants. The streets are beginning to be quiet, as the whores, bullies, and thieves have retired to their apartments; noisy drunken mechanics are got to their lodgings; coachmen, watchmen and soldiers are mostly asleep; and the fishwomen gone to Billingsgate to wait the tide for the arrival of the mackerel boats.

Hour V. From four till five o'clock on Sunday morning
Publicans in the Fields and villages near London beginning to open their houses for the reception of early customers, who had rather arise and go a-walking than dress themselves to go to their parish church. Fish-dealers very busy in cheating each other during high-mackerel market at Billingsgate. Early risers, with pipes stuck in their jaws, walking towards Hornsey-Wood, Dulwich Common, Chelsea, Mary-bone, and Stepney, in order to take large morning draughts, and secure the first fuddle of the day.

Young virgins who are to be married in a few hours, kicking, tossing, and rolling about their beds for want of sleep, having strongly possessed themselves with the thoughts of their intended husbands, and how they are to behave the following night. Drunken husbands, whose money is all spent and credit quite exhausted, going with sorrowful relenting faces home to their half-starved disconsolate families. Poor servant-maids plagued in their bed-chambers with the pressing and wheedling persuasiveness of their lewd and infirm masters. Careful old mothers of families, whose pangs and infirmities prevent their taking natural rest, lying in bed, considering how their circumstances are, and what method is best to take for the future. Young people, lately entered into the bonds of matrimony, playing as they lie in bed, in order to bring on a *Good-morrow*, before they arise to walk two or three miles about the Fields adjacent to London.

The wives and servant-girls of mechanics and day-labourers, who live in courts and alleys where one cock supplies the whole neighbour-hood with water, taking the advantage before other people are up, to fill their tubs and pans with a sufficiency to serve them the ensuing seven days. Firemen of the several Insurance Offices of London and West-minster who have been called up to their duty the foregoing night, in the public-houses of the alarmed neighbourhood, giving in their names to the foremen, whose account is afterwards signed by some of the principal frightened inhabitants, for the inspection and satisfaction of their several directors.

Young men and women who had rather do *any thing*, than serve their Maker or their Neighbour, calling each other up to walk in the Fields, give abusive language to sober people they meet, gather cowslips, and get drunk before breakfast.

Hour VI. From five till six o'clock on Sunday morning
People about the City and Suburbs, as have a board before their cham-
ber-windows crowded with a number of flower-pots filled with Angelica,
Southernwood, Pinks, Roses, etc., getting water, and giving them a
morning's refreshment. Consumptive people, who live at the cowhouses nearest the City, getting warm milk from the kine, mixed
with sugar, rum, etc., as a restorative to their health. News-collectors
who are in bed, instead of their prayers are inventing stories of rapes,
robberies, riots, etc., to fill up the newspapers of the ensuing week.
Poor people with fruit, nosegays, buns, etc., making their appearance
on Holborn Hill, Charing-Cross, the Strand, Cheapside, Tower Hill,
etc.

Tailors, shoemakers, staymakers, mantua-makers, milliners, glove-
washers and hoop-petticoat-makers, begin to arise, in order to break the
fourth Commandment, *Remember to*, etc. Bells tolling, and the streets
begin to fill with old women and Charity children who attend the service
of the Church. Poor labouring men who have been pestered with their
wives' uneasiness the past night, instead of taking any rest, are obliged
to get up, put on part of their clothes, and go *a-nighting*, i.e. fetching
midwives, nurses, and gossips. Poor women and lame men, whose
bread depends chiefly on sweeping the passages to churches, chapels,
and meetings, trimming their brooms and going to their respective
stands.

Hour VII. From six till seven o'clock on Sunday morning
Pork-men busy in their shops and cellars, in salting and putting into
brine what meat was left the night before, to prevent its stinking and
going to putrefaction. Gentlemen of small fortunes, who keep little
private houses within eight or ten miles of London, preparing to go to
them in post-chaises or other light carriages, and carrying with them a
cargo of mutton, beef, and veal, and in return at night bring home a
quantity of beans, pease, lettuces, and other vegetables for the use of
their families in Town. A knocking at pawnbroker's doors by twelve-
penny harlots to redeem some wearing apparel which they are obliged
to put on, as they are sent for to some bagnio on fresh duty. Great
numbers of people of all nations, opinions, circumstances, and sizes of
understanding, going to the Bantering Booth on Windmill-Hill, Upper
Moorfields, to hear their beloved Apostle, Mr Wesley.

The wives of poor journeymen mechanics getting up to buy a little
soap, and wash their husbands a shirt, stock, handkerchief, and stockings, that they may appear in the afternoon like *Christians* though they
live like *Brutes*. Gossiping women lighting candles at each others'
apartments, at which time they are complaining of their husbands,

telling what late hours they kept, and that they came home fuddled, without any money in their pockets.

Servant women in public-houses, who have just got up, running about with their stockings about their legs, caps and petticoats half off, drinking of gin, taking of snuff, lighting of candles for gossiping neighbours, and playing with fellows who have been drinking, swearing, and playing at cards all the past night.

Hour VIII. From seven till eight o'clock on Sunday morning
Poor devils of women, with empty bellies, naked backs, and heads intoxicated with Geneva, standing and gossiping with each other in the street, whose discourse always begins and ends with wishing the Compliments of the Season, it being Whit-Sunday. Laundresses in all the Inns of Court very busy in sweeping out the outer chambers, laying out linens, brushing clothes, and getting shoes cleaned for their masters, for the use of the ensuing day. Some few elderly women of small fortunes at their private devotions, for want of company.

Journeywomen mantua-makers, clear-starchers, quilters, and servant-maids out of place, running up scores at chandlers-shops for teas, sugars, rolls, butter, and quarterns of Geneva; but, if credit is denied, they come a second time, and leave a shift, cap, apron, or pocket as a pledge till the money is paid. Common people going to quack-doctors and petty barbers in order to be let blood (and perhaps have their arms lamed) for threepence. The whole cities of London, Westminster, and the borough of Southwark, covered by a cloud of smoke, most people being employed in lighting fires.

Poor women, whose husbands are confined for debt in Ludgate, the Compters, Marshalsea, King's Bench, or any other prison for debtors, preparing to carry them some clean linen, a little money, and some small provision to keep them the ensuing week.

Hour IX. From eight till nine o'clock on Sunday morning
Tradesmen who follow the amusement of angling, preparing to set out for Shepperton, Carshalton, Epping Forest, and other known places of diversion, to pass away the first two or three days of the week. Old people and children looking through the rails on London Bridge, to see the barges, hoys, and boats go through with the tide. Women pretty far advanced in years, telling each other the misfortunes of their past lives, as they walk, or rather creep, home from the morning lectures. Lawyers (whose laundresses have finished their business and gone from their chambers) are lacing on the stays of their female bed-fellows, and giving them money to get rid of their company.

Servants to ladies of quality are washing and combing such lap-dogs

1. Times of the Day: Morning

2. Times of the Day: Noon

3. Times of the Day: Evening

4. Times of the Day: Night

as are to go to church with their mistresses that morning. Handsome whores hurrying home from the bagnios in hackney-coaches and chairs, to the houses of their keepers, that they may change their clothes and linen, and go upon fresh service. Kept mistresses are as lazy in their beds as lifeguardsmen and common soldiers are in their quarters. Beggars planting themselves about the church doors, that with their forced cries and sham sores they may seize upon the parishioners going to Divine Service.

Hour X. From nine till ten o'clock on Sunday morning
Pupils belonging to surgeons in the hospitals of St Bartholomew, St Thomas, St George, Guy, the London Infirmary, etc., going about their several wards, and letting blood, mending broken bones, applying plasters, etc., and doing whatever else they think necessary for their poor patients. Surgeons with their pupils going to the homes of reputable patients, laying plasters to sore breasts, broken shins, and other parts.

Gardeners, who live at gentlemen's houses near London, mowing and sweeping the grass-plats and rolling the gravel walks, to make them fit for the reception of their masters and mistresses. Chambermaids dressing their ladies, telling them every story they hear in the house and back-biting all their servants, excepting their favourite footman, who they are in some notion of making a fool of a husband of. Spruce apprentices admiring themselves at their masters' shop doors, and appointing their afternoon's ramble. Citizens who take a walk in the morning with an intent to sleep away the afternoon, creeping to Sadler's Wells or Newington, in order to get drunk during the time of Divine Service.

Churchwardens, Select Vestrymen, and Overseers of the Poor, and other tun-bellied Parochial officers, going towards church, where the time is spent more in considering who will succeed them, what sums of money they have deceived the parish of by their office, and the pleasure of having the Warder stand at the door with a silver-headed staff, than for any act of real piety or devotion as becomes the place. The Beadles of parishes begin to come into great power, which holds among the shoe-boys, nosegay women, and common beggars all the time of Divine Service. Quakers flock into their meetings with well-dressed hats, stiff-starched neckerchiefs, hypocritical countenances, and indifferent consciences. Gateways and alleys filled with boys playing marbles, pitch-and-hussle, and such like diversions. The Charity children begin to make their weekly processions to their several parish churches, with Bibles under their arms, and making bows and curtsies to all their Trustees they meet on the way.

Hour XI. From ten till eleven o'clock on Sunday morning
Young men and women, who are willing to be married according to Act of Parliament, going to the churches of the parishes in which they reside, in order to hear themselves asked, during the time of prayers. The churchyards about London, as Stepney, Pancras, Islington, etc., filled with people reading the tombstones and eating currants and gooseberries. Ladies flocking to public worship, where they spend the prayer time in quarrelling for the hassocks and the upper ends of the pews. Fine fans, rich brilliants, white hands, envious eyes, and enamelled snuff-boxes displayed in most places of Divine Service all over London. People of fashion humbling themselves in fine lace and tissue, and enduring the intolerable fatigue of Divine Service with wonderful seeming patience.

Poor women going to chandlers' shops and fetching half-pecks of coal in dirty towels and woollen aprons, for firing to dress dinner with. The pumps crowded with milk-people, who are cleaning their pails with wisps of hay, scouring sand, and soap-boilers' lees, against the afternoon. Poor parentless children, who have not any friends to take care of them, going about the fields and ditches where wild-honey-suckles, nettles, and thistles grow, with bottles in their hands, and catching of bees, wasps, lady-birds, blue-bottles, and other winged insects.

Hour XII. From eleven till twelve o'clock on Sunday noon.
Gentlemen's coachmen and footmen drinking at the adjacent public-houses, while the families are at Divine Service. The wives of genteel merchants, under pretence of going to prayers in their apartments, take a nap and a dram, after which they chew lemon peel to prevent being smelt. Old women propping up each other as they sleep under pulpits in sermon time. Ladies about St James's reading plays and romances, and making paint for their faces. Poor people that lodge in low-rented houses going to each other and after paying their awkward compliments, borrowing saucepans and stewpans for the dressing of peas, beans, bacon, and mackerel for dinner.

Hour XIII. From twelve till one o'clock on Sunday noon.
A general church delivery from the morning service all over London, excepting the Chapel Royal at St James's and the Temple Church and a few other places where Divine Service is not ended till one o'clock. Idle apprentices who have played under gateways in the street during the hour of Divine Service, begging the text of old women at the church doors to carry home to their inquisitive masters and mistresses. Young tradesmen, half-starved gentlemen, merchants' clerks, petty offices in

the Customs, Excise, and news-collectors, very noisy over their half-pints and diminutive dumplings in tavern kitchens about Temple Bar and the Royal Exchange.

Vintners and publicans joyfully open their doors after the recess of business for two hours. Common servants in a great bustle in their dark, dirty kitchens, preparing dinner for their noisy, voracious, and dainty masters. Measly pork, rusty bacon, stinking lamb, rotten mutton, stinked veal, and coddled cow, with yellow greens, sooty pottage, and greasy pudding, sold at the common cooks' shops about the skirts of the Town. Hackney coaches flying about the streets with whole families, new-married couples, uncles, aunts, and cousins, to dine with their relations and acquaintance. Poor mechanics of more merit than fortune, sitting down to dinner on wholesome, homely food and quiet consciences. Ladies pretty far advanced in years, and just returned from receiving the Sacrament, abusing the footmen for non-attendance, and threshing their maids for delaying dinner. Apprentice boys who keep pigeons unknown to the family they live with, taking the advantage of their masters being at dinner, to get out of their trap-doors to feed and fly them. All the common peoples' jaws in full employment.

Hour XIV. From one till two o'clock on Sunday afternoon
The friends of criminals under sentence of death in Newgate presenting money to the turnkeys to get to the sight of them, in order to take their last farewell, and present them with white caps with black ribbons, prayer-books, nosegays, and oranges, that they may make a decent appearance up Holborn, on the road to the other world.

Young people who are rowing boats about the River Thames, between Woolwich and Richmond, taking spells of the oar to relieve each other, while they refresh themselves with the tongue, ham, bread, butter, wine and punch which they took on board. People of indifferent circumstances, who have just clothes sufficient to appear clean in, and intend to take a walk in the Fields, or see some relations or friends, dressing and pleasing themselves with thinking on their afternoon's ramble.

Young married women, who have casually met at their friends' houses, retiring from the rest of the company to a private place backwards, where they compare *Notes*, and talk of their new husbands. Foolish husbands praising there wives before their faces, which only heightens their pride, and brings themselves under petticoat government. Poor undone dogs of husbands, who were foolish enough to spend all their money the preceding night, and not make a reserve by hiding some in the Family Bible, bottom of the chamber-pot, or top of the bed's tester (where they may be sure wives never search) on their knees to borrow a sixpence of their termagant helpmates for the use of the afternoon.

Hour XV. From two till three o'clock on Sunday afternoon
Citizens who have pieces of ground in the adjacent villages, walking to them with their wives and children, in order to drink tea, punch, or bottled ale; after which they load themselves with flowers for beaupots, and roots, salads, and other vegetables, to bring home to supper. Young handsome ladies demanding adoration instead of paying it in church. City cheesemongers, grocers, and other tradesmen, who did not take a nap after dinner, snoring in churches and meeting–houses. The paths of Kensington, Highgate, Hampstead, Islington, Stepney, and Newington, found to be much pleasanter than those of the Gospel.

Hour XVI. From three till four o'clock on Sunday afternoon
Boys belonging to farmers and cow-keepers near Town, driving the kine into the fields after milking, that they may go and sweep out the cow-stalls, and proceed to play. Women servants half-naked in their bed-chambers, looking into broken pieces of glass, and vainly attempting by the power of soap and towel to alter their sad-coloured complexion. Poor men such as labourers, hay-makers, and cow-keepers' men, sitting under hay-ricks in the fields and farmyards, and lousing their breeches.

Divers citizens who are too fat and lazy to walk in the Fields, are fast asleep on settees or in easy-chairs, by way of taking a nap after dinner. Ladies of quality picking their teeth, and hearing their husbands' oaths without any disturbance of mind. Poor women at their looking-glasses, viewing their apparel, and seeing that the wrinkles are out which they got at the pawnbrokers.

Misers, who have locked themselves up in their chambers, are counting over their money and looking over bills, bonds, leases, notes and assignments, being fearful of losing them, lest they should be robbed. Widows, whose husbands are to be buried in the evening, are dressing themselves in their weeds, and humming over tunes in a room by themselves, being pleased that they are their own mistresses. Abundance of witty sayings, smart repartees, and fag ends of scandal, flung across the tables between the servants of nobility while they sit at dinner. Servants in common tradesmen's houses, receiving orders from their mistresses (who are just awakened from their afternoon naps) to put on the tea-kettle, and then begin to shell peas for supper.

Hour XVII. From four till five o'clock on Sunday afternoon
Some hundreds of people, mostly women and children, walking backward and forward on Westminster Bridge, for the benefit of the air;

looking at the boats going up and down the river; and sitting on the resting-benches to pick up new acquaintance. The servants of nobility and gentry, whose day it is to go abroad, meeting their acquaintance according to appointment in the Fields, and giving and taking Green Gowns [rolling on the grass] from each other, and retiring to public-houses to drink ale and cyder, and treat the girls with veal, ham, and cakes, now they have them abroad.

The apprentices of poor merchants, who are just returned from church and have told their masters the text, are begging to go and see their parents the remainder of the evening. Poor women, who live in courts, yards, and alleys in the suburbs, bringing their chairs into the streets, where they sit with their constant gossips, and pass their verdict on people going into and coming out of the Fields.

Poor honest women at their bedsides, praying and coaxing their husbands to arise and take a walk with them in the Fields. Common whores and thieves, who have been out on their different occupations the preceding night, contriving as they lie in bed who they shall delude or rob the ensuing evening. The tap-rooms of the prisons are filling with the friends of prisoners who are come to see them, where they pay an extravagant price for pricked wine and muddy sour beer, since they cannot sell punch or spirituous liquors.

Hour XVIII. From five till six o'clock on Sunday evening
Well-dressed gentlemen and ladies of quality drove out of St James's Park, Lincoln's Inn Gardens, and Gray's Inn Walks by milliners, mantua-makers, sempstresses, stay-makers, French barbers, dancing-masters, gentlemen's gentlemen, tailors' wives and butchers' daughters.

The public-houses and bun-houses, which have been opened on the Surrey Shore since the finishing Westminster Bridge, very full of customers, noise, smoke, and children. Servant-maids and other young wenches, who intend to go the ensuing day to Greenwich in order to roll down Flamstead-Hill, go to country-dancing, be treated by apprentice-boys, and be debauched by anybody, are looking out their ribbands, caps, stockings, and other apparel for that purpose.

The inhabitants who have the conveniency of flat leaded roofs on the top of their houses (especially such as have prospects of the Thames) taking the advantage of the fineness of the weather, and drinking beer, tea, and punch, and smoking tobacco there, till the dusk of the evening. Old women and children, who have filled their pockets with pieces of bread at dinner-time, are feeding the ducks in St James's Park, and the swans at New-River-Head.

Night-walkers washing their smocks, caps, aprons, and handker-chiefs, against the evening, that they may appear clean in their walks.

Great numbers of footmen near the gate the entrance to Hyde Park, wrestling, cudgel-playing, and jumping; while others who have drank more than their share are swearing, fighting, spewing, sleeping, etc., till their ladies return from [riding in] the Ring.

Vintners' wives and daughters dressed up in their best apparel behind their bars, that they may wheedle old fools, country esquires, and conceited young fellows into large reckonings. A great number of coal-heavers, glasshouse-men, pothouse-men, carmen, Billingsgate porters, and common labourers, washing their dirty carcasses at the several stairs leading to the river. People who have drank too freely in the afternoon, are inclinable to sleep an hour before they give a fresh attack to the liquor.

The back garrets of gentlemen's and tradesmen's houses in a general confusion with gowns, petticoats, shifts, stockings, etc., of women servants, who have been dressing to go to visit their acquaintance.

Hour XIX. From six till seven o'clock on Sunday evening
Mackerel just come up with the tide which will not keep till the ensuing day, selling in great quantities very cheap among crowds of people at Whitechapel-Bars, Bishopsgate-church, Fore-street, High Holborn, Charing Cross, the borough of Southwark, and other public places. Children in back alleys and narrow passages very busy at their doors, shelling peas and beans for supper, and making boats, as they call them, with bean-shells and deal-matches. New milk and biscuits plentifully attacked by old women, children, and fools, in St James's Park, Lamb's Conduit-Fields, and St Giles's Fields. Westminster Abbey crowded with people who are admiring the monuments and reading their inscriptions. Country people, who are travelling to London on business, well pleased at viewing St Paul's church at a distance.

The pasture-fields near the suburbs, especially those about Islington, filling with oxen, calves, sheep, and lambs for the ensuing market in Smithfield. Fools and powdered fops, who have spent the day in talk and dress, admiring their pretty persons in the glasses of coffee-houses, and reading such pamphlets as are taken in by the subscription of the customers. City apprentices complaining to their fond mothers of the ill-treatment they receive from the masters, mistresses, and fellow servants; but are careful not to mention the provocation they give them. Men who keep hay-farms about this Metropolis ordering their servants to prevent the too great devastation of new-mown hay by people who are tumbling about the fields.

Hour XX. From seven till eight o'clock on Sunday evening
The drawers [barmen] at Sadler's Wells, and the Prospect House near

Islington, Jenny's Whim at Chelsea, the Spring Gardens at Newington and Stepney, the Castle at Kentish Town, and the Angel at Upper Holloway, in full employment, and every room in those houses full with talk and smoke. Dusty one-horse chaises, with young spendthrifts and whores in ribbands, cotton gowns, and high-crowned hats, who have spent all their money on the road, are limping through the streets.

The taverns about the Royal Exchange filled with merchants, underwriters, and principal tradesmen, who oftentimes do as much business on the Sunday evening as they do when they go upon the Exchange. A general ringing of bells on board the vessels in the river, in order to set the night's watch. The turnkeys of prisons locking all fast, that they may drink with the prisoners' friends. A great number of poor people looking for coals at low-water mark on the sandbank near Cuper's Stairs on the Surrey shore.

Sober people, who are willing to indulge their melancholy thoughts, sitting at their back windows and listening to the bells tolling for the interment of persons departed this transitory life. Nurses, whose bread depends on the care of young infants, are feeding them, putting on their night-dresses, and hushing them to sleep.

Hour XXI. From eight till nine o'clock on Sunday evening
As it is now twilight, reputable young fellows, as students in the law, merchants' clerks, non-commissioned officers, dependent nephews and grandsons, coasting commanders, and mechanics' sons, who have been unhappily scarred in the wars of Venus, are repairing to their several quack doctors and surgeons' pupils, to get safe, easy, and speedy cure for their several disorders.

About the same time, young women, whose unhappy minute has been taken the advantage of by pretended lovers, rakes of quality, lewd masters, lecherous fornicators, and drinking spirituous liquors, are repairing to persons of their own sex who live about Ludgate-hill and St Martin's Lane and put out hand-bills for the cure of all disorders incident to women.

Cold beef and carrot most vigorously attacked in taverns and public-houses by hungry acquaintance just come out of the Fields. Ministers, physicians, and lawyers meet at taverns, and enter into high dispute about pre-eminence. Undertakers who have had a body to bury from their own houses, which they have sold to be anatomised, are interring a coffin full of rubbish, and suffer a funeral service to be devoutly performed over it. Black eyes and broken heads exhibited pretty plentifully in the streets. A multiplicity of lies told by old men and travellers in public-houses, concerning the troubles, travels and adventures of their lives.

47

Great struggling at the Paris-Garden Stairs, and the Barge-house Stairs in Southwark, to get into the boats that ply to and from Blackfriars and the Temple. A great number of men and boys who have spent the day in angling in the Narrow River, and have caught nothing, are returning to London with empty pockets, baskets, and stomachs. Great slaughter made among gooseberry pies and tarts by apprentice boys at their masters' and parents' houses. Young highwaymen venturing out upon the road, to attack such coaches, chaises, and horsemen as they think are worth meddling with in their return to London. Great swearing in the stables of inns and yards where horses are let out to hire, upon the changing of bridles, over-riding, half-starving, and breaking the knees of such cattle as have been rode upon the preceding day. Brewers' servants and women who go out washing for their livelihood, and are to be at work by one o'clock in the morning, thinking of going to bed. Divers hard-working men who have spent all their money, going to bed, that they may save the expense of a supper and candle.

Hour XXII. From nine till ten o'clock on Sunday night
The streets hardly wide enough for numbers of people who are reeling to their habitations. Sailors lately come from abroad, in close conversation with whores, punch, and bottled ale, at the public-houses in Rotherhithe, Limehouse, Wapping, and St Catherine's. The public-houses about the verge of the town which have been crowded with customers all day, now begin to be pretty empty. Great hallowing and whooping in the Fields by such persons who have spent the day abroad and are now returning home half-drunk. Bakers who have been carousing all the afternoon abroad, begin to strip and enter on their business for the ensuing week.

Hour XXIII. From ten till eleven o'clock on Sunday night
Men of spirit and condition, who have been over-rated by hackney coachmen in the demand of their fares, taking the numbers of their coaches, and going to their houses, with the full intention of prosecuting them before the Commissioners as far as the law directs. Some nurses and watchers in the hospitals getting together, when they think a poor patient is near making his exit, and taking the pillows from under their heads, that they may go quietly out of the world a few hours sooner than they otherwise would have done; in the meanwhile they search their pockets, carrying away what is valuable, and vouch for each other, that they found nothing but a tobacco-box, pocket-piece ['lucky' coin], and almanack, or some other trifling thing about them.

Link-boys who have just money sufficient to buy a torch taking their stands at Temple Bar, London Bridge, Lincoln's Inn Fields, Smithfield, the City Gates, and other public places, to light, knock down and rob people who are walking about their business. Mrs Mary Daggle-Ass and other ladies of her profession cursing and roaring at her wenches and drawers, to drown the dismal cries and groans of departing maiden-heads. Destitute whores and runaway apprentices, who have neither lodging, money, nor friends, carrying hay, etc. into empty houses to make themselves beds. The lamplighters of the several wards preparing to go out and give the lamps within their rounds a trimming. The slaves who do business for nightmen [removers of ordure, etc.] preparing their teams of horses, to come into the City and follow their occupation.

Hour XXIV. From eleven till twelve o'clock on Sunday night
The high roads near this Metropolis kept free from thieves of all denominations by the perpetual ringing of the bells fastened to the ears and collars of higglers' horses, who are bringing goods to the markets. Street-robbers and house-breakers patrolling about the streets, looking sharp after the watchmen, and considering who they may knock down and rob, or what houses they may break open.

Carcass-butchers, who have been most part of the day slaughtering calves, sheep, and lambs, hanging them out at their doors in White-chapel and Cowcross, and bringing them to the markets for the ensuing day's sale. People of quality leaving off gaming, in order to go to supper.

The streets begin to swarm with whores and pickpockets. Smith-field in an uproar with drovers who are driving in oxen, sheep, lambs, and hogs, for the ensuing market. Night-houses begin to fill with whores, thieves, drunkards, foolish tradesmen, and lumberers. Abundance of 'I wish you a good night' bestowed by friends on each other, after spending the evening together. One-third of the inhabitants of London, Westminster, and Southwark fast asleep, and almost penniless. The whole body of the watch with their staves and lanthorns ready to cry the hour, 'Past twelve o'clock'.

Low Life; or, One Half of the World knows not how the Other Half Live . . .,
3rd edn (1764).

(c) WOMEN OF THE TOWN

Having gone 'round the clock' in *Low Life* we may very well have gained the impression that in eighteenth-century London 'women of the town' (a much-favoured collective term in those days for prostitutes, streetwalkers, whores, harlots, etc.) were to be found everywhere, at all hours of the day and night.

There cannot be the least doubt that this was indeed the case. Even though *Low Life* should not be accepted as altogether authoritative, the pages of *Tom Jones* and *Peregrine Pickle* and *The Beggar's Opera*, of some of Dr Johnson's essays, and the descriptions of such foreign visitors as the German J. W. von Archenholz (to say nothing of such English trippers as the Birmingham tradesman, William Hutton), afford a wealth of supporting evidence.

Even in the pages of *The Wealth of Nations* the prostitute makes her appearance – and in a very surprising context, too, at the conclusion of a paragraph on the dietary value of potatoes. 'The chairmen, porters, and coal-heavers in London, and those unfortunate women who live by prostitution' – so the sentence runs – 'the strongest men and the most beautiful women perhaps in the British dominions, are said to be, the greater part of them, from the lowest rank of people in Ireland, who are generally fed with this root.'

But it is in 'The Harlot's Progress', the first and most popular of Hogarth's series of domestic chronicles, that the London eighteenth-century whore is represented with the most true to life attention to every detail.

I

Hogarth's 'The Harlot's Progress'

(Plates 5 to 7)

This series of prints gives the history of a prostitute. The story commences with her arrival in London . . . at the Bell Inn, in Wood Street; and the heroine may possibly be the daughter to the poor old clergyman who is reading the direction of a letter close to the York waggon, from which vehicle she has just alighted. In attire [she is] neat, plain, and unadorned; in demeanour, artless, modest, diffident; [she is] in the bloom of youth, and more distinguished by native innocence than elegant symmetry; her conscious blush and downcast eyes attract the attention of a female fiend who panders to the vices of the opulent and libidinous.

Coming out of the door of the inn we discover two men, one of whom is eagerly gloating on the devoted victim. This is a portrait, and said to be a strong resemblance of Colonel Francis Chartres, whose epitaph was written by Doctor Arbuthnot: in that epitaph his character is most emphatically described. ('Here continueth to rot the body of Francis Chartres; who, with an inflexible constancy and inimitable uniformity of life, persisted in spite of age and infirmities, in the practice of every human vice, excepting prodigality and hypocrisy . . .') The attendant represents John Gourlay, the colonel's favourite and confidential pimp.

The old procuress, immediately after the girl's alighting from the waggon, addresses her with the familiarity of a friend rather than the reserve of one who is to be her mistress . . . this is the portrait of a woman infamous in her day (Mother Needham, who stood in the pillory on 5 May 1734 and was so roughly treated by the populace that she died a few days afterwards. The crime for which she suffered was, *keeping a disorderly house*).

The balcony, with the linen hanging out to dry; the York waggon, which intimates the county that gave birth to our young adventurer; parcels lying on the ground, and a goose directed 'To my lofen coosin in Tems Street in London', prove the particular attention Hogarth paid to the *minutiae*. The initials M.H. on one of the trunks give us the name of the heroine of this drama – (Margaret, or Kate) Hackabout was a character then well known, and infamous for her licentiousness and debauchery.

From the inn she is taken to the house of the procuress, divested of her homespun garb, dressed in the gayest style of the day, and the tender hue of her complexion encrusted with paint and disguised by patches. She is then introduced to Colonel Chartres, and by artful flattery and liberal promises becomes intoxicated with the dreams of imaginary greatness.

Quarrels with her Jew Protector

Entered into the path of infamy, the next scene exhibits our young heroine the mistress of a rich Jew, attended by a black boy, and surrounded with the pompous parade of tasteless profusion. Her mind being now as depraved as her person is decorated, she keeps up the spirit of her character by extravagance and inconstancy. An example of the first is exhibited in the monkey being suffered to drag her rich headdress round the room; and of the second, in the retiring gallant. The Hebrew is represented at breakfast with his mistress, but having come earlier than was expected, the favourite has not departed. To secure his retreat, is an exercise for the invention of both mistress and maid. This is accomplished by the lady finding a pretence for quarrelling with the Jew, kicking down the tea-table, and scalding his legs, which, added to the noise of the china, so far engrosses his attention, that the paramour assisted by the servant, escapes discovery.

On the toilet-table we discover a mask, which well enough indicates where the lady had passed part of the preceding night, and that masquerades, then a very fashionable amusement, were much frequented by women of this description; a sufficient reason for their being avoided by those of an opposite character.

Under the protection of this disciple of Moses she could not remain long. Riches were his only attraction, and though profusely lavished on this unworthy object, her attachment was not to be obtained, nor could her constancy be secured; repeated acts of infidelity are punished by dismission; and her next situation shows that, like most of the sisterhood, she had lived without apprehension of the sunshine of life being darkened by the passing cloud, and made no provision for the hour of adversity.

Apprehended by a Magistrate

We here see this child of misfortune fallen from her high estate! Her magnificent apartment is quitted for a dreary lodging in the purlieus of Drury Lane: she is at breakfast, and every object exhibits marks of the most wretched penury; her silver tea-kettle is exchanged for a tin-pot and her highly decorated toilet gives place to an old leaf-table, strewed with the filthy relics of her last night's revel, and ornamented with a broken looking-glass. Around the room are scattered tobacco-pipes, gin measures, and pewter pots – emblems of the habits of life into which she is initiated, and the company which she now keeps. This is further intimated by the wig-box of James Dalton, a notorious street-robber, who was afterwards executed. In her hand she displays a watch, which it is not unfair to suppose she stole from her last night's gallant. In addition to the evils of poverty, we see, by the phials and pill-boxes in the window, intimations of that common attendant upon promiscuous prostitution well enough described as 'the curse and punishment of lawless love'.

The dreary and comfortless appearance of every object in this wretched receptacle, the bit of butter on a piece of paper (this paper is a pastoral letter from Gibson Bishop of London, and intimates that the writings of grave prelates were sometimes to be found in chandlers' shops), the candle in a bottle, the basin upon a chair, the punch-bowl and comb upon the table, and the tobacco-pipes strewed upon the unswept floor, give an admirable picture of the style in which this pride of Drury Lane ate her matin meal. There is some whimsicality in placing the two ladies under a canopy, formed by the unnailed valance of the bed, and crowned by the wig-box of a highwayman.

A magistrate (Sir John Gunston, a justice of the peace very active in the suppression of brothels), cautiously entering the room with his attendant constables, commits her to a house of correction. Imagine her then, with her worthless and infamous servant, notwithstanding all her cries, promises, and entreaties, hurried through the streets to Bridewell; her shame and mortification enhanced by the shouts and jeers of an attendant populace, and there put to hard labour, in the hope that, joined with hard fare, it may produce a reformation.

Scene in Bridewell

The situation in which the last plate exhibited our wretched female was sufficiently degrading, but in this her misery is greatly aggravated. We now see her suffering the chastisement due to her follies: reduced to the wretched alternative of beating hemp or receiving the correction of a savage taskmaster. She is exposed to the derision of all around. Even her own servant, who is well acquainted with the rules of the place, appears little disposed to show any return of gratitude for recent obligations, though even her shoes, which she displays while tying up her garter, seem by their gaudy outside to have been a present from her mistress.

The civil discipline of the stern keeper has all the severity of the old school. With the true spirit of tyranny, he sentences those who will not labour to the whipping-post, to a kind of picketing suspension by the wrists, or having a heavy log fastened to their leg. With the last of

53

these punishments he at this moment threatens the heroine of our story; nor is it likely that his obduracy can be softened except by a well-applied fee.

To show that neither the dread nor the endurance of the severest punishment will deter from the perpetration of crimes, a one-eyed female, close to the keeper, is picking a pocket. The torn card may probably have been dropped by the well-dressed gamester, who has exchanged the dice-box for the mallet, and whose laced hat is hung up as a companion trophy to the hoop-petticoat.

One of the girls appears scarcely in her teens. Vice is not confined to colour, for a *black* woman is ludicrously exhibited as suffering the penalty of those frailties which are imagined peculiar to the *fair*.

The figure chalked as dangling on the wall, with a pipe in his mouth, is intended as a caricatured portrait of Sir John Gunston, and probably the production of some would-be artist whom the magistrate had committed to Bridewell. The inscription upon the pillory, 'Better to work than stand thus', and that on the whipping-post, near the laced gambler, 'The reward of idleness', are judiciously introduced.

Expires while the Doctors are Disputing
Released from Bridewell, this victim to her own indiscretion breathes her last sad sigh and expires in all the extremity of penury and wretchedness. The two quacks, whose injudicious treatment has probably accelerated her death, are vociferously supporting the infallibility of their respective medicines, and each charging the other with having poisoned her. While the maidservant is entreating them to cease quarrelling, and assist her dying mistress, the nurse plunders her trunk of the few poor remains of her former grandeur. Her little boy turning a scanty remnant of meat hung to roast by a string; the linen hanging to dry; the coals deposited in a corner; the candles, bellows, and gridiron hung upon nails; the furniture of the room, and indeed every accompaniment, exhibit a dreary display of poverty and wretchedness. Over the candles hangs a cake of Jew's bread, once perhaps the property of her Levitical lover, and now used as a fly-trap. On the floor lies a paper inscribed 'Anodyne Necklace', at that time deemed a sort of charm against the disorders incident to children, and near the fire, a tobacco-pipe and a paper of pills.

The Funeral
The adventures of our heroine are now concluded. The preparations for her funeral are as licentious as the progress of her life, and the contagion of her example seems to reach all who surround her coffin. One of them is engaged in the double trade of seduction and thievery; a second is

contemplating her own face in a mirror. The female who is gazing at the corpse displays some marks of concern; but if any other part of the company are in a degree affected, it is at best but a maudlin sorrow, kept up by glasses of strong liquor. The depraved priest does not seem likely to feel for the dead that hope expressed in our liturgy. (The woman seated next to the divine was intended for Elizabeth Adams, who, on 10 September 1737, at the age of thirty, was executed for a robbery which had been attended with circumstances that aggravated the crime.)

It must be acknowledged that there are in this plate some things which are violations of propriety and custom; such is her child, but a few removes from infancy, being habited as chief mourner, to attend his parent to the grave; rings presented, and an escutcheon hung up in a garret at the funeral of a needy prostitute. . . . The woman looking into the coffin has more beauty than we generally see in Hogarth's works. The undertaker's gloating stare, his companion's leer, the internal satisfaction of the parson and his next neighbour, are contrasted by the Irish howl of the woman at the opposite side, and evince Hogarth's thorough knowledge of the operation of the passions upon the features.

JOHN IRELAND, *Hogarth Illustrated* (1791), vol. I, pp. 1-25.

2

'The Willing Ladies'

The manner in which the two sexes approached each other in London surprised me, as being different from what I had ever observed.

Before I had been one hour there, a gentleman remarked, as two ladies were passing along, 'They were girls of the town.' I replied, You must be mistaken, they appear ladies of beauty, elegance, and modesty. I could have laughed at his ignorance. But before I had been one day, he had reason, I found, to laugh at mine.

Some of the finest women I saw in London were of this class. I conversed with many of them. They could all swear, talk indecently, and drink gin. Most of them assured me, they had not a penny in the world. I considered them as objects of pity more than of punishment; and would gladly have given a trifle to each, but found it could not be done for less than ten thousand shillings.

Of all professions, this seems the most deplorable, and the most industriously pursued. That diligence is exercised to starve in this, which would enable them to live in another.

Many causes tend to furnish the streets of London with evening game; as, being destitute of protection in early years; being trepanned by the artful of our sex, or the more artful of their own; accidental distress, without prospect of relief; disappointment of places, or of love. But the principal cause is idleness. To the generality of the world, ease is preferable to labour. Perhaps it is difficult to produce an instance of a girl, of an industrious turn, going upon the town. It is seldom an act of choice, but of necessity. Inclination seems no part of the excitement. This is much the same as in the rest of women. It is not the man they want, but the money. They suffer what they do not relish, to procure the bread they do. In the connections between the sexes, the heart is not of the party. Their language, like that of the leech, is *give*; and like it, they squander their profits and become lean. Their price is various, but always a little more than they can get.

Various degrees of prudence may easily be seen, even among these fallen beauties, by their dress and their manners. But in this profession, produce does not increase with age; for I could observe, the dress and the wearer grew old together.

Some are elegantly attired, others extremely showy with trifles, and the use of spirits had burnt holes in the apparel of numbers, which are never repaired by the needle, or a flourishing trade.

A genteel figure, and one of the handsomest women I had even seen, approached me; a few insignificant remarks opened a conversation, as is customary with those who have nothing to say, but who understand intentions better than words.

And pray, Madam, what could you do with an old fellow?

'O, my dear Sir, I love an old man better than a young one.'

Provided he is better furnished in the – pocket. And so you take anything in your arms, if you can but take the cash in your fingers.

'It is a cold night, and I wish to take you.'

But I have no *fire* about me.

'Let me lead you, Sir, to my apartments.'

Perhaps I shall find one there; or rather, like the Israelites, be led by a pillar of fire.

'Let me drink your health, Sir.'

Perhaps you are able to destroy health without drinking.

'Do, Sir, favour me with a glass.'

I have not one drop of spirits, or they should be much at your service.

'But you have *that* which will purchase them.'

And *that* I will give you with pleasure.

'Shall I see you again?'

If you take a journey to Birmingham.

* * *

'Let me go with you, Sir', says a smart young lass, as she laid hold of my arm.

If you please, Madam, and welcome; but really I do not know myself where I am going. I am like some others in this city, only a street-walker.

'I will do anything to oblige you, sir.'

You are extremely civil, Madam.

'I will strip myself, if you chuse.'

Perhaps you will strip me.

'Indeed, Sir, I shall be upon honour.'

I did not know, Madam, that that word was written upon your bed.

'O you joker. Please to give me something to drink your health.'

Take that then, and I wish it may preserve your's. A curtesy divided us for ever.

w. HUTTON, *A Journey from Birmingham to London* (1785), pp. 73–82.

3

'Fifty Thousand Prostitutes'

London is said to contain 50,000 prostitutes, without reckoning kept mistresses. The most wretched of these live with *matrons*, who lodge, board, and clothe them. The dress worn by the very lowest of them is silk, according to the custom which luxury has generally introduced into England. Sometimes they escape from their prison, with their little wardrobes under their arms, and trade on their *own bottoms*, when, if they are unfortunate or happen not to be economical, they are soon dragged to gaol by their creditors.

The uncertainty of receiving payment makes the housekeepers charge them double the common price for their lodgings. They hire by the week a first floor, and pay for it more than the owner gives for the whole premises, taxes included. They are so much their own mistresses that if a justice of the peace attempted to trouble them in their apartments they might turn him out of doors, for as they pay the same taxes as the other parishioners they are consequently entitled to the same privileges.

Their apartments are elegantly, and sometimes magnificently furnished; they keep several servants, and some have their own carriages. Many of them have annuities paid them by their seducers, and others settlements into which they have surprised their lovers in the moment of intoxication. The testimony of these women, even of the lowest of them, is always received as evidence in the courts of justice . . .

Besides the immense number of women who live in ready-furnished apartments, there are many noted houses in the neighbourhood of St James's where a great number are kept for people of fashion . . .

There is also in London a species of houses called Bagnios. These do not keep women, but they are instantly brought in chairs; and only those who are celebrated for their fashion, their elegance and their charms have the honour of being admitted. This kind of entertainment is very expensive, and yet sometimes the bagnios are full all night long. For the most part, they are situated within a few paces of the theatres, and are surrounded by taverns.

A tavern-keeper in Drury Lane prints every year an account of the women of the town entitled *Harris's List of Covent-Garden Ladies*. In it the most exact description is given of their names, their lodgings, their faces, their manners, their talents, and even their tricks. It must of course happen that there will be sometimes a little degree of partiality in these details; however, notwithstanding this, 8,000 copies are sold annually . . .

The higher classes of these females are uncommonly honest; you may entrust them with a purse crammed with gold, without running any risk whatever. They can never be prevailed upon to grant favours to the lover of one of their companions, even if they are sure that the circumstances will be kept a profound secret. During the elections for members of Parliament it is not unusual to see these ladies refuse to barter their favours for large sums of money, and reserve their charms for the purchase of votes in favour of certain patriots whom they esteem.

Let it be recollected, however, that I speak only of a few, for it is very uncommon to find such precious qualities among those vile prostitutes whose kind of life stifles in their breasts every seed of virtue. At all seasons of the year they sally out towards the dusk, arrayed in the most gaudy colours, and fill the principal streets. They accost the passengers and offer to accompany them; they even surround them in crowds, stop and overwhelm them with caresses and entreaties. The better kind, however, content themselves with walking about till they themselves are addressed . . .

I have beheld with a surprise mingled with terror, girls from eight to nine years old make a proffer of their charms; and such is the corruption of the human heart, that even they have their lovers . . .

J. W. VON ARCHENHOLZ, *A Picture of England* (1789), vol. 2, pp. 89–102.

4

Dr Johnson's Pity

These forlorn creatures, the women of the town, were once, if not virtuous, at least innocent; and might still have continued blameless and easy, but for the arts and insinuations of those whose rank, fortune, or education, furnished them with means to corrupt or to delude them. Let the libertine reflect a moment on the situation of that woman, who, being forsaken by her betrayer, is reduced to the necessity of turning prostitute for bread, and judge of the enormity of his guilt by the evils which it produces.

It cannot be doubted but that numbers follow this dreadful course of life, with shame, horror, and regret; but where can they hope for refuge? Their sighs, and tears, and groans, are criminal in the eye of their tyrants, the bully and the bawd, who fatten on their misery, and threaten them with want or a gaol, if they show the least design of escaping from their bondage. . . . There are places, indeed, set apart, to which these unhappy creatures may resort, when the diseases of incontinence seize upon them; but if they obtain a cure, to what are they reduced? Either to return with the small remnants of their beauty to their former guilt, or perish in the streets with nakedness and hunger.

How frequently have the gay and thoughtless, in their evening frolics, seen a band of these miserable females, covered with rags, shivering with cold, and pining with hunger; and without either pitying their calamities, or reflecting upon the cruelty of those who perhaps first seduced them by caresses of fondness, or magnificence of promises, go on to reduce others to the same wretchedness by the same means?

DR S. JOHNSON, *The Rambler*, no. 107, 26 March 1751.

(d) THE FATAL PASSION FOR DRINK

Whatever may have been their habits in earlier times, it was in the reign of the first Elizabeth that Englishmen first gained the reputation of being (as Iago puts it in *Othello*) 'most potent in potting'. As the years passed, they certainly lived up to it. Even under Cromwell, a writer could refer to England as the dizzy island, and its inhabitants as being steeped in liquors, drinking as though they were sponges or had tunnels in their mouths. As might be expected the permissive atmosphere of the Restoration period encouraged hard drinking, particularly when toast-giving came into vogue, and even after the introduction of coffee-drinking had begun to exercise some countervailing influence. Then after the revolution of 1689 successive governments, out of jealousy of the French, imposed duties on foreign wines and spirits, and encouraged the production of home-produced spirits, beer and ale, with consequent advantage to the growers of wheat and barley.

At the beginning of the eighteenth century, the great mass of the people were beer-drinkers, but there was a growing taste for gin which from about 1724 became an absolute mania. 'Small as is the place which this fact occupies in English history', wrote the historian W. E. H. Lecky, 'it was probably, if we consider all the consequences that have flowed from it, the most momentous in that of the eighteenth century – incomparably more so than any event in the purely political or military annals of the country. The fatal passion for drink was at once, and irrevocably, planted in the nation.'

Drunkenness was something that all classes had learnt to live with and indeed to indulge in, but there was something about the orgy of spirit drinking that appalled all those who had any concern for the health and welfare of the people. The attitude of these men of good will is powerfully expressed in Henry Fielding's *Inquiry into the Causes of the late Increase of Robbers*, that the great novelist wrote out of his experiences as a magistrate at Bow Street police court. As will be seen, he recognised the existence of a 'new kind of drunkenness'.

The governing classes took alarm, and in 1736 and 1743 acts of parliament were passed, with a view to restricting the distilling and the retailing of gin, which had both been practically uncontrolled. Riots stimulated by the vested interests in the gin trade prevented any real improvement, and Hogarth's 'Gin Lane', published in 1751, depicts the horror at its height. In that same year, however, the efforts of Fielding, Hogarth, and other shamers of the public conscience had a considerable measure of success, when Henry Pelham's government passed an act restricting the activities of both distillers and gin-retailers. Even so, however, the pages of *Low Life* show that 'Geneva shops' still managed to do a large trade, within or without the law.

Henry Fielding's grim warning is given below, followed by John Ireland's descriptive pieces on Hogarth's prints, 'Beer Street' and 'Gin Lane', which are reproduced in our Plates 14 and 15.

I

'A New Kind of Drunkenness'

A new kind of drunkenness, unknown to our ancestors, is lately sprung up amongst us, and which, if not put a stop to, will infallibly destroy a great part of the inferior people. The drunkenness I here intend is that acquired by the strongest intoxicating liquors, and particularly by that poison called *Gin*; which I have great reason to think is the principal sustenance (if it may be so called) of more than a hundred thousand people in this metropolis. Many of these wretches there are who swallow pints of this poison within the twenty-four hours; the dreadful effects of which I have the misfortune every day to see, and to smell too. But I have no need to insist on my own credit, or on that of my informers; the great revenue arising from the tax on this liquor (the consumption of which is almost wholly confined to the lowest order of people) will prove the quantity consumed better than any other evidence.

Now, besides the moral consequences occasioned by this drunkenness, with which, in this treatise, I profess not to deal; how greatly must this be supposed to contribute to those political mischiefs which this essay proposes to remedy? This will appear from considering, that however cheap this vile potion may be, the poorer sort will not easily be able to supply themselves with the quantities they desire; for the intoxicating draught itself disqualifies them from using any honest means to acquire it, at the same time that it removes all sense of fear and shame, and emboldens them to commit every wicked and desperate enterprise. Many instances of this I see daily; wretches are often brought before me, charged with theft and robbery, whom I am forced to confine before they are in a condition to be examined; and when they have afterwards become sober, I have plainly perceived, from the state of the case, that the *Gin* alone was the cause of the transgression, and have been sometimes sorry that I was obliged to commit them to prison.

But beyond all this ... is that dreadful consequence which must attend the poisonous quality of this pernicious liquor to the health, the strength, and the very being of numbers of his majesty's most useful subjects. ... And though, perhaps, the consequence of this poison, as it operates slowly, may not so visibly appear in the diminution of the strength, health, and lives of the present generation; yet let a man cast his eyes but a moment towards our posterity, and there the dreadful consequences must strike on the meanest capacity, and must alarm, I think, the most sluggish degree of public spirit.

What must become of the infant who is conceived in Gin? With the poisonous distillations of which it is nourished both in the womb and at the breast. Are these wretched infants (if such can be supposed, capable of arriving at the age of maturity) to become our future sailors, and our future grenadiers? Is it by the labour of such as these that all the emoluments of peace are to be procured us, and all the dangers of war averted from us? Doth not this polluted source, instead of producing servants for the husbandman or artificer, instead of providing recruits for the sea or the field, promise only to fill almshouses and hospitals, and to infect the streets with stench and diseases?

HENRY FIELDING, *An Inquiry into the Causes of the late Increase of Robbers, etc.,* sec. II (1751).

2

Beer Street

(*Plate 14*)

This admirable delineation is a picture of John Bull in his most happy moments. ... The neighbourhood is St Martin's Lane. In the left corner, a butcher and a blacksmith are each of them grasping a foaming tankard of porter. By the *King's Speech* and the *Daily Advertiser* on the table before them, they appear to have been studying politics, and settling the state of the nation.

The blacksmith, having just purchased a shoulder of mutton, is triumphantly waving it in the air. Next to him, a drayman is whispering soft sentences of love to a servant-maid, round whose neck is one of his arms; in the other hand a pot of porter. Two fishermen, furnished with a flagon of the same liquor, are chanting a song of Mr Lockman's on the British Herring Fishery. A porter, having put a load of waste paper on the ground is eagerly quaffing this best of barley wine.

On the front of a house in ruins is inscribed, 'Pinch, Pawnbroker'; and through a hole in the door a boy delivers a full half-pint. In the background are two children. They have joined for three-pennyworth to recruit their spirits and repair the fatigue they have undergone in trotting between two poles, with a ponderous load of female frailty.

Two paviors are washing away their cares with a heart-cheering cup. In a garret window, a trio of sailors are employed in the same way; and on a house-top are four bricklayers, equally joyous.

Each of these groups seem hale, happy, and well-clothed; but the artist, who is painting a glass bottle from an original which hangs before him, is in a truly deplorable plight; at the same time that he carries in his countenance a perfect consciousness of his talents in this creative art.

JOHN IRELAND, *Hogarth Illustrated*, vol. 2, pp. 330–2.

3

Gin Lane

(*Plate 15*)

From contemplating the health, happiness, and mirth flowing from a moderate use of a wholesome and natural beverage, we turn to this nauseous contrast, which displays human nature in its most degraded and disgusting state.

Upon the steps sits a retailer of gin and ballads, with a bottle in one hand and a glass in the other. Having bartered away his waistcoat, shirt, and stockings, and drank until he is in a state of total insensibility, he is a perfect skeleton. A few steps higher a thoroughly intoxicated woman is taking snuff, and so negligent of the infant at her breast that it falls over the rail into an area, and dies. Another of the fair sex (*far left*) has drank herself to sleep; as an emblem of her slothful disposition a snail is crawling from the wall to her arm. Close to her we discover one of the lords of creation gnawing a bare bone, which an equally ravenous bull-dog endeavours to snatch from his mouth.

A working carpenter is depositing his coat and saw with a pawnbroker, and a tattered female offers at the same shrine her culinary utensils, among them a tea-kettle – pawned to procure money to purchase gin. An old woman, having drank until she is unable to walk, is put into a wheelbarrow, and in that situation is solaced with another glass. With the same poisonous and destructive compound, a mother in the corner (*right*) drenches her child. Near her are two Charity-girls of St Giles's, pledging each other in the same corroding compound. The scene is completed by a quarrel between two drunken cripples; while one of them uses his crutch as a quarter-staff, the other aims a stool at the head of his adversary.

This, with a crowd waiting for their drams at a distiller's door, completes the catalogue of the quick living. Of the dead, there are two, besides an unfortunte child whom a drunken madman has impaled on a spit. One, a barber, who having probably drank gin until he has lost his reason, has suspended himself by a rope in his own ruinous garret; the other, a beautiful woman, whom, by the direction of the parish beadle, two men are depositing in a coffin. From her wasted and emaciated appearance, we may fairly infer, she also fell a martyr to this destructive and poisonous liquid. On the side of her coffin is a child lamenting the loss of its parent.

The large pewter measure hung over a cellar (*bottom left*), on which is engraved 'Gin Royal', was once a common sign. The inscription on this cave of despair, 'Drunk for a penny – dead drunk for twopence – clean straw for nothing' is worthy of observation; it exhibits the state of our metropolis at that period.

The scene of this horrible devastation is laid in a place which was properly enough called the Ruins of St Giles's. Except the pawnbroker's, the distiller's, and the undertaker's, the houses are literally ruins; but these doorkeepers to Famine, Disease, and Death, living by the calamities of others, are in a flourishing state.

JOHN IRELAND, *Hogarth Illustrated*, vol. 2, pp. 333–6.

CHAPTER 3

ENGLISH TRADESMEN

(a) 'A NATION OF SHOPKEEPERS'

Who was it that first called the English 'a nation of shopkeepers'? Napoleon's may be the first name to suggest itself: he is said to have used it in conversation on St Helena. But many years earlier it had appeared in *The Wealth of Nations*, a book which the Emperor is believed to have had on his shelves.

The passage in which it occurs forms part of Adam Smith's sustained argument against the commercial policy adopted by the government of his day, which was inspired by the concept that the British colonies in the West Indies and North America constituted a kind of private estate to be maintained and developed for the sole benefit of British merchants and manufacturers. 'To found a great empire for the sole purpose of raising up a people of customers [it runs], may at first sight appear a project fit only for a nation of shopkeepers. It is, however, a project altogether unfit for a nation of shopkeepers; but extremely fit for a nation whose government is influenced by shopkeepers.'

The use of 'shopkeepers' in this connection is peculiar: clearly Adam Smith had some other people in mind beyond the butcher and baker and candlestick-maker – the people whom he refers to as merchants and manufacturers or as tradesmen, the business community in general. Economically speaking, these might be considered the backbone of the country; and yet, extraordinary to relate, Smith's attitude towards them is one of intense suspicion, a dislike of almost pathologic intensity.

Scattered through the pages of *The Wealth of Nations* are the most scathing reflections on their character and conduct. Thus he writes of the 'mean rapacity, the monopolising spirit, of merchants and manu-facturers', and of the 'clamour and sophistry' they exhibit when maintaining that *their* interest is the interest of the whole people. He stigmatises them as 'an order of men who have generally an interest to deceive and even to oppress the public', and alleges that 'people of the same trade seldom meet together even for merriment and diversion, but the conversation ends in a conspiracy against the public'. Towards the end of a paragraph in which he remarks that 'a gentleman drunk with ale has scarce ever been seen among us', he describes the plea that we should buy port in preference to Spanish sherry, because the Portuguese are the better customers, as one of 'the sneaking arts of underling tradesmen'.

Almost one might suppose that this is some forerunner of Karl Marx, denouncing the iniquities of the bourgeoisie. Nothing of the kind, however. His contempt for the businessman was at least equalled by that he had for 'that insidious and crafty animal, vulgarly called a statesman or politician'. From beginning to end and all the time, his political economy is definitely capitalistic; and notwithstanding his gibes and sneers, he had not the least hesitation in recognising in the common run of merchants and manufacturers the agents and instruments of Divine Providence.

All the same, in seeking to discover what sort of man the tradesman was, we shall be well advised to look elsewhere.

In eighteenth-century England traders of one kind and another formed an important and rapidly growing section of the community, and it is a matter for congratulation that we know so much about them. This is mainly through the writings of Daniel Defoe, and in particular his *Complete English Tradesman*, of which the first edition was published in 1726.

Defoe knew what he was writing about: he was a tradesman born and bred and for a number of years a practising one. Born in London in 1660 he was the son of a butcher who had a shop in St Giles's, Cripplegate, and on Sundays was a regular attendant at a Nonconformist place of worship; the Nonconformists, or Dissenters, it should be noted, were in those days the backbone of the trading interest, since so many other avenues of profitable employment were closed to them. As a youth Daniel went into business as a dealer in hosiery, but after some years went bankrupt. Later he was manager of a tile-factory at Tilbury, in Essex, but this, too, was a failure. He had many other jobs, but before the close of the century he had revealed a marked gift for popular pamphleteering, and until his death in 1731 he was constantly engaged in journalistic activity.

In Queen Anne's reign he travelled far and wide in England and Scotland, partly as some sort of commercial traveller but also as an agent of the government in finding out what people were thinking and doing. The fruits of this incessant journeying were embodied in his *Tour thro' the Whole Island of Great Britain* (1724–6), a guide-book packed with factual information such as travellers on business were most in need of. By this time he was famous as the author of *Robinson Crusoe, Moll Flanders*, and other works of factually-based fiction, besides pamphlets beyond counting on a great variety of topics.

Much of his immense literary output is concerned with matters of business, in particular the book above mentioned, of which the full title runs: *The Complete English Tradesman, in Familiar Letters directing*

him in all the several Parts and Progressions of Trade. Circulated for the
Instruction of our Inland Tradesmen, and especially of Young Beginners.

This book has had its critics, who have commented sourly on Defoe's worldly-wise attitude, his businessman's morality, his rather sly piety; but all the same, it contains a deal of sound practical guidance and good sense, and the 'young beginners' at least can have found little to complain about. More than a hundred years after its publication, it was considered still sufficiently up to date to be issued in a new edition.

I

'On the Dignity of Trade in England'

Our tradesmen are not, as in other countries, the meanest of our people. Some of the greatest and best and most flourishing families, among not the gentry only but even the nobility, have been raised from trade, owe their beginning, their wealth, and their estates to trade; and I may add, those families are not at all ashamed of their original, and, indeed, have no occasion to be ashamed of it.

As to the wealth of the nation, that undoubtedly lies chiefly among the trading part of the people. How ordinary it is to see a tradesman go off the stage, even but from mere shopkeeping, with from ten to forty thousand pounds' estate to divide among his family! How many noble seats, superior to the palaces of sovereign princes in some countries, do we see erected within a few miles of this city by tradesmen, or the sons of tradesmen! In how superior a port or figure do our tradesmen live, to what the middling gentry either do or can support! No wonder that the gentlemen of the best families marry tradesmen's daughters, and put their younger sons apprentices to tradesmen! In short, trade in England makes gentlemen.

As our soldiers by the late war [under the Duke of Marlborough] gained the reputation of being some of the best troops in the world, and our seamen are, and very justly so, esteemed the best sailors in the world, so the English tradesman may in a few years be allowed to rank with the best gentlemen in Europe.

DANIEL DEFOE, *Complete English Tradesman* (1726: reprint of 1838), pp. 73–5.

2

'Tradesmen' Defined

In the north of Britain and likewise in Ireland, when you say a tradesman you are understood to mean a mechanic, such as a smith, a carpenter, a shoemaker, and the like.

But in England, and especially in London and the south part of
Britain, shopkeepers, whether wholesalers or retailers of goods, are
called tradesmen; such are our grocers, mercers, linen and woollen
drapers, tobacconists, haberdashers (whether of hats or small wares),
glovers, hosiers, milliners, booksellers, stationers, and all other shopkeepers who do not actually work upon, make or manufacture the goods
they sell. On the other hand, those who make the goods they sell,
though they do keep shops to sell them, are not called tradesmen but
handicraftsmen, such as smiths, shoemakers, founders, joiners, carpenters, carvers, turners, and the like. Others who only make, or cause
to be made, goods for other people to sell, are called manufacturers.

As there are several degrees of people employed in trade below these,
such as workmen, labourers, and servants, so there is a degree of
traders above them, whom we call merchants; where it is needful to
observe, that in other countries, and even in the north of Britain and
Ireland, the shopkeepers are called merchants. But in England the
word merchant is understood of none but such as carry on foreign
correspondences, importing the goods and growth of other countries
and exporting the growth and manufactures of England to other
countries or, to use a vulgar expression, because I am speaking to and
of those that use that expression, such as trade beyond sea. In England
these, and these only, are called merchants.

DANIEL DEFOE, *Complete English Tradesman*, p. 6.

3

Business Morality

There is some difference between an honest man and an honest tradesman. There are some latitudes which a tradesman is and must be

allowed, and which by the custom and usage of trade he may give himself a liberty in; and whatever some pretenders to strict living may say, yet that tradesman shall pass with me for a very honest man notwithstanding. Those liberties are such as these.

1. The liberty of asking more than he will take. I know some people have condemned this practice as dishonest, and the Quakers for a time stood to their point in the contrary practice; but time and the necessities of trade made them wiser, and they by degrees came to ask, and abate, and abate again, just as other honest tradesmen do.

Indeed, it is the buyers that make this custom necessary; for they, and especially those who buy for immediate use, will first pretend positively to tie themselves up to a limited price, and bid them a little and a little more, till they come so near the sellers' price, that they, the sellers, cannot find it in their hearts to refuse it, notwithstanding their first words to the contrary.

2. Another trading licence is that of appointing and promising payments of money, which men in business are oftentimes forced to make and forced to break, without any scruple; nay, and without any reproach upon their integrity.

Custom indeed has driven us beyond the limits of our morals in many things which trade makes necessary; so that if our yea must be yea and our nay nay; if no man must go beyond or defraud his neighbour; if our conversation must be without covetousness and the like – why, then, it is impossible for tradesmen to be Christians, and we must shut up shop and leave off trade, and in many things must leave off living.

Complete English Tradesman, pp. 55–7.

4

Shopping List of a Country Grocer

All our manufactures are so useful to and depend on one another so much in trade, that the sale of one necessarily causes the demand of the other in all parts. For example, suppose a middling tradesman is going to live in some market-town and to open his shop there; suppose him to deal in groceries and such sort of ware as country grocers sell. Suppose he lives in Sussex, where very few, if any, manufactures are carried on . . . in Horsham, which is a market-town in or near the middle of the county.

For his clothing of himself – for we must allow him to have a new suit of clothes when he begins the world – the cloth comes out of Wiltshire, and his stockings, of worsted, from Nottingham. Come we next to his wife; and she, being a good honest townsman's daughter, is not dressed over fine, yet she must have something decent, being newly married too, and especially, as times go, when the burghers' wives of Horsham, or any other town, go as fine as they do in other places: allow her, then, to have a silk gown, with all the necessaries belonging to a middling tolerable appearance, and yet nothing at all extravagant. For example:

Her gown, a plain English mantua-silk, manufactured in Spitalfields. Her petticoat the same. Her binding, a piece of chequered stuff, made at Bristol and Norwich. Her under-petticoat, a piece of black calla-manco, made at Norwich – quilted at home if she be a good housewife, but the quilting of cotton from Manchester, or cotton-wool from abroad. Her inner-petticoats, flannel and swanskin, from Salisbury and Wales. Her stockings from Tewkesbury, if ordinary – from Leicester if woven. Her lace and edgings from Stony Stratford the first and Great Marlow the last. Her muslin from foreign trade; likewise her linen, being somewhat finer than the man's. Her wrapper, or morning-gown, a piece of Irish linen, printed at London. Her black hood, a thin English lustring [glossy silk cloth]. Her gloves, lamb's skin, from Berwick and Northumberland, or Scotland. Her ribands, being but very few, from Coventry or London. Her riding-hood of English worsted, made at Norwich.

Come next to the furniture of their house. The hangings are made at Kidderminster, dyed in the country and painted or watered at London. The chairs if of cane are made at London; the ordinary matted chairs, perhaps in the place where they live. Tables, chests of drawers, etc., are made at London; as also, looking-glass. Bedding: the curtains from Taunton and Exeter, or from Norwich; the ticking and feathers from the west country; the blankets from Witney in Oxfordshire; the sheets, of good linen, from Ireland. The rugs from Westmorland and Yorkshire. Kitchen utensils and chimney furniture: almost all the brass and iron from Birmingham and Sheffield, earthenware from Stafford, Nottingham, and Kent. Glass ware from Sturbridge in Worcestershire, and London.

As what is thus wanted is but in small quantities, there are shop-keepers in every village, or at least in every considerable market-town, who do not send to where the goods are made but correspond with wholesale dealers in London, who not only furnish them with great quantities of goods but give them large credits; and at these shops the people who want them are easily supplied.

Complete English Tradesman, pp. 78–9.

5

'Hundreds of Thousands' of Shopkeepers

I have endeavoured to make some calculation of the number of shop-keepers in this kingdom, but I find it is not to be done – we may as well count the stars; not that they are equal in number neither, but it is impossible, unless any one person corresponded so as to have them numbered in every town or parish throughout the kingdom.

I doubt not they are some hundreds of thousands, but there is no making an estimate – the number is in a manner infinite.

Complete English Tradesman, p. 78.

6

Getting the Goods to Market

The carriage of goods in England is chiefly managed by horses and waggons, the number of which is not to be guessed at ...

It is true, our coasting trade is exceedingly great and employs a prodigious number of ships, as well as from all the shores of England to London as from one part to another. But as to our river navigation, we have but a very few navigable rivers compared with those of other countries, nor are many of them navigable to any considerable length from the sea; as, the northern Ouse but to York, the Orwell but to Ipswich, the Yare but to Norwich, the Tyne not above twelve miles above Newcastle, the Tweed not at all above Berwick, the Great Avon but to Bristol, the Exe but to Exeter, and the Dee but to Chester.

In a word, our river-navigation is not to be named for carriage with the vast bulk of carriage by pack-horses and by waggons; nor must the carriage by pedlars on their backs be omitted.

This carriage is the medium of our inland trade. For example: the Taunton and Exeter serges come chiefly by land; the clothing, such as the broadcloth and drugget from Wilts, Gloucester, Worcester, and Shropshire, comes all by land-carriage to London, and goes down again by land-carriage to all parts of England; the Yorkshire clothing trade, the Manchester and Coventry trades, all by land, not to London only but to all parts of England by horse-packs – the Manchester men being, saving their wealth, a kind of pedlars, who carry their goods themselves to the country shopkeepers everywhere, as do now the Yorkshire and Coventry manufacturers also.

Complete English Tradesman, pp. 77–8.

I

Choose the Right Place for Your Shop

Some tradesmen, especially retailers, ruin themselves by fixing their shops in such places as are improper for their business. . . . Many trades, particularly in the city of London, have their peculiar streets and proper places for the sale of their goods, where people expect to find such shops, and consequently when they want such goods, go thither for them: as the booksellers in St Paul's Churchyard, about the Exchange, Temple, and the Strand; the mercers on both sides Ludgate, in Gracechurch and Lombard streets; the shoemakers in St Martin's le Grand, and Shoemaker Row; the coachmakers in Long-Acre, Queen Street, and Bishopsgate; butchers in Eastcheap, and such like.

For a tradesman to open his shop in a place unresorted to, or where his trade is not agreeable, and where it is not expected, it is no wonder if he has no trade. Pray, what would a bookseller make of his business at Billingsgate, or a mercer in Tower Street or near the Custom House, or a draper in Thames Street? What retail trade would a milliner have among the fishmongers' shops on Fishstreet-Hill . . . ?

When a shop is ill chosen, the tradesman starves; he is out of the way, and business will not follow him that runs away from it . . .

Complete English Tradesman, pp. 23–4.

2

Fitting Out the Shop

It is a modern custom to have tradesmen lay out two-thirds of their fortune in fitting up their shops. . . . I mean, in painting and gilding, in fine shelves, shutters, pediments, columns, and the like . . .

It will hardly be believed, that in 1710 (let the year be recorded) the fitting up of a pastry-cook's shop should cost upwards of £300. That this was the case I have good authority for. It consisted of the following particulars: Sash windows, all of looking-glass plates, twelve inches by sixteen. All the walls lined with tiles, and the back shop with tiles in panels painted in forest-work and figures. Two large pier looking-glasses, one chimney-glass in the shop, and one very large, seven feet high, in the back shop. Two large branches of candlesticks, one in the shop and one in the back room. Three great glass lanterns in the shop, and eight small ones. Twenty-five sconces against the wall, with a large pair of silver candlesticks in the back room. Six fine large silver salvers to serve sweetmeats. Twelve large high stands of rings to place small dishes for tarts, jellies, etc. Painting the ceiling and gilding the lanterns, the sashes, and the carved work.

These, with some odd things to set forth the shop and make a show, besides small plate, china basins and cups, amounted to above £300. Add to this the more necessary part, which was: Building two ovens, about £25, and £20 in stock for pies and cheesecakes. So that, in short, here was a trade which might be carried on for about thirty or forty pounds' stock, required three hundred pounds to fit up the shop and make a show to invite customers.

Complete English Tradesman, pp. 62–3.

3

Mind Your Own Business!

Nothing can give a greater prospect of thriving to a young tradesman than his own diligence; let the man have the most perfect knowledge of his trade, and the best situation for his shop, yet without application nothing will go on. Hark how the people talk of such conduct as the slothful negligent trader discovers in his way.

'Such a shop', says the customer, 'stands well, and there is a good stock of goods in it, but there is nobody to serve but a 'prentice-boy or two and an idle journeyman; one finds them always at play together, rather than looking out for customers; and when you come to buy, they look as if they did not care whether they showed you anything or no. One never sees a master in the shop, if we go twenty times, nor anything that bears the face of authority.

'Then, it is a shop always exposed, it is perfectly haunted with thieves and shop-lifters; they never see anybody but raw boys in it, that mind nothing, and the diligent devils never fail to haunt them, so that there are more outcries of "Stop thief!" at their door, and more constables fetched to that shop, than to all the shops in the row.

'There was a brave trade at that shop in Mr ——'s time; he was a true shopkeeper; you never missed him from seven in the morning till twelve, and from two till nine at night, and he throve accordingly – he left a good estate behind him.

'But I don't know what these people are; they say there are two partners of them, but there had as good be none, for they are never at home, nor in their shop. One wears a long wig and a sword, I hear, and you see him often in the Mall and at court, but very seldom in his shop or waiting on his customers; and the other, they say, lies a-bed till eleven o'clock every day; just comes into the shop and shows himself, then stalks about to the tavern to take a whet, then to Child's coffee-house to hear the news; comes home to dinner at one, takes a long sleep in his chair after it, and about four o'clock comes into the shop for half an hour or thereabouts; then to the tavern, where he stays till two in the morning, gets drunk, and is led home by the watch, and so lies till eleven again. ... And what will it all come to? They'll certainly break [go bankrupt]; they can't hold it long.'

Complete English Tradesman, p. 16.

4

'No Flesh and Blood' Behind the Counter

A tradesman behind his counter must have no flesh and blood about him, no passions, no resentment; he must never be angry – no, not so much as to seem to be so.

If a customer tumbles five hundred pounds' worth of goods and scarce bids money for anything – nay, though they really come to his shop with no intent to buy, only to see what is to be sold ... it is all one; the tradesman must take it, and must answer as obligingly to those that give him an hour or two's trouble and buy nothing, as he does to those who in half the time pay out ten or twenty pounds. The case is plain. It is his business to get money, to sell and please; and if some do give him trouble and do not buy, others make him amends and do buy.

Let it be easy or hard, it must be done, and it is done. There are men who have, by custom and usage, brought themselves to it. Nothing could be meeker and milder than when they are behind the counter, and yet nothing more furious and raging in every other part of life. Nay, the provocations they have met with in their shops have so irritated their rage that they would go upstairs from their shop and fall into frenzies and beat their heads against the wall.

Nay, I heard once of a shopkeeper that when he was provoked by the impertinence of his customers, beyond what his temper could bear, he would go upstairs and beat his wife and kick his children like dogs, and be as furious for two or three minutes as a man chained down in Bedlam. When the fit was over he would sit down and cry faster than the children he had abused; and would go down into his shop again and be as humble, as courteous, and as calm as any man whatever.

Complete English Tradesman, pp. 24–7.

5

A Tradesman's Pleasures

I know nothing is more frequent than for a tradesman, when company invites or an excursion from business presses, to say, 'Well, come, I have nothing to do; there is no business to hinder, there's nothing neglected, I have no letters to write', and the like; and away he goes to take the air for the afternoon, or to sit and enjoy himself with a friend – all of them things innocent and lawful in themselves; but here is the crisis of a tradesman's prosperity. In that very moment business presents, a valuable customer comes to buy, an unexpected bargain offers to be sold; another calls to pay money, and the like . . .

The tradesman's pleasure should be in his business; his companions should be his books; and if he has a family, he makes his excursions upstairs, and no farther; when he is there, a bell or a call brings him down; and while he is in his parlour, his shop or warehouse never misses him, his customers never go away unserved, his letters never come in and are unanswered.

None of my cautions aim at restraining a tradesman from diverting himself, as we call it, with his fireside, or keeping company with his wife and children. That tradesman who does not delight in his family will never delight long in his business; for as one great end of an honest tradesman's diligence is the support of his family, so the very sight of, and above all, his tender and affectionate care for his wife and children is the spur of his diligence; that is, it puts an edge upon his mind, and makes him hunt the world for business as hounds hunt the woods for their game.

Complete English Tradesman, p. 33.

6

'Can You Pay the Charges?'

When a young tradesman in Holland or Germany goes a-courting, I am told, the first question the young woman asks of him, or perhaps her friends for her, is, 'Are you able to pay the charges?', that is to say, in English, 'Are you able to keep a wife when you have got her?' The question would be but a gross way of receiving a lover here, according to our English good breeding, but there is a great deal of reason in the inquiry, that must be confessed.

When a tradesman marries, there are necessary expenses. First, furnishing the house; and let this be done with the utmost plainness, so as to be decent, yet it calls for ready money, and that ready money by so much diminishes his stock in trade. Secondly, servants. If the man was frugal before, it may be he shifted with a shop and a servant in it, an apprentice or a journeyman, and so his expenses went on small and easy. But when he brings home a wife, besides the furnishing of his house, he must have a formal house-keeping, even at the very first; and as children come on, more servants, that is maids or nurses, that are as necessary as the bread he eats – especially if he multiplies apace, as he ought to – in this case let the wife be frugal and managing, let her be unexceptionable in her expense, yet the man finds his charge mount high, and perhaps too high for his gettings, notwithstanding the additional stock obtained by her portion [dowry]. It is a little hard to say it, but it is very true, there is many a young tradesman ruined by marrying a good wife, before they had inquired whether, as above, they could pay the charges . . .

Complete English Tradesman, pp. 35–6.

7

A Dialogue between a Tradesman and his Wife

A tradesman was very melancholy for two or three days, and his wife, with all her arts, entreaties, anger, and tears, could not get it out of him; only now and then she heard him fetch a deep sigh, and at another time say, he wished he was dead, and the like expressions. At last, she began the discourse with him in a respectful, obliging manner, but with the utmost importunity, thus:

Wife My dear, what is the matter with you?

Husband Nothing.

Wife Nay, don't put me off with an answer that signifies nothing, for I am sure something extraordinary is the case – tell me, I say, tell me. (*Then she kisses him.*)

Husband I tell you nothing is the matter – what should be the matter? (*He kisses her*)

Wife Come, my dear, I must not be put off so. Come, don't distract yourself alone; let me bear a share of your grief, as well as I have shared in your joy.

Husband Why, then, I will tell you; indeed, I am not going to break [go bankrupt], and I hope I am in no danger of it, at least as yet.

Wife Well, you are not going to break, that is, not just now, not yet; but, my dear, if it may happen, may not some steps be taken to prevent it for the present, and save us from it at last too?

Husband What steps could you think of, if that were the case?

Wife Indeed, it is not much that is in a wife's power, but I am ready to do what lies in me, and what becomes me; and first, pray let us live lower. Do you think I would live as I do, if I thought your income would not bear it? No, indeed.

Husband What will you do to prevent it? Let's see, what can you do?

Wife Why, first, I keep five maids and a footman. I shall immediately give three of my maids warning, and the fellow also, and save you that part of the expense.

Husband How can you do that? You can't do your business.

Wife There's nobody knows what they can do till they are tried. Two maids may do all my house-business, and I'll look after my children myself. ... In order to abate the expense of living, I will keep no visiting days; I'll drop the greatest part of the acquaintance I have; I'll lay down our treats and entertainments and the like needless occasions of expense.

Husband But this, my dear, will make as much noise almost as if I were actually broke.

Wife No, leave that part to me. Why, I'll go into the country. I'll put off our usual lodgings at Hampstead and give out that I am gone to spend the summer in Bedfordshire, at my aunt's, where everybody knows I used to go sometimes; they can't come after me thither.

Husband And what must I do? I know not where to begin.

Wife Why, you keep two horses and a groom, you keep rich company, and you sit long at the Fleece every evening. I need say no more; you know where to begin well enough.

Husband It is very hard; I have not your spirit, my dear.

Wife I hope you are not more ashamed to retrench than to have your name in the *Gazette* . . .

Complete English Tradesman, pp. 36–8.

8

Keep Your Books Posted

A tradesman's books, like a Christian's conscience, should always be kept clean and clear; and he that is not careful of both will give but a sad account of himself either to God or man. . . . I recommend it to a tradesman to take exact care of his books, as I would to every man to take care of his diet and temperate living; for though, according to some, we cannot, by all our care and caution, lengthen our life, yet, by temperance and regular conduct we may make that life more comfortable, more agreeable, and pleasant, by its being more healthy and hearty; so, though the exactest book-keeping cannot be said to make a tradesman thrive, because his profit and loss do not depend upon his books, or the goodness of his debts depend upon the debtor's accounts being well posted, yet this must be said, that the well-keeping of his books may be the occasion of his trade being carried on with the more ease and pleasure, and the more satisfaction, by having numberless quarrels, and contentions, and law-suits, which are the plague of a tradesman's life, prevented and avoided.

A tradesman without his books, in case of a law-suit for a debt, is like a married woman without her certificate. How many times has a woman been cast, and her cause not only lost but her reputation and character exposed, for want of being able to prove her marriage, though she has been really and honestly married, and has merited a good character all her days? And so in trade, many a debt has been lost, many a sum of money paid over again, especially after the tradesman has been dead, for want of his keeping his books carefully and exactly when he was alive, by which negligence, if he has not been ruined when he was living, his widow and children have been ruined after his decease.

Complete English Tradesman, p. 68.

9

Beware of Gossip!

A tradesman's credit and a virgin's virtue ought to be equally sacred from evil tongues; and it is a very unhappy truth that, as times now go, they are neither of them regarded among us as they ought to be.

The tea-table among the ladies, and the coffee-house among the men, seem to be places devoted to scandal, where the characters of all kinds of persons and professions are handled in the most merciless manner.

It seems a little hard that the reputation of a young lady, or of a new married couple, or of people in the most critical season of establishing the characters of their persons and families, should lie at the mercy of the tea-table; nor is it less hard that the credit of a tradesman, which is the same thing in its nature as the virtue of a lady, should be tossed about, shuttle-cock like, from one table to another in the coffee-house, till they shall talk all his creditors about his ears, and bring him to the very misfortune which they reported him to be near, when at the same time he owed them nothing who raised the clamour, and nothing to all the world but what he was able to pay.

And yet how many tradesmen have been thus undone; and how many more have been put to the full trial of their strength in trade, and have stood by the mere force of their good circumstances, whereas had they been unfurnished with cash to have answered their whole debts, they must have fallen with the rest.

Complete English Tradesman, p. 47.

10

Learn the 'Cant' of Business

There are many advantages to a tradesman of having a general knowledge of the terms of art and the cant, as I call it, of every business. . . .
Thus, if you go to a garden to buy flowers, plants, trees, and greens, if
you know what you go about, know the names of flowers or greens, the
particular beauties of them, when they are fit to remove and when to
slip and draw and when not, what colour is ordinary and what rare, when
a flower is rare and when ordinary – the gardener presently talks to you
as to a man of art, a friend to a florist, shows you his exotics, his green-
house and his stores; what he has set out, and what he has budded, and
the like. But if he finds you have none of the terms of art, know little
or nothing of the names of plants or the nature of planting, he picks
your pocket instantly, shows you a fine trimmed fuz-bush for a juniper,
sells you common pinks for painted ladies, an ordinary tulip for a rarity,
and the like.

Thus I saw a gardener sell a gentleman a large yellow auricula, that
is to say, a *running away*, for a curious flower, only because he discovered at his coming that he knew nothing of the matter. The same
gardener sold another person a root of white painted thyme for the
right *Marum Syriacum*; and thus they do every day.

Complete English Tradesman, pp. 12–13.

11

The Woman who Learnt her Husband's Business

A tradesman has begun the world about six or seven years. He has by
his industry and good understanding in business just got into a flourishing trade, by which he clears £500 or £600 a year; and if it should please
God to spare his life for twenty years or more, he would certainly be a
rich man. But in the middle of his prosperity he is snatched away by a
sudden fit of sickness, and his widow is left in a desolate, despairing
condition, having five children, and big with another. But the eldest of
these is not above six years old, and though a boy, yet he is utterly

incapable to be concerned in the business. So the trade which, had his father lived, would have been an estate to him, is like to be lost, and perhaps go all away to the eldest apprentice, who, however, wants two years of his time. Now, what is to be done for this unhappy family?

'Done!' says the widow; 'why, I will never let the trade fall so, that should be the making of my son, and in the meantime the maintenance of all my children.'

'Why, what can you do, child?' says her father; 'you know nothing of it. Mr —— did not acquaint you with his business.'

'That is true,' says the widow; 'he did not, because I was a fool, and did not care to look much into it. He did not press me to it, because he was afraid I might think he intended to put me upon it; but he often used to say, that if he should drop off before his boys were fit to come into the shop, it would be a sad loss to them.'

'But what does that signify now, child?' adds the father; 'You see it is so now, and cannot be helped.'

'Why,' says the widow, 'I used to ask him if he thought I could carry it on for them, if such a thing should happen. He shook his head and answered, "Yes, I might, if I had good servants, and if I would look a little into it beforehand."'

'And why did you not take the hint then,' says her father, 'and acquaint yourself a little with things, that you might have been prepared for whatever might happen?'

'Why, so I did,' says the widow, 'and have done for above two years past. He used to show me his letters and his books, and I know where he bought everything; and I know a little of goods, too, when they are good, and when bad, and the prices; also I know all the country-people he dealt with, and have seen most of them, and talked with them. He used to bring them up to dinner sometimes, and he would prompt my being acquainted with them, and would sometimes talk of his business with them at table, on purpose that I might hear it; and I know a little how to sell, too, for I have stood by him sometimes, and seen the customers and him chaffer with one another.'

'And did your husband like that you did so?' says the father. 'Yes,' says she, 'he loved to see me do it, and often told me that if he were dead, he believed I might carry on the trade as well as he.'

'But he did not believe so, I doubt,' says the father.

'I do not know as to that, but I sold goods several times to some customers, when he has been out of the way. Nay, I have served a customer sometimes when he has been in the warehouse, and he would go away to his counting-house on purpose, and say, "I'll leave you and my wife to make the bargain" and I have pleased the customer, and him too.'

'Well,' says the father, 'do you think you could carry on the trade?'

'I believe I could, if I had but an honest fellow of a journeyman for a year or two to write in the books, and go abroad among customers.'

'Well, you have two apprentices; one of them begins to understand things very much, and seems to be a diligent lad.'

'He comes forward, indeed, and will be very useful, if he does not grow too forward, upon a supposition that I shall want him too much; but it will be necessary to have a man to be above him for a while.'

'Well,' says the father, 'we will see to get you such a one.'

In short, they got her a man to assist to keep the books, go to Exchange, and do the business abroad; and the widow carried on the business with great application and success, till her eldest son grew up, and was first taken into the shop as an apprentice to his mother. The eldest apprentice served her faithfully, and was her journeyman four years after his time was out; then she took him in partner to one-fourth of the trade, and when her son came of age, she gave the apprentice one of her daughters, and enlarged his share to a third, gave her own son another third, and kept a third for herself to support the family. Thus the whole trade was preserved, and the son and son-in-law grew rich in it, and the widow, who grew as skilful in the business as her husband was before her, advanced the fortunes of all the rest of her children very considerably. This was an example of the husband's making the wife (but a little) acquainted with his business . . .

Complete English Tradesman, pp. 71–2.

CHAPTER 4

'PRENTICE BOYS

In England from time immemorial the principal trades and handicrafts were carried on by a three-fold order of masters, journeymen, and apprentices. The last named were the raw recruits, who from about the age of fourteen were put to serve a master who, in return for a premium, was expected to teach the youth his trade. On satisfactory completion of the term, the young man ranked as a journeyman, working for wages, whence he might rise to become a master in his turn.

Adam Smith strongly criticised the apprenticeship system. It interfered with a man's right to employ his 'strength and dexterity in what manner he thinks proper without detriment to his neighbour', it gave no security against 'insufficient workmanship', and it had no tendency to 'form young people to industry'. As he put it, 'an apprentice is likely to be idle, and almost always is so, because he has no immediate interest to be otherwise. . . . They who are soonest in a condition to enjoy the sweets of labour are likely soonest to conceive a relish for it, and to acquire the early habit of industry.'

No doubt his views on the subject were coloured by his contact with James Watt who, when Smith was a professor at Glasgow, was forbidden by the Corporation of Hammermen to practise his craft of mathematical instrument-maker in the town because he had not served as apprentice to one of their members. Smith had thereupon taken the matter up, with the result that Watt was provided by the university with a workshop in its precincts, where he carried out those experiments on steam-power that were of such vital importance in the development of the steam-engine.

Gradually Smith's arguments gained ground, but it was not until 1814 that the statutory ban on anyone practising a trade or handicraft (other than in one of the new towns, such as Manchester, Birmingham, and Wolverhampton) who had not served a seven years' apprenticeship, was repealed. Throughout Adam Smith's time the Act of Apprentices of 1563 remained in full force, and the 'prentice boys constituted a large (and often unruly) element of the population. Information on apprenticeship requirements and opportunities was eagerly sought, and Daniel Defoe in his *Complete English Tradesman* and R. Campbell in his *London Tradesman* included chapters on the subject, from which the passages given below have been taken.

The young apprentice in love is encountered in that charming old ballad *Sally in our Alley*, of which both the words and the music were written by Henry Carey (1693?–1743), who in the course of his hard-pressed existence produced over 200 light poems, songs, and dramatic pieces.

But it is in Hogarth's series of engravings, 'Industry and Idleness', (1747) (*see* Plates 9–12), that we may see the London 'prentice drawn from life by one whose art was ever actuated by a moral purpose. The great satirical artist described them as follows; 'Industry and Idleness exemplified in the conduct of two fellow-apprentices; where the one by taking good courses ... becomes a valuable man and an ornament to his country; and the other, by giving way to idleness, naturally falls into poverty, and ends fatally.'

I

The Young Tradesman's Education

The first part of a trader's beginning is ordinarily when he is very young, I mean, when he goes as an apprentice, and the notions of trade are scarcely got into his head, for boys go as apprentices while they are but boys. During the first years he of course learns to weigh and measure either liquids or solids, to pack and make bales, trusses, packages, etc., and do the coarser and laborious part of the business. But in the latter part of his time he is taken from the counter and from sweeping the warehouse, into the counting-house, where he sees the bills of parcels of goods bought, and thereby knows what everything costs at first hand, what gain is made of them, and if a miscarriage happens, what loss too, by which he is led of course to look into the goodness of the goods, and see the reason of things.

If the youth slips this occasion, and goes out of his time without obtaining such skill as this in the goods he is to deal in, he enters into trade without his most useful tools. For want of this knowledge of the goods, he is liable to be cheated and imposed upon in the most notorious manner by the sharp-sighted world, for his want of judgement is a thing that cannot be hid. The merchants or manufacturers of whom he buys presently discover him; the very boys in the wholesalemen's warehouses and in the merchants' warehouses, will play upon him, sell him one thing for another, show him a worse sort when he calls for a better, and, asking a higher price for it, persuade him it is better; and when they have bubbled him, they triumph over his ignorance when he is gone.

The next thing I recommend to an apprentice is to acquaint himself with his master's chapmen – I mean of both kinds, as well those he sells to as those he buys off. I need not explain myself not to mean by this the chance customers of a retailer's shop, for there can be no acquaintance, or very little, made with them; I mean the country shop-keepers, or others, who buy to sell again, or export as merchandise.

Next, the apprentice when his time is near expiring ought to acquaint himself with the books, that is to say, to see and learn his master's method of book-keeping, that he may follow it if the method is good, and may learn a better method in time if it is not.

A tradesman's books are his repeating-clock, which upon all occasions are to tell him how he goes on, and how things stand with him in the world. If they are not duly posted, and if everything is not carefully entered in them, the debtor's accounts kept even, the cash constantly balanced, and the credits all stated, the tradesman is like a ship at sea steered without a helm; he is all in confusion, and knows not what he does or where he is; he may be a rich man or a bankrupt – for, in a word, he can give no account of himself to himself, much less to anybody else.

The last article, and in itself essential to a young tradesman, is to know how to buy. If his master is kind and generous, he will let him into the secret of it of his own free will, and that before his time is fully expired; but if that should not happen, as often it does not, let the apprentice lose no opportunity to get into it, whether his master approves of it or no.

DANIEL DEFOE, *Complete English Tradesman*, pp. 7–9.

2

Advice to the Young Apprentice

How to behave during his Apprenticeship, in order to acquire his Business, obtain the good-will of his Master, and avoid the many Temptations to which Youth are liable in this great City.

The apprentice must be diligent in his business, and consider that it is a crime against moral honesty to trifle away his time when he should be employed in his master's work. He ought to apply closer in his master's absence than in his presence.

He must interfere as little as possible in the domestic concerns of his house. He must avoid tattling between servants, or carrying stories between husband and wife. He ought to be ready to do his mistress all the good offices in his power, and if he has any complaints to make of her, let him endeavour to have them taken notice of by the master himself, without making the complaint.

He must keep his master's secrets, both in relation to his Craft and dealings and to the private affairs of his family. He must carry no tales to his neighbour's house, or entertain his friends at the expense of his master and mistress's reputation.

He ought to take his master's advice and reasonable correction with the same submission as if he was his father.

A lad grown to some years must carefully avoid idle company and alehouses; the time he spends there must be stolen from his master or encroach upon those hours necessary for rest. Late hours destroy his health, and give him a habit of drinking and a love of company, the great bane of all tradesmen. That time his master can spare him, or can be taken from the hours of rest, he ought to employ in learning to write, read, cast accounts, drawing, or any other qualification suitable to his station.

Women are another strong temptation to apprentices to go astray. The blood runs warm in their young veins, and they are naturally prone to gratify the new-grown appetite. Against this evil the young apprentice must exert all the force of reason, interest, and religion; he must consider, he risks his health and plunges himself into a sea of diseases when he embraces a common woman – not only his health but his morals; their arts, their blandishments and snares are such that, sooner or later, they tempt their votaries from one degree of vice to another, till ruin, diseases, and a shameful end finishes their catastrophe.

As to what is called lawful love – courting a woman to make a wife of – that desire ought to be checked in the bud, for an apprentice is never completely miserable till he has got a wife. He ought to consider marriage as a matter not to be undertaken rashly at any age, but on no account till he is settled in a way of providing for a family. If he cannot save when single, how can he propose to maintain a family upon his wages? What a dreadful thing is it for a man to see a wife and children in want, and he unable to support them! It is worse than death to an honest man.

Great care ought to be taken in the choice of company. Idle, profligate fellows ought to be shunned; we soon partake of the manners of those we converse with; their vices become familiar to us, and by degrees steal insensibly upon our minds and convert us into one of themselves.

5. The Harlot's Progress: (*above*) Ensnared by a procuress; (*below*) Quarrels with her Jew protector

6. The Harlot's Progress: *(above)* Apprehended by a magistrate
(below) Scene in Bridewell

7. The Harlot's Progress: (*above*) Expires while the doctors are disputing; (*below*) The funeral

8. The Rake's Progress: Tavern Scene

Above all, gambling must be avoided; even gaming for amusement is pernicious to the mind of youth; the habit soon grows ungovernable, and draws us by degrees to love gaming for the sake of money which we formerly loved only for diversion; and when that spirit once possesses us, all sense of honesty is lost, we are uneasy when we are not engaged in play, suffer all the tortures of the unhappy when Fortune has been unfavourable, and to repair the breach made by our folly, run all lengths that craft, despair, and villainy can suggest.

Reverence for Religion and a conscientious discharge of the duties of it I place last, not as contributing the least to our happiness but that in it all other considerations are centred ...

R. CAMPBELL, *The London Tradesman*, pp. 312–17.

3

'Sally in Our Alley'

[Henry Carey explained the genesis of the following in a note: 'A shoemaker's apprentice making holiday with his sweetheart treated her with a sight of Bedlam [lunatic asylum], the puppet shows, the flying chairs, and all the elegancies of Moorfields; from whence proceeding to the Farthing Playhouse he gave her a collation of buns, cheesecakes, gammon of bacon, stuffed beer, and bottled ale; through all which scenes the author dogged them (charmed with the simplicity of their courtship), from whence he drew this little sketch of nature.']

> Of all the girls that are so smart
> There's none like pretty Sally;
> She is the darling of my heart,
> And she lives in our alley.
> There is no lady in the land
> Is half so sweet as Sally;
> She is the darling of my heart,
> And she lives in our alley ...
>
> When she is by, I leave my work,
> I love her so sincerely;
> My master comes like any Turk,
> And bangs me most severely:
> But let him bang his bellyful,
> I'll bear it all for Sally;
> She is the darling of my heart,
> And she lives in our alley.

Of all the days that's in the week
 I dearly love but one day –
And that's the day that comes betwixt
 A Saturday and Monday;
For then I'm drest all in my best
 To walk abroad with Sally;
She is the darling of my heart,
 And she lives in our alley.

My master carries me to church,
 And often I am blamèd
Because I leave him in the lurch
 As soon as text is namèd;
I leave the church in sermon-time
 And slink away to Sally;
She is the darling of my heart,
 And she lives in our alley ...

My master and the neighbours all,
 Make game of me and Sally,
And, but for her, I'd better be
 A slave and row a galley;
But when my seven long years are out,
 O, then, I'll marry Sally;
O, then we'll wed, and then we'll bed –
 But not in our alley!

4

Hogarth's 'Industry and Idleness'

(*Plates 9–12*)
The first view we have of the two heroes of our history is at the looms
of their master, a silk weaver in Spitalfields. The assiduity of one of
these artisans, Master Francis Goodchild, is manifested in his countenance and attention to the business he is engaged in. Over his head
hang those excellent old ballads, *Turn again, Whittington, Lord Mayor
of London*, and *The Valiant Apprentice*. On the floor near him is the
'Prentice's Guide, a book which our citizen probably presented to every
young man he had under his care; for we see the same title on a muti-
lated volume at the feet of Mr Thomas Idle, who, being asleep, has
dropped his shuttle, which a cat is playing with. On the wall hangs the
ballad of *Moll Flanders*, and very near him is a tobacco-pipe and a

porter pot. His appearance is consonant to his disposition: hair un-
combed, collar unbuttoned, and worn-out coat, are strong indications
of negligence and sloth. With angry eye and cane uplifted, the master,
just entering the room, seems very well disposed to punish his indolence
and drowsiness; but these habits are too strongly rooted to be eradicated
by chastisement.

The Industrious 'Prentice his master's favourite
From attention to business and propriety of conduct, the industrious
apprentice has gained the confidence of his employer. He is now in
the counting-house, entrusted with the management of the business; has
the day-book, purse, and keys in his hands, and attentively listens to the
directions of his friendly master, who, with a face expressive of the
highest partiality and regard, familiarly leans upon his shoulder. A
partnership, on the eve of taking place, is covertly intimated by a pair
of gloves upon the writing-desk. A city porter is bringing in a bale of
goods. The mastiff that attends him is violently opposed by the domestic
cat.

The Industrious 'Prentice marries his master's daughter
The reward of industry is success. Our prudent and attentive youth
is now become partner with his master, and married to his daughter.
To show that plenty reigns in this mansion, a servant distributes the
remains of the table to a poor woman, and the bridegroom pays one of
the drummers who, according to ancient custom, attend with their
thundering gratulations the day after a wedding. A performer on the
bass viol, and a herd of butchers armed with marrow-bones and
cleavers, form an English concert! A cripple, with the ballad *Jesse, or
the Happy Pair*, represents a man known by the name of Philip in the
Tub, who had visited Ireland and Holland, and was a general attendant
at weddings.

The Idle 'Prentice in a garret with a prostitute
Meanwhile the Idle Apprentice has been turned away from his employment and sent to sea. He is now returned from his voyage, and is
exhibited in a garret with a common prostitute. By the pistols, watches,
etc., which lie upon and near the bed, it seems evident that the source of
his present subsistence is from robbery on the highway. Horror and
dismay are strongly depicted in his agitated and terrified face. To
prevent surprise, the door is locked, double bolted, and barricaded with
planks; notwithstanding these precautions, the noise occasioned by a
cat having slipped down a ruinous chimney throws him into the utmost
terror. Not so his depraved companion; solely engrossed by the plunder

upon the bed, she looks with delighted eyes at a glittering earring. The broken jug, pipe, knife, plate, dram-bottle, glass, and pistols, are very properly introduced; and the rat renders this filthy and disgusting scene still more nauseous. The lady's hoop, hanging on the wall is a good specimen of the fashion of that day, when this cumbrous, inconvenient, and ungraceful combination of whales' bones was worn by women of the lowest as well as the highest rank.

The Idle 'Prentice betrayed by a prostitute

The idle and incorrigible outcast, mature in vice and lost to society, is here represented in a night-cellar – in a house near Water Lane, Fleet Street, known by the name of 'Blood Bowl House' from the scenes of riot and murder which were there perpetrated. In this cavern of vice and infamy he is dividing the spoil produced by robbery with one of his wretched accomplices, when the woman that seems his favourite and in whose garret we have just seen him, deliberately betrays him. The officers of justice are entering, and he is on the point of being seized. The corpse of a gentleman who has been murdered is with unfeeling indifference being put down a cavity made in the floor for the purposes of concealment. A scene of riot, likely to terminate in blood, passes in the background. A rope hanging immediately over a fellow who is asleep, should not be overlooked. Some cards scattered on the floor show the amusements of this earthly Pandemonium.

The Industrious 'Prentice, Alderman of London; the Idle one brought before him and impeached by his accomplice

He who was an industrious apprentice is now an alderman and a magistrate (and in due course will become Lord Mayor); he who was once his fellow-'prentice is now brought before him, handcuffed and accused of robbery, aggravated by murder. Shocked at seeing the companion of his youth in so degraded a situation, he instinctively covers his eyes. Agitated, terrified, self-convicted, and torn by remorse, the wretched culprit is unable to support his frame. Did he not lean upon the bar, he would sink to the earth. His distressed and heartbroken mother intercedes with the swollen and important constable to use his interest for her unhappy son. A number of watchmen attend the examination, and one of them holds up the sword and pistols which were found on the prisoner. A young woman bribes the swearing-clerk to befriend the one-eyed wretch who has turned evidence against his accomplice, by suffering him to take the usual oath with his left hand laid upon the book instead of his right (a little circumstance considered at the Old Bailey as a complete excuse for false swearing). The alderman's clerk is making out a warrant of commitment directed to the turn-key of Newgate prison.

The Idle 'Prentice executed at Tyburn

After a life of sloth, wretchedness and vice, the career of our degraded character terminates at Tyburn. His pale and ghastly look denotes the remorse and horror of his mind; and it must embitter his last moments to hear a Grub Street orator proclaim his dying speech. The chaplain of Newgate leads the procession in a coach, but the criminal's spiritual concerns are left to an enthusiastic follower of John Wesley, who zealously exhorts him to repentance. On the right side of the print we see his afflicted mother. In a cart above her is a curious trio of females: an old beldam, breathing out a pious ejaculation and swallowing a bumper of spirits at the same moment; a young woman taking a glass from beneath; and a third dissuading a fellow from ascending the vehicle. While a vendor of gingerbread expatiates on the excellence of his cakes, a minor pickpocket purloins his handkerchief. A female enraged at a man oversetting her orange-barrow, is literally tearing his eyes out. To show the reverence which an English mob have for any-thing that bears the appearance of religion, an inmate of St Giles's seizes a dog by the tail, and is on the point of throwing it at the Metho-dist parson.

A female pugilist, near the centre of the print, is so earnest in punish-ing a fellow who has offended her, that she neglects her child, which, lying on the ground, is probably destined to be crushed to death. A tall butcher has suspended an old legal periwig on the end of his cudgel; in this, the artist might intend to display an emblem of the sanguinary complexion which marks our courts of justice. The porter with his pipe; a cripple; the soldier sunk knee-deep in a bog, and two boys laughing at him, are well imagined. We must not overlook a gentleman [the hangman] emphatically called the 'Finisher of the law', who sedately smokes his best Virginia on the gallows. In the background we have a view of Highgate and Hampstead hills.

JOHN IRELAND, *Hogarth Illustrated* (1791), vol. I, pp. 253–81.

CHAPTER 5

SOME LONDON SHOPKEEPERS

When Daniel Defoe 'calculated' that there were 'some hundreds of thousands of shopkeepers in this kingdom', we may be sure that he had in mind a whole heap of places that we should never think of calling 'shops'. For example, in his description of the great fair held at Sturbridge, near Chesterton, in Cambridgeshire, which lasted from the middle of August to the middle of September and attracted a host of people from far and wide, he speaks of the tents and booths in which goods were displayed as 'shops', when 'stalls' would to us seem the appropriate word.

By the beginning of the eighteenth century, when Defoe flourished, Sturbridge fair was in its decline, as were most of the other fairs that were held annually in various parts. For most people in those days the equivalent of a 'shopping spree' was a visit to the market in the nearest market-town – for which reason Defoe was always careful to mention in his *Tour* which towns held regular markets and on what days of the week, just as today the same information is included in bus and train time-tables. For the rest, there were in the larger villages little 'stores' where tea and sugar, sheep-dip and cattle medicines, boots and shoes, petticoats and smocks and hats, candles and soap, needles and thread, perhaps a printed ballad or two and a months-old newsletter from London, were mixed in messy and smelly confusion. Then much business was done by pedlars, chapmen, barrow-pushing hawkers, and other itinerant traders.

In some of the larger towns in the provinces, such as Bristol, Norwich, and Leeds, and such favourite pleasure resorts as Bath and Tunbridge Wells, there were quite a number of what we should regard as shops – more or less permanent establishments, open for business on every week-day, and with glass windows through which one might glimpse Mr Grocer or Mr Draper bustling about between his counter and his stock in trade.

But for shops as for so many other things there was no place to compare with London. As early as Norman times the city's narrow and pestilence-ridden streets were crammed with shops of one kind or another. In Shakespeare's day the business tide had started to flow beyond the ancient walls, and following upon the Great Fire of 1666 Fleet Street and the Strand were lined with shops on both sides. Defoe was staggered by the cost of shop fittings in 1710, and sixty years later the French traveller P. J. Grosley was in ecstasies over the London shops, which 'make a most splendid show, greatly superior to any thing of the kind in Paris'.

By then the shopping districts had spread westward to Leicester Square and Piccadilly, and even to Oxford-street, although as late as the beginning of George III's reign in 1760 this was still on the edge of the country. The City still maintained its pre-eminence, however, as the principal shopping centre of the metropolis (and indeed, of the country), and the London shopkeepers whom we are about to meet in the following 'documents' all had their places of business within sound of Bow Bell.

I

Favourite Shops of the Fair Sex

The *Mercer* deals in silks, brocades, and an innumerable train of trifles for the ornament of the fair sex. He must be a very polite man, and skilled in all the punctilios of City good breeding; he ought by no means to be an awkward, clumsy fellow: such a creature would turn the lady's stomach in a morning, when they go their rounds to tumble silks they have no mind to buy. He must dress neatly and affect a Court air, however far distant he may live from St James's.

Our Mercer must have a good deal of the Frenchman in his manners, as well as a large parcel of French goods in his shop; he ought to keep close intelligence with the fashion-office at Paris, and supply himself with the newest patterns from that changeable people. Nothing that is mere English goes down with our modern ladies: from their shift [chemise] to their top-knots they must be equipped from *Dear Paris*.

The Mercer who intends to succeed in his business ought to humour the ladies, and accommodate himself to their taste and understanding as much as a Rational Creature can.

The business requires a very considerable stock; ten thousand pounds, without a great deal of prudent management, makes but a small figure in their way. Nor will the profits, though reasonable, admit of the expense of a Nobleman. A City and a country-house, a pack of hounds in the country, and a Doxy [mistress] in a corner of the Town, coaches, horses, gaming, and the polite vices of St James's, cannot be afforded out of the profits of silk and velvet.

95

A lace-man must have a well-lined pocket to furnish his shop with all sorts of gold and silver lace, gold and silver buttons, shapes for waistcoats, lace and net work for robings and women's petticoats, fringes, bugles, spangles, gold and silver wire, twist, etc.

His chief talent ought to lie in a nice taste in patterns of lace, etc. He ought to speak fluently, though not elegantly, to entertain the Ladies, and be a master of a handsome bow and cringe; should be able to hand a lady to and from her coach without being seized with the palpitation of the heart at the touch of a delicate hand, the sight of a well-turned and much exposed limb, or a handsome face.

But above all, he must have confidence to refuse his goods in a handsome manner to the extravagant Beau who never pays, and patience as well as stock to bear the delays of the sharping Peer, who pays but seldom.

With these natural qualifications, five thousand pounds in his pocket, and a set of good customers in view, a young man may commence Lace-man. If he trusts moderately and with discretion, lives with economy, and minds his business more than his mistress, he may live to increase his stock; but otherwise I know no readier road to a jail than a Lace-man's business.

Milliners are concerned in making and providing the Ladies with smocks, aprons, tippets, handkerchiefs, neckaties, ruffles, mobs, caps, with as many Etceteras as would reach from Charing-Cross to the Royal Exchange. They find them in gloves, muffs, and ribbons; they sell quilted petticoats and hoops of all sizes; and lastly, some of them deal in habits for riding and dresses for the masquerade. In a word, they furnish everything to the Ladies that can contribute to set off their beauty, increase their vanity, or render them ridiculous.

The milliner must be a neat needlewoman in all its branches, and a perfect connoisseur in dress and fashion. She imports new whims from Paris every post, and puts the ladies' heads in as many different shapes in one month as there are different appearances of the moon. The most noted of them keep an agent in Paris, who has nothing else to do but to watch the motions of the Fashions and procure intelligence of their changes, which she signifies to her principals with as much zeal and secrecy as an ambassador would the important discovery of some political intrigue.

Milliners have vast profits of every article they deal in, yet give but poor, mean wages to every person they employ under them.

Hoop-petticoat makers I placed the Hoop-petticoat in the Milliner's branch, but upon recollection I choose to afford this seven-fold fence a section by itself, since I am bound to do honour to every thing that concerns the Fair, and if I lumped it with the rest of their wardrobe I might be suspected an enemy to this female entrenchment.

When this ingenious contrivance came into fashion has much perplexed the learned . . . but sufficient for us to know that about the middle of the last century they were revived under the denomination of Farthingales, and were less in their dimensions.

As to their use, I dare not divulge the secrets of the Fair. They have kept it inviolably, nay, better than we have kept the Freemason's sign; for I defy all the male creation to discover the secret use the Ladies designed them for. Some apparent advantages flow from them which every one may see; but they have a cabalistical meaning which none but such as are within the Circle can fathom.

We see they are friends to men, for they have let us into the secrets of Ladies' Legs, which we might have been ignorant of to Eternity without their help; they discover to us indeed a Sample of what we wish to purchase, yet serve as a Fence to keep us at an awful distance.

Hoop petticoats are made of striped holland, silk, or check (according to the quality of the Fair to be inclosed), supported with rows of whalebone or rattan. They are chiefly made by women: they must not be polluted by the unhallowed hands of a rude Male. The work is harder than most needlework, and requires girls of strength. A mistress must have a pretty kind of Genius to make them fit well and adjust them to the reigning mode; but in the main, it is not necessary she should be a Witch.

The Stay-maker is employed in making stays, jumps [short coats], and bodices for the ladies. He ought to be a very polite tradesman, as he approaches the ladies so nearly, and possessed of a tolerable share of assurance and command of temper to approach their delicate persons in fitting on their stays, without being moved or put out of countenance. He is obliged to inviolable secrecy when he is obliged by art to mend a crooked shape, to bolster up a fallen hip, or distorted shoulder.

The delicate shape we so much admire in *Miranda* is entirely the workmanship of the stay-maker; to him she reveals all her natural deformity, which she industriously conceals from the fond lord who was caught by her slender waist. Her shape she owes to steel and whalebone, her black locks to her tire-woman, and her florid complexion to paint and pomatum. She is like the jack-daw in the fable, dressed out in borrowed plumes; and her natural self, when deposited in the bridal-bed, is a mere lump of animated deformity, fitter far for the undertaker than to be initiated in the mysteries of connubial joy.

How necessary a qualification is it in that kind of tradesman to keep the deformed secret? and how dangerous to the repose of the Fair Sex would it be to blab the misshapen truth? I am surprised that ladies have not found out a way to employ women stay-makers rather than trust our sex with what should be kept as inviolable as Freemasonry. But the work is too hard for women; it requires more strength than they are capable of, to raise walls of defence about a lady's shape, which is liable to be spoiled by so many accidents.

The Matua-maker's business is to make night-gowns, mantuas [loose outer gowns], and petticoats, etc., for the ladies. She is sister to the tailor, and, like him, must be a perfect connoisseur in dress and fashions; and, like the stay-maker, she must keep the secrets she is entrusted with, as much as a woman can.

For though the stay-maker does his business as nicely as possible and conceals all deformities with the greatest art, yet the mantua-maker must discover them at some times; she must see them, and pretend to be blind, and at all times she must swear herself to an inviolable secrecy. She must learn to flatter all complexions, praise all shapes, and, in a word, ought to be complete mistress of the art of dissimulation. It requires a vast stock of patience to bear the tempers of most of their customers, and no small share of ingenuity to execute their innumerable whims.

Mantua-makers' profits are but inconsiderable, and the wages they give their journeywomen small in proportion; they may make a shift with great sobriety and economy to live upon their allowance, but their want of prudence and general poverty has brought the business into small reputation.

R. CAMPBELL, *The London Tradesman* (1747), pp. 147–8, 197–9, 206–8, 211–13, 224–6, 227.

2

'Mr Fashioner' – of Clothes, and Men

No man is ignorant that a Tailor is a person that makes our clothes; to some he not only makes their dress but in some measure may be said to make themselves.

There are numbers of beings in and about this Metropolis who have no other identical existence than what the tailor, milliner, and periwig-maker bestow upon them. Strip them of these distinctions, and they are quite a different species of beings – have no more relation to their dressed selves than they have to the Great Mogul, and are as insignificant in society as Punch, deprived of his moving wires and hung upon a peg.

From all this I would infer, that Mr Fashioner is not such a despicable animal as the world imagines; that he is really a useful member in society, and consequently that, though according to the vulgar saying, it takes nine tailors to make one man, yet you may pick up nine men out of ten who cannot make a complete tailor.

The tailor's fancy must always be upon the wing, and his wit not woolgathering but fashion-hunting. He ought to have a quick eye to steal the cut of a sleeve, the pattern of a flap, or the shape of a good trimming at a glance; any bungler may cut out a shape when he has a pattern before him, but a good workman takes it by his eye in the passing of a chariot, or in the space between the door and a coach.

He must be able, not only to cut for the handsome and well-shaped but to bestow a good shape where Nature has not designed it; the hump-back, the wry-shoulder, must be buried in flannel and wadding, and the coat must be *de gage* though put over a post. He must study not only the shape but the common gait of the subject he is working upon, and make the clothes fit easy in spite of a stiff gait or awkward air.

In a tailor's shop there are always two sorts of workmen. First, the foreman, who takes measure when the master is out of the way, cuts and finishes all the work, and carries it home to the customer. This is the best workman in the shop, and his place the most profitable, for besides his cabbage [remnants of cloth] he has generally a guinea a week, and the drink-money given by the gentleman on whom he waits to fit on their clothes. The next class is the mere working tailor. Not one in ten of them know how to cut out a pair of breeches. They are employed only to sew the seam, to cast the button holes, and prepare the work for the finisher. Their wages, by Act of Parliament, is twenty pence in one season of the year, and half a crown the other; however, a good hand has half a crown and three shillings. They are as numerous as locusts, are out of business about three or four months in the year, and generally as poor as rats. The house of call runs away with all their earnings, and keeps them constantly in debt and want.

The house of call is an ale-house, where they generally use, the landlord knows where to find them, and masters go there to enquire when they want hands. Custom has established it into a kind of law, that the house of call gives them credit for victuals and drink while they are unemployed; this obliges the journeymen on the other hand, to spend all the money they earn at this house alone. The landlord, when once he has got them in his debt, is sure to keep them so, and by that means binds the poor wretch to his house, who slaves only to enrich the publican.

The London Tradesman, pp. 191–3.

3

Success-Story of a City Bookseller

[James Lackington (1746–1815) was the son of a journeyman shoemaker in Wellington, Somersetshire, and was apprenticed at fourteen to a shoemaker at Taunton. He subsequently worked at his trade at Bristol and other places, joined the Methodists, and educated himself by much reading of good books. In 1770 he married a country girl, and three years later moved to London, where in 1774 he opened a shoemaker's shop and bookstall combined in Featherstone-street, St Luke's, in the City. Before long he was able to concentrate on secondhand-book selling, moved to larger premises in Chiswell-street, and eventually, after a hard struggle and many vicissitudes, established himself as the City's largest bookseller in Finsbury Square. He travelled widely in search of stock, and visited Scotland in 1787 and 1790. In 1798 he disposed of his interest in the business, and retired to Budleigh Salterton in Devonshire. His *Memoirs of the Forty-five First Years* of his life was published in 1792, and went into a number of editions.]

It was some time in 1780 when I resolved from that period to give no person whatever any credit. I had observed that where credit was given, most bills were not paid within six months, many not within a twelvemonth, and some not for two years. Indeed, many tradesmen have accounts of seven years standing, and some bills are never paid. The losses sustained by the interest on the money in long credits, and by those bills that were not paid at all; the inconveniences attending not having the ready-money to lay out in trade to the best advantage, together with the great loss of time in keeping accounts and collecting debts, convinced me, that if I could establish a ready-money business *without any exceptions*, I should be enabled to sell every article very cheap.

When I communicated my ideas on this subject to some of my acquaintances I was much laughed at and ridiculed; and it was thought that I might as well attempt to rebuild the tower of Babel as to establish a large business without giving credit. But notwithstanding this discouragement, I determined to make the experiment; and began by plainly marking in every book facing the title the lowest price that I would take for it; which being much lower than the common market prices, I not only retained my former customers but soon increased their numbers. In the first three years after I refused to give credit to any person, my business increased much, and as the whole of my profit (after paying all expences) was laid out in books, my stock was continually enlarged, so that my Catalogues in 1784 were very much augmented in size. The first contained twelve thousand, and the second thirty thousand volumes; this increase was not merely in numbers, but also in value, as a very great part of these volumes were *better*, that is, books of an higher price. I now sell more than one hundred thousand volumes annually . . .

As I never had any part of the *miser* in my composition, I always proportioned my expenses according to my profits; that is, I have for many years expended two-thirds of the profits of my trade; which proportion of expenditure I never exceeded. In the beginning, I opened and shut my own shop, and welcomed a friend by a shake of the hand. About a year after, on such occasions I beckoned across the way for a pot of good porter. A few years after that, I sometimes invited my friends to dinner, and provided them a roasted fillet of veal; in a progressive course the ham was introduced, and a pudding was the next addition made to the feast. For some time a glass of brandy and water was a luxury; a glass of Mr Beaufoy's raisin wine succeeded; and as soon as two-thirds of my profits enabled me to afford good red port, it immediately appeared; nor was sherry long behind.

It was some years before I discovered that a lodging in the country was very conducive to my health. The year after, my country lodging was transformed into a country house; and in another year the inconveniences attending a stage coach were remedied by a chariot. For four years Upper Holloway was to me an elysium; Surrey next appeared the most beautiful county in England, and Upper Merton the most rural village in Surrey. So now Merton is selected as the seat of occasional philosophical retirement.

But in every step of my progress, envy and malevolence has pursued me close. When by the advice of that eminent physician, Dr Letsom, I purchased a horse, and saved my life by the exercise it afforded me, the old adage, 'Set a beggar on horseback and he'll ride to the Devil', was deemed fully verified; but when Mrs Lackington mounted another, 'they were very sorry to see people so young in business run on at so great a rate!' The occasional relaxation which we enjoyed in the country was censured as an abominable piece of pride; but when the *carriage* and *servants* in *livery* appeared, 'they would not be the first to hurt a foolish tradesman's character; but if (as was but too probable) the docket was not already struck, the *Gazette* would soon settle that point'.

But I have been lately informed that these *good-natured* and *compassionate* people have found it necessary to alter their story. It seems that at last they have discovered the secret springs from whence I drew my wealth; however, they do not quite agree in their accounts, for although some can tell you the very *number* of my fortunate lottery ticket, others are as positive that I found bank-notes in an old book, to the amount of many thousand pounds, and if they please, can even tell you the title of the very fortunate old book that contained this treasure. But I assure you, upon my honour, that I found the whole of what I am possessed of, in SMALL PROFITS, bound by INDUSTRY, and clasped by ECONOMY.

Memoirs of the Forty-five First Years of the Life of James Lackington,
7th edn (1794), pp. 210–14, 256–9, 268.

4

Mr Treacle's Complaint

———————

To the Idler Sir, I have the misfortune to be a man of business; that, you will say, is a most grievous one; but what makes it the more so to me, is, that my wife has nothing to do: at least she had too good an education, and the prospect of too good a fortune in reversion when I married her, to think of employing herself either in my shop-affairs, or the management of my family.

For my part, I have enough to mind, in weighing my goods out, and waiting on my customers; but my wife, though she could be of as much use as a shopman to me, if she would put her hand to it, is now only in my way. She walks all the morning sauntering about the shop with her arms through her pocket-holes, or stands gaping at the door-sill, and looking at every person that passes by. She is continually asking me a thousand frivolous questions about every customer that comes in and goes out; and all the while I am entering any thing in my day-book, she is lolling over the counter, and staring at it, as if I was only scribbling or drawing figures for her amusement. Sometimes, indeed, she will take a needle; but as she always works at the door or in the middle of the shop, she has so many interruptions, that she is longer hemming a towel, or darning a stocking, that I am in breaking forty loaves of sugar and making it up into pounds.

In the afternoon I am sure likewise to have her company, except she is called upon by some of her acquaintance; and then as we let out all the upper part of our house, and keep only a little room backwards for ourselves, they either keep such a chattering, or else are calling out every moment to me, that I cannot mind my business for them.

My wife, I am sure, might do all the little matters our family requires, and I could wish that she would employ herself in them; but instead of that, we have a girl to do the work, and look after a little boy about two years old, which I may fairly say is the mother's own child. The brat must be humoured in every thing: he is therefore suffered constantly to play in the shop, pull all the goods about, and clamber up the shelves to get at the plums and sugar. I dare not correct him; because, if I did, I should have wife and maid both upon me at once. As to the latter, she is as lazy and sluttish as her mistress; and because she complains she has too much work, we can scarcely get her to do anything at all. Nay, what is worse than that, I am afraid she is hardly honest; and as she is instructed to buy in all our provisions, the jade, I am sure, makes a market-penny out of every article.

But to return to my deary. – The evenings are the only time, when it is fine weather, that I am left to myself; for then she generally takes the child out to give it milk in the park. When she comes home again, she is so fatigued with walking, that she cannot stir from her chair; and it's an hour, after shop is shut, before I can get a bit of supper, while the maid is taken up in undressing and putting the child to bed.

But you will pity me much more when I tell you the manner in which we generally pass our Sundays. In the morning she is commonly too ill to dress herself to go to church; she therefore never gets up till noon; and what is still more vexatious, keeps *me* in bed with her, when I ought to be busily engaged in better employment. It is well if she can get her things on by dinner time; and when that is over, I am sure to be dragged out by her, either to Georgia, or Hornsey Wood, or the White Conduit House. Yet even these near excursions are so very fatiguing to her that besides what it costs me in tea and hot rolls, and syllabubs, and cakes for the boy, I am frequently forced to take a hackney-coach, or drive them out in a one-horse chair. At other times, as my wife is rather of the fattest, and a very poor walker, besides bearing her whole weight upon my arm I am obliged to carry the child myself.

Thus, Sir, does she constantly drawl out her time, without either profit or satisfaction; and, while I see my neighbours' wives helping in the shop, and almost earning as much as their husbands, I have the mortification to find, that mine is nothing but a deadweight upon me.

In short, I do not know any greater misfortune can happen to a plain hard-work-tradesman, as I am, than to be joined to such a woman, who is rather a clog than a helpmate to him.

– and Mrs Treacle's Rejoinder

Sir, I am the unfortunate wife of the grocer whose letter you published, in which he complains, like a sorry fellow, that I loiter in the shop with my needlework in my hand, and that I oblige him to take me out on Sundays, and keep a girl to look after the child. Sweet Mr Idler, if you did but know all, you would give no encouragement to such an unreasonable grumbler. I brought him three hundred pounds, which set him up in a shop, and bought-in a stock, on which, with good management, we might live comfortably; but now I have given him a shop, I am forced to watch him and the shop too.

I will tell you, Mr Idler, how it is. There is an alehouse over the way with a ninepin alley, to which he is sure to run when I turn my back, and there loses his money, for he plays at ninepins as he does every thing else. While he is at this favourite sport, he sets a dirty boy to watch his door, and call him to his customers; but he is long in coming, and so rude when he comes, that our custom falls off every day.

Those who cannot govern themselves, must be governed. I have resolved to keep him for the future behind his counter, and let him bounce at his customers if he dares. I cannot be above stairs and below at the same time, and have therefore a girl to look after the child and dress the dinner; and, after all, pray who is to blame?

On a Sunday, it is true, I make him walk abroad, and sometimes carry the child; I wonder who should carry it! But I never take him out till after church-time, nor would I do it then, but that, if he is left alone, he will be upon the bed. On a Sunday, if he stays at home, he has six meals, and, when he can eat no longer, has twenty strategems to escape from me to the alehouse; but I commonly keep the door locked, till Monday produces something for him to do . . .

The Idler (ed. DR S. JOHNSON), nos 15 and 28 (1758).

5

London Tradesmen: Past and Present

What a contrast between a tradesman or citizen of former times, and those of our days!

To go no farther back than forty or fifty years, a thriving tradesman was almost as stationary as his shop; he might at all times be found there. 'Keep your shop, and your shop will keep you', was a maxim continually in his mind. Born within the sound of Bow-Bell, he rarely ventured out of it, except perhaps once or twice in a summer, when he indulged his wife and family with an expedition to Edmonton or Hornsey. On this occasion, the whole family, dressed in their Sunday clothes, were crowded together in a landau or coach hired for the day. On Easter or Whitsunday he might likewise treat himself to a ride on a Moorfields hack, hired at eighteen pence a ride, through what was then called the Cuckolds Round.

If in holiday time a friend was invited to dinner, which was not often the case, his fare was a large plum-pudding, with a loin of veal, the fat spread on a toast, well sauced with melted butter, a buttock of beef, or, if the guest was of the Common Council, possibly a ham or chickens. The drink was elder or raisin wine made by his wife, and strong ale in a silver tankard. The meat was brought up in new-scoured pewter; the apprentice cleaned the best knives, and the maid, with her hands before her, waited at table, serving every guest with a low curtsey. His wife was dressed in her best silk damask gown, with flowers as large as a fire-shovel, so stiff that it would have stood alone – probably left her by her mother or grandmother.

These tradesmen paid their bills when due, and would have conceived themselves ruined, had a banker's runner called twice for a draft; and after going through all parish and ward offices, as well as those of their [livery] company, terminated their days in rural retirement, at Turnham-Green, Hackney, or Clapham Common; from whence they could now and again make a trip, in their one-horse chaise, to visit the shop where they had acquired their fortune.

The daughters of these men were taught all kinds of needle-work, and at a certain age were initiated into all the culinary secrets of the family, preserved in a manuscript handed down from their great-grandmother. The boys, instead of losing their time in an imperfect acquisition of a little Latin, were well grounded in Cocker's and

Wingate's Arithmetic, and were perfect adepts in the rule-of-three and practice.

A tradesman of the present day is as seldom found in his shop as at church. A man of any spirit, he says, cannot submit to sit kicking his heels there; it is consequently left to the care of his apprentices and journeymen, whilst he goes to the coffee-house to read the news, and settle the politics of the parish.

His evenings are spent at different clubs and societies. On Monday he has a neighbourly meeting, consisting of the most substantial inhabitants of the parish; this it would be extremely wrong and unsocial to neglect. On Tuesday he goes to the Sols or Bucks, among whom he has many customers. Wednesday he dedicates to a disputing club, in order to qualify himself to make speeches in the Vestry, or at Common Council. As a man of taste and cultivator of oratory, he forms an acquaintance with some of the under players, from whom on benefit nights he takes tickets, and at other times receives orders. If he has the misfortune to sing a good song, at least a night in the week is devoted to private concerts, of gentlemen performing for their own amusement at some public-house. As a good husband, he cannot refuse to accompany his wife and daughters to the monthly assembly, held at a tavern in St Giles's or Soho, and sometimes to a card party, to play an innocent game at shilling whist.

During two or three of the summer months, he and his family take a *tower*, as they term it, to Margate, Brighton, or some other of the watering-places, where, to make a handsome appearance, and look like themselves, they are dressed in every expensive piece of trippery then in vogue.

If a friend is invited to take a family dinner, nothing less than two courses will go down; besides the footman, the porter and errand-boy exhibit in liveries. Claret and Madeira are the liquors.

On a tradesman of this sort entering into the holy state of matrimony, his wife's drawing and dressing-rooms must be furnished according to the newest fashion, with carpets, curtains, looking-glasses, girandoles [chandeliers], and all the fashionable appendages.

If he has a family, the young ladies, as they are always styled, are sent to a boarding-school, where they are taught to dance, to jabber a few mispronounced French phrases, and to thrum two or three tunes on the pianoforte; but not a single stitch of plain-work, for fear of making them hold down their heads, or spoiling their eyes; and as to housewifery, they could as soon make a smoke-jack as a pudding.

The education of the male part of the family is not more sensible. At school they are taught the Latin grammar, and advance in that language to Corderius and Cornelius Nepos, which is forgotten in three months after they leave school. This, with a little French, dancing, and blowing a tune on the German flute, completes the piece.

This style of living is for a while supported by paper credit, and assisted by two or three tradesmen of the same description, who jointly manoeuvre drafts of accommodation, and run through all the mazes of that art denominated swindling; till at length, overpowered by the accumulated expenses of renewals, interest, and forbearance money, this gentleman-like tradesman makes his appearance in the *Gazette*, preceded by a 'Whereas', and falls to rise no more, but terminates his life in the Marshalsea or King's Bench [prison], his lady in the parish workhouse, his daughters, if handsome, in a brothel, and his sons, unable to procure a livelihood by industry, make their exit at Newgate, or are sent on their travels at the national expense – to Botany Bay.

FRANCIS GROSE, *Olio* (The Grumbler, Essay 7) (1796).

CHAPTER 6

COUNTRY CHARACTERS

Although Adam Smith was born in a town (admittedly a very small one) and lived for most of his life in towns and cities, in *The Wealth of Nations* there is very much more about fields and farms than about factories and workshops.

As passage after passage more than suggests, he had an intimate acquaintance with country scenes and people, and it is not without interest to speculate where he got his information. Some of it, no doubt, dated from that first journey of his into England, when as a youth of seventeen he rode all the way to Oxford. Hardly had he crossed the border than he was noting how much better cultivated the English countryside was than what he had left behind in Scotland; while as for the livestock, whereas the Scottish kine were thin and scraggy, the English oxen were great fat beasts. We may imagine him passing on his way droves of Scotch cattle on the way to Norfolk pastures for fattening before ending up at Smithfield; and (who knows?) it may have been the recollection of the shaggy mob in charge of the wild-looking Highland drovers that, years later in the quiet of his study at Kirkcaldy, prompted the observation that 'Live cattle carry themselves to market'.

Somewhere or other the sight of a squatter's hut on the edge of a common may have led him to remark that 'as the poorest family can often maintain a cat or a dog, without any expense, so the poorest occupiers of land can commonly maintain a few poultry, or a sow and a few pigs, at very little'.

Turn the page, and we are told that where a farmer can get only a low price for his butter he will not think it worth his while to have a particular room or building for a dairy but 'will suffer the business to be carried on amidst the smoke, filth, and nastiness of his own kitchen, as was the case of almost all the farmers in Scotland thirty or forty years ago, and as is the case of many of them still'.

Then it was, perhaps, the recollection of a Fifeshire peasant 'plough-ing the ground with a team of horses or oxen' that led to his protest against the generally held view that 'the common ploughman is the pattern of stupidity and ignorance'. True, 'he is less accustomed to social intercourse than the mechanic who lives in a town', and 'his voice and language are more uncouth and more difficult to be understood by those who are not used to them'; but, on the other hand, 'his understanding, being accustomed to consider a greater variety of objects, is generally much superior to that of the other, whose whole attention from morning till night is commonly occupied in performing one or two very simple operations'.

Some surprise may be felt that Adam Smith makes no particular mention of that 'agricultural revolution' that takes up so much space in the economic histories, and the course of which was spanned by his life. More surprise, surely, should be felt that Arthur Young has very little to say about it either. In the one case as in the other, the reason for the omission may well be that they would have jibbed at the use of 'revolutionary' to describe what was going on. Changes, yes, plenty of them: changes in land ownership and occupation and use, changes in farming practice, changes in the relationships of the classes engaged in agriculture; but these might all be seen as developments of what had been going on for a very long time.

The substitution of compactly individual farms for the open-field system, and the enclosure of many hundreds of thousands of acres of commonlands, waste, and woodland, had been in progress since the Middle Ages. Adam Smith recognised the fact, even though he makes only one mention of 'enclosures' in his book, and that is a rather oblique one. 'The advantage of enclosure is greater for pasture than for corn', he remarks. 'It saves the labour of guarding the cattle, which feed better too when they are not liable to be disturbed by their keeper or his dog.'

About the part played by landed proprietors he is more precise. Of landlords as a class he had little good to say: 'landlords, like all other men, love to reap where they never sowed', to quote one of his most remembered apophthegms. But for those who *did* 'sow', i.e. employed their capital in improving their estates, he had nothing but praise. He had special commendation for 'country gentlemen and farmers', since they of all people were the least subject to 'the wretched spirit of monopoly' and 'have no secrets, such as those of the greater part of manufacturers . . . but are generally rather fond of extending as far as possible any new practice which they have found to be advantageous'. But here again it was not a matter of 'revolution', with its connotation of dramatic suddenness and well-nigh universal impact, but slow and gradual change. 'Evolution', was the word that Smith and Young might have chosen, if it had entered into their everyday vocabulary.

Arthur Young (1741–1820) was the younger son of a country parson, the rector of the little village of Bradfield, near Bury St Edmunds in Suffolk. He went to school at Lavenham, and in 1758 was apprenticed to a merchant at King's Lynn. But he had no taste for commercial pursuits, and when in the year following his father died, he quitted what he called his 'most detestable situation' and faced the world 'without education, pursuit, profession, or employment'.

At first he tried authorship, in which he received no encouragement from Dr Johnson. Then he became a farmer, starting with the management of the family farm at Bradfield Hall, and proceeding to a farm of 300 acres in Essex, where he spent his time and his wife's money in unprofitable experiments, and finally a smaller farm at North Mimms in Hertfordshire. He failed to make a living in all of them. But he always managed to learn something from his mistakes; and moreover, he possessed a restlessly inquisitive intelligence which stood him in good stead when towards the end of the 1760s he set out on what became a series of tours of the English countryside, on horseback or in a hired chaise, in course of which he covered some thousands of miles. Wherever he went he made careful note of anything and everything that he thought of interest and likely to be of value to such of 'the nobility, gentry, landlords, farmers, and others', who were concerned about agricultural progress.

The results of these indefatigable journeyings he published between 1768 and 1771 in volumes – *A Six Weeks' Tour through the Southern Counties of England and Wales, A Six Months' Tour through the North of England,* and *A Farmer's Tour through the West of England* – which are not only among the classics of English topography but our chief sources of information on what is usually denominated the agricultural revolution.

In the preface to the second edition of his *Northern Tour* he explains how he went about it. To begin with, he inserted advertisements in the

London and country papers, inviting all those who were acquainted
with any particular improvements in the counties he proposed to visit
to inform him of them, 'with exact directions to the places where the
improvements, etc., might be examined'. The response was not as
encouraging as he had wished, but he persevered. On the whole, 'gentlemen' were much more useful than 'common farmers', although some
of these gave him some 'very sensible accounts of common practices'.
He found that 'a practical knowledge of agriculture was as requisite to
such an undertaking as plenty of patience'. He goes on:

'My business was likewise so very unusual, that some art was required
to gain intelligence from farmers, etc., who were startled at the first
attack. I found that even a profusion of expense was often necessary to
gain the end I had in view: I was forced to make more than one honest
farmer half drunk, before I could get sober, unprejudiced intelligence.
I met with some farmers who gave me accounts too improbable to
credit; whether from ignorance, or an intention to deceive, I know not;
but always I repeated my inquiries upon those occasions, until I gained
the truth.'

But although he did quite well out of his *Tours* and his many other
writings, his farm in Hertfordshire held him for nine years as in 'the
jaws of a wolf'. He was always in debt, in spite of what he 'earned by
the sweat of my brow, and almost my heart's blood'. In 1773 he got a
job reporting the debates in parliament for the *Morning Post* at five
guineas a week; and for some years he used to walk home every Saturday
seventeen miles to his farm at North Mimms, and back again to London
on the Monday morning. More than once he seriously contemplated
emigrating to America.

In 1776 he made a tour of Ireland, and a little later took a farm near
his old home in Suffolk. Then in 1784 he started the *Annals of Agriculture*, which he continued to edit until 1809. Although the magazine's
circulation was never so large as he thought it ought to be, it was read
by most people of consequence in agriculture – among them King
George III, or 'Farmer George' as he was familiarly styled, who
occasionally contributed articles to its columns signed Ralph Robinson,
the name of his Majesty's shepherd at Windsor. 'Mr Young', the king
is reported to have said once, 'I conceive myself more indebted to you
than to any man in my dominions.'

On the death of his mother in 1785 Young became the owner of
Bradfield Hall, but his appetite for travel was still keen, and he several
times visited France, when he was enabled to witness the *ancien régime*
just before it was engulfed in the French revolution. On the second
visit, in 1788, Young's old mare became completely blind. His reaction

to this catastrophe warms the heart. 'After riding her 3,700 miles', he declared, 'humanity did not allow me to sell her', and they returned home together.

In 1793 Young was appointed secretary of the newly established Board of Agriculture, at a salary of £400 a year. His latter years were clouded with blindness and domestic troubles. So lived and died this greatest of agricultural journalists, the man who above all others was responsible for the elevation of agriculture into a science.

I

Carrying Out the Enclosures

There is scarcely any point in rural economics more generally acknowledged than the great benefits of inclosing open lands. Some authors, it is true, have attacked them as supposititious, and asserted them to be a national disadvantage, of trivial use to the proprietors, but very mischievous to the poor. My residence in this part of Yorkshire brought to my knowledge some particulars respecting the merits of inclosure, and the means commonly pursued in the execution, which are not to be found in any act of Parliament whatever, but which are certainly of importance in weighing and deciding the advantages of the measure.

The proprietors of large estates generally agree upon the measure, adjust the principal points among themselves, and fix upon their attorney before they appoint any general meeting of *all* the proprietors. The small proprietor, whose property in the township is perhaps his all, has little or no weight in regulating the clauses of the act of Parliament, has seldom if ever an opportunity of putting a single one in the bill favourable to his rights, and has as little influence in the choice of commissioners; and of consequence they have seldom any great inducement to be attentive to his interest.

The division and distribution of the lands are totally in their [the commissioners] breasts, and as the quality of the soil as well as the number of acres is concerned, the business is extremely intricate, and requires uncommon attention; but on the contrary is often executed in an inaccurate and blundering manner. Nor is there any appeal from their allotments but to the commissioners themselves however carelessly or partially made. Thus is the property of the proprietors, and especially the poor ones, entirely at their mercy; every passion of resentment, prejudice, etc., may be gratified without control, for they are vested with a despotic power known in no other branch of business in this free country. There is no remedy against the impositions or blunders of the commissioners but that which, perhaps, is as bad as the disease, viz. filing a bill in chancery . . .

A. YOUNG, *Northern Tour* (1771), vol. I, p. 222.

2

A Million Acres

In the last 30 or 40 years 900 bills of inclosure have passed the House of Commons. Upon a moderate calculation they have been the means of improving about a million of acres. The greater part of land before cultivated, but in the constraint and imperfection of the open-field system, in which mankind were so long content to abide by the inconvenience which the barbarity of their ancestors had neither knowledge to discover nor government to remedy. . . . Many of those improvements were in wastes; and if we value the whole at 30s an acre before inclosure, it will not probably be under-rated. By that simple regulation, which annexes to property the power of improving it, the produce doubles, so that the same land now yields £3 from which the more scanty harvests were before reaped at a greater expense. Hence, therefore, these million of acres have been made to yield, at a very modest calculation, a million and a half a year more than in their unimproved state . . .

A. YOUNG, *Annals of Agriculture* (1790), vol. I, p. 72.

3

The Peasant in the Pot-house

Nothing can be clearer than the vast importance which these poor people attach to the object of possessing land, though no more than to set a cottage on. . . . When we sit by our firesides and think how a poor labourer can afford to build a comfortable cottage, enclose some land, break up and cultivate a rough waste, acquire some livestock, and get many conveniences about him, we defy calculation; there must be some moving principle at work which figures will not count, for in such an inquiry we see nothing but impossibilities. But we forget a thousand animating principles of human feeling. Such effects could not possibly have been produced without years of great industry and most economical saving – to become independent, to marry a girl and fix her in a spot they can call their own, instigates to a conduct not a trace of which would be seen without the motive ever in view. With this powerful impulse they will exert every nerve to earn, call into life and vigour every principle of industry, and exert all the powers of frugality to save. Nothing less can account for the spectacle, and such animating prospects will account for anything.

Go to an alehouse kitchen of an old enclosed country, and there you will see the origin of poverty and poor rates. For whom are they to be sober? For whom are they to save? (Such are the questions.) 'For the parish? If I am diligent, shall I have leave to build a cottage? If I am sober, shall I have land for a cow? If I am frugal, shall I have half an acre of potatoes? You offer no motives; you have nothing but a parish officer and a workhouse! – Bring me another pot.'

  A. YOUNG, *Annals of Agriculture* (1801), vol. 36, pp. 507–9.

4

Robert Bakewell's Art of Stock Breeding

[Robert Bakewell (1725–95), of Dishley, Leicestershire, was outstandingly successful as a breeder of cattle (Leicestershire long-horns), sheep (Leicesters), and draught horses. As has been well said of him, he produced beef and mutton for the millions.]

Mr Bakewell's breed of cattle is famous throughout the kingdom. He has in this part of his business many ideas which I believe are perfectly new, or that have been hitherto neglected. His principle is to gain the beast, whether sheep or cow, that will weigh most in the valuable joints: there is a great difference between an ox of 50 stone, carrying 30 in roasting pieces, and 20 in boiling ones – and another carrying 30 in the latter and 20 in the former. And at the same time that he gains the shape, that is, of the greatest value in the smallest compass, he asserts, from his long experience, that he gains a breed much hardier and easier fed than any others. These ideas he applies equally to sheep and oxen.

In the breed of the latter, the old notion was, that where you had much and large bones, there was plenty of room to lay flesh on; and accordingly the graziers were eager to buy the largest boned cattle. This whole system Mr Bakewell has proved to be an utter mistake. He asserts, the smaller the bones, the truer will be the make of the beast – the quicker she will fat – and her weight, we may easily conceive, will have a larger proportion of valuable meat; *flesh*, not *bone*, is the butcher's object.

The breed which Mr Bakewell has fixed on as the best in England is the Lancashire, and he thinks he has improved it much, in bringing the carcass of the beast into a truer mould; and particularly by making them broader over the backs. The shape which should be the criterion of a cow, a bull, or an ox, and also of a sheep, is that of a hogshead, or a firkin; truly circular with small and as short legs as possible; upon the plain principle that the value lies in the barrel, not in the legs.

Another particularity is the amazing gentleness with which he brings up these animals. All his bulls stand still in field to be examined; the way of driving them from one field to another, or home, is by a little swish; he or his men walk by their side, and guide him with the stick wherever they please, and they are accustomed to this method from being calves. A lad, with a stick three feet long, and as big as his finger, will conduct a bull away from other bulls, and his cows from one end of the farm to the other. All this gentleness is merely the effect of management, and the mischief often done by bulls is understandably owing to practices very contrary – or else to a total neglect.

The general order in which Mr Bakewell keeps his cattle is pleasing; all are fat as bears; and this is a circumstance which he insists is owing to the excellence of the breed. His land is no better than his neighbours, at the same time that it carries a far greater proportion of stock.

In the breed of his sheep, Mr Bakewell is as curious, and I think, if any difference, with greater success, than in his horned cattle; for better made animals cannot be seen than his rams and ewes: their bodies are as true barrels as can be seen; round, broad backs; and the legs not above six inches long. The breed is originally Leicestershire, but Mr Bakewell thinks, and very justly, that he has much improved it.

In the breed of stallions for getting cart-horses, Mr Bakewell is also very attentive: he has those at present that he lets out from 25 to 150 guineas the season. He conceives the true make of a cart-horse to be nearly that described above for an ox – thick and short bodies, and very short legs. He makes them all particularly gentle, and apprehends that bad drawing horses can be owing to nothing but bad management. He has one stallion that leaps at 5 guineas a mare.

A. YOUNG, *The Farmer's Tour through the East of England* (1771), vol. 1, pp. 110–20.

5

Lord Rockingham, Statesman and Farmer

Wentworth, the palace of the Marquis of Rockingham [1730–82; prime minister 1765–6 and 1782], situated between Rotherham and Barnsley, is in every respect one of the finest places in the kingdom. But the husbandry of the Marquis is much more worthy of attention than any palace.

Upon turning his attention to agriculture, his Lordship found the husbandry of the West Riding of Yorkshire extremely deficient in numerous particulars. It was disgusting to him to view so vast a property cultivated in so slovenly a manner. Large tracts of land, both grass and arable, yielded but a trifling profit, for want of draining. The pastures and meadows were laid down in ridge and furrow, a practice highly destructive of profit and detestable to the eye. The culture of turnips was become common, but without hoeing, so that the year of fallow was the most capital one of slovenliness and bad husbandry. The implements used were insufficient for a vigorous culture, the general knowledge of manures was extremely imperfect, and the practice void of spirit.

From the beginning, his Lordship conducted himself upon the soundest of principles, that of practising himself those methods which reason told him were the best; he determined to set the example of good husbandry, as the only probable means of being successful.

In the pursuit of this end his conduct was judicious and spirited. He has upwards of 2,000 acres in his hands, and began their improvement with draining such as were wet, rightly considering this part of husbandry as the *sine quâ non* of all others. His method was the most perfect that experience has hitherto brought to light, that of covered drains.

The improvement by these drains (which last for ever) is almost immediately manifest; land which before poached [was cut up] with the weight of a man will now bear without damage the tread of an ox; land that used to be flowed with rain, and quite poisoned by it, now lies perfectly dry throughout the year.

His Lordship's management in laying down and keeping his grass lands is worthy of universal imitation. The success is so very great, that in several large fields I viewed the after-grass was eight and nine inches high, soon after clearing a crop of hay of two tons per acre, and this the first year of the lay. Adjoining several of these new lays, some of the old pastures are to be seen yet in tenants' hands; they are poisoned with superfluous water and overrun with every species of trumpery and weeds, the grass of a poor sort, and the quantity trifling.

But Lord Rockingham in scarce anything has acted with greater spirit than the improvement of the turnip culture, for the disgust he felt at seeing the common slovenly management of the farmers in respect to this crop made him determine to introduce the excellent practice of hoeing, common in many of the southern parts of the kingdom. With this view he attempted to persuade his tenants to come into the method, described the operations, pointed out its advantages, clearly explained the great consequence of increasing the size of the roots . . . yet with a set of men of contracted ideas, used to a stated road, with deviations neither to the right nor left, it had very little effect: turnips continued to be sown, but were never hoed. His Lordship then finding that discourse and reasoning could not prevail over the obstinacy of their understandings, determined to convince their eyes. He sent into Hertfordshire for a husbandman used to hoeing turnips, and gave directions for his management of a large crop. This he continued several years, and by degrees introduced the practice which is now the common practice of all the good common farmers.

In the introduction of new implements and the improvement of old ones, his Lordship was equally attentive. In the article of manuring also, this excellent cultivator set an example of good husbandry. The composts at Wentworth are formed of all sorts of manures, particularly farm-yard dung and manures purchased at the neighbouring towns, such as soap-boilers' ashes, coal ashes, horn shavings, curriers' shavings, &c. And sometimes mole-hills, turf, and lime are added; layers of these are formed one on another, and after remaining a few months are turned over . . . mixed again, and so repeated until the substances are thoroughly rotted.

I cannot take my leave of these pursuits, so truly worthy of a British nobleman, of a philosopher, and of a man, without remarking how greatly the example calls for imitation. Those who have declined the employments and amusements of agriculture under the false idea of their being mean and unworthy of great riches and high rank, should consider the example I have endeavoured to sketch; will they find the character of a statesman and a patriot sullied by the addition of that of a farmer?

A. YOUNG, *Northern Tour* (1771), vol. I, pp. 245-316.

6

A Sussex Farmer at Home

I shall not quit Sussex without making an observation upon the comforts which I have long remarked to be the natural inheritance of a farmer who has the enjoyment of a considerable business. The style of living to which I allude is this: A large, roomy, clean kitchen, with a rousing wood fire on the hearth, and the ceiling well hung with smoked bacon and hams; a small room for the farmer and his family, opening into this kitchen, with glass in the door, or the wall, to see that things *go right*. When company is in the house, the fire in a parlour, very well furnished.

4. A country fair; from an aquatint by W. H. Pyne.
The Costume of Great Britain (1808)

At table, great plenty of plain things, with a bottle of good port after dinner, and at least a hogshead of it in his cellar. . . . On his table some books of piety and common literature. The *Annals of Agriculture* not there so often as they ought to be.

In the stable a good nag, for his own riding, but not good enough for hunting, a recreation too common, but not to be approved! as it is apt to lead into a dissipated, idle, drinking, and expensive life. The only country amusement allowable is shooting. In equipage he goes no further than a one-horse chaise for his wife.

[But] sometimes I see a piano forte in a farmer's parlour, which I always wish was burnt; a livery servant is sometimes found, and a post chaise to carry their daughters to assemblies; these ladies are sometimes educated at expensive boarding-schools, and the sons often at the University, to be made parsons. But all these things imply a departure from that line which separates these different orders of beings [gentlemen and farmers]. Let these things, and all the folly, foppery, expense, and anxiety, that belong to them, remain among gentlemen: a wise farmer will not envy them.

A. YOUNG, *Annals of Agriculture* (1792), vol. 17, pp. 151–7.

7

James Croft, Miner-Farmer

Miners in general are a tumultuous, sturdy set of people, greatly impatient of control, very insolent, and much devoid of industry. Those employed in the lead mines of Craven [West Riding of Yorkshire] and in many collieries can scarcely, by any means, be kept to the performance of a regular business; upon the least disgust they quit their service and try another. No bribes can tempt them to any industry after the first performance of their stated work, which leaves them half the day for idleness or rioting at the alehouse.

Mr Danby [of Swinton, near Rotherham] partaking of these inconveniences in common with his neighbours, struck upon a remedy which sufficiently displays his knowledge of human nature. 'If', said he, 'I can give these fellows a better notion of a local property and happiness, I shall gain a power over them, which I can easily turn to their good and the benefit of their families, as well as to my own convenience.'

Observing some of the men (that had a little industry in them) to cultivate their gardens better than their comrades, he made them an offer of inclosing from the moor a field for each, contiguous to their gardens, that they might raise their own corn instead of buying it. Which was accordingly done, and no additional rent taken for it. By degrees others applied for the same favour, which was always readily granted, and there is now not a collier without his farm, each from three or four to twenty acres. Most of them keep a cow or two, and a galloway [small horse]; raise the corn they eat; are well fed, well clothed, industrious and happy. Their time is spent at home instead of the alehouse; those young fellows who formerly were riotous and debauched, now marry, settle, and become the honest fathers of a laborious and valuable race of children. Nothing is so much desired as a little farm, which, being the reward for industry and sobriety, becomes an incitement to a continued good behaviour. And the whole colliery, from being a scene of idleness, insolence, and riot, is converted into a well-ordered and decently-cultivated colony.

The best intelligence I gained was of James Croft, one of the colliers. Thirteen years ago he began his husbandry by taking an acre of moor, which he pared and burnt, spread lime among the ashes and sowed it with oats. He next planted half with potatoes, and sowed the other half with maslin [mixed rye and wheat]; the crops middling. After another liming, sowed it with oats, the crop 35 bushels. . . . After the oats were off, he mixed some lime and earth together and spread it over the land. The grass came up very finely, and has been exceeding good ever since, and improving every year; it is now worth 20s an acre. His next effort was an addition of eight acres; these were exceeding stony, so that one acre cost him two months to clear and fill up the holes. He threw these lands into a better husbandry than what he used before . . . turnips . . . oats . . . grass, sometimes rye. Potatoes he has regularly cultivated.

Two years ago he took in eight acres more, on which he is now hard at work. He has five acres of grass. His flock of cattle is three milch cows, a heifer, and his galloway; their winter food hay, turnips, and straw. He makes 6 lb of butter per cow per week. [Yet] his work in the colliery has been regular, equal in every respect to the other men and in some superior. His hour of going to the mines is 12 o'clock at night, the work and time of meals are over at noon the next day. Nor has he ever received the least assistance of any kind, or ever expended one shilling in hiring the labour of another man. Some assistance in weeding potatoes, in harvest, etc., he has received from his family, but of four or five children he has only one son of about fourteen years of age, who works with him constantly in the colliery.

From the time of leaving off work in the mine till that of sleeping, he has regularly spent in unremitted labour on his farm. He has never had more than four hours sleep, and of moonlight or bright starlight nights, seldom so much. The regular severe labour of the colliery has not been sufficient to bow down the spirit of this poor fellow; he applies the remainder of the day, and even steals from the night, to prosecute his favourite works of husbandry.

A. YOUNG, *Northern Tour* (1771), vol. 2, pp. 261–70.

8

Mr Coke's Husbandry at Holkham

Mr Coke [Thomas William Coke (1752–1842); created Earl of Leicester of Holkham in 1837] resides in the midst of the best husbandry in Norfolk, where the fields of every tenant are cultivated like gardens. . . . The views which instigated Mr Coke in the culture of his farm were of the most liberal and public-spirited nature. Convenience might have been answered on a much smaller tract of land, but the experiments which he wished to make could convince the farmers only by being on the largest scale. Pleasure, as well as public good, attended the pursuit . . .

The scale of his agriculture will appear from the particulars of his farm: 3,000 acres. £2,000 rent. 400 acres plantation; 400, sainfoin; 500, turnips; 300, barley; 130, oats; 30, wheat; 40, pease. 800 Norfolk ewes, 100 of Bakewell's breed, besides lambs. 600 wethers. 120 fat oxen, 12 working ditto. 30 cows. 8 carters, servants. 40 labourers.

Work on Sundays
To name Mr Coke's management in this respect in harvest, will, I hope, be sufficient to excite a general imitation. His men go to church in the morning; and then immediately to the field, where their useful and honest industry will, I trust, be found as acceptable in the sight of God, as the more common dissipation in an ale house kitchen, to say nothing of the drunkenness, broils, and gaming which usually take place . . .

I cannot quit the management of this spirited improver without relating an anecdote, not less to his honour than any of the preceding circumstances.

A Lesson in Ploughing
Upon a journey made into Gloucestershire, finding that a tenant of his brother Lord Sherborn, Mr Pacey of Northleach, was an active and intelligent farmer, that stepped much beyond the common herd in the

ill-cultivated county, he could not see him using six horses in a plough, upon a soil, and for work which two would stir in Norfolk; he, however, did more than give advice; for, on his return to Holkham, he singled out an active ploughman that could also hoe turnips, and sent him to Mr Pacey, with a pair of horses and a Norfolk plough, desiring him to keep both man and horses as long as he pleased.

A man ploughing with a pair in that country, and without a driver, was a phenomenon rare enough to collect the whole neighbourhood; he did the work well, ploughed the land clean, and in a husband-like manner, at one-third of the common strength and expense.

Mr Pacey was completely convinced that the project was feasible; dismissed his supernumerary horses and bullocks, and practised the Norfolk tillage; and, when Mr Coke went again to see him, returned him the warmest thanks, with assurances that the experiment had saved him one hundred and fifty pounds a year, and, in memory of the original transaction, had the original Norfolk plough painted and hung up in his barn, as the instrument of his conversion from prejudice and custom. It hung there a sign of his own merit and his neighbours stupidity; for, strange to say, the practice has scarcely travelled beyond his own hedges.

A. YOUNG, *Annals of Agriculture* (1784), vol. 2, pp. 353–5, 379–81.

I

Mr and Mrs Strudwick

Anne Hurst was born at Witley in Surrey; there she lived the whole period of a long life, and there she died. As soon as she was thought able to work, she went to service: there, before she was twenty, she married James Strudwick, who, like her own father, was a day-labourer. With this husband she lived a prolific, hard-working, contented wife, somewhat more than fifty years. He worked more than threescore years on one farm; and his wages, summer and winter, were regularly a shilling a day. He never asked more: nor was he ever offered less. They had between them seven children, and lived to see six daughters married, and three of them the mothers of sixteen children; all of whom were brought up, or are bringing up, to be day-labourers.

Strudwick continued to work till within seven weeks of the day of his death; and at the age of fourscore, in 1787, he closed, in peace, a not inglorious life; for, to the day of his death, he never received a farthing in the way of parochial aid. His wife survived him about seven years; and though bent with age and infirmities, and little able to work, excepting as a weeder in a gentleman's garden, she also was too proud either to ask or receive any relief from her parish. For six or seven of the last years of her life, she received twenty shillings a year from the person who favoured me with this account, which he drew up from her own mouth.

With all her virtue, and all her merit, she yet was not much liked in her neighbourhood: people in affluence thought her haughty, and the Paupers of the parish, seeing, as they could not help seeing, that her life was a reproach to theirs, aggravated all her little failings. Yet, the worst thing they had to say of her was, that she was proud; which, they said, was manifested by the manner in which she buried her husband. Resolute, as she owned she was, to have the funeral, and everything that related to it, what she called decent, nothing could dissuade her from having handles to his coffin, and a plate on it, mentioning his age. She was also charged with having behaved herself crossly and peevishly towards one of her sons-in-law, who was a mason, and went regularly every Saturday evening to the ale-house, as he said, *just to drink a pot of beer.* James Strudwick, in all his life, as she often told this ungracious son-in-law, never spent five shillings in any idleness; luckily (as she was sure to add) he had it not to spend.

A more serious charge against her was, that, living to a great age, and but little able to work, she grew to be seriously afraid that, at last, she might become chargeable to the parish (the heaviest, in her estimation, of all human calamities); and that thus alarmed, she did suffer herself more than once, during the exacerbations of a fit of distempered despondency, peevishly (and, perhaps, petulantly) to exclaim that God Almighty, by suffering her to remain so long upon earth, seemed actually to have forgotten her.

SIR F. M. EDEN, *State of the Poor* (1797), vol. I, pp. 578–9 (note).

2

Old George Barwell

3 October 1785. It having always appeared to me incomprehensible how a common farm labourer who perhaps does not earn more than six or seven shillings a week, rears a large family, as many a one does, without assistance – I desired old George Barwell, who has brought up five or six sons and daughters, to clear up the mystery.

He acknowledges that he has frequently been 'hard put to it'. He has sometimes barely had *bread* for his children: not a morsel for himself! having often made a dinner off *raw hog peas*: saying, that he has taken a handful of peas, and ate them with as much satisfaction as he had eaten better dinners; adding, that they agreed with him very well, and that he was able to work upon them as upon other food: closing his remarks with the trite maxim – breathed out with an involuntary sigh – 'Ay, no man knows what he can do, till he's put to it.'

Since his children have been grown up and able to support themselves, the old man has saved, by the same industry and frugality which supported his family in his younger days, enough to support himself in old age! What a credit to the species!

19 March 1786. Last week died George Barwell, whose honesty, industry, and good sense were such as rarely centre in a farm labourer. He died worth a hundred pounds, a fortune which he of course accumulated in the wane of life, dying at the age of seventy-three. In evidence of his strict honesty, he owed only sixpence, and he thought of it, in his moments of recollection, until the hour he died; entreating

his children to remember to pay it; and even in delirium he thought
about his work. He thought more justly, and more clearly, than any
unlettered man I ever conversed with.

w. MARSHALL, *Rural Economy of the Midland Counties* (1796), vol. 2,
pp. 197–8, 247.

3

'Captain Sally' and her 'Man Mary'

Mrs Sarah Spencer was the daughter of a gentleman in Sussex . . . and
though she had been well, and genteelly, educated, and with such views
as are common to people in her sphere of life, yet, on the demise of her
father, she found her whole fortune did not amount to quite £300. Her
sister Mary, a woman of perhaps not inferior goodness of heart, though
certainly of very inferior abilities, was left in a similar predicament.

Their persons, though not uncomely, were not so attractive as to
flatter them that, without fortunes, they could marry advantageously;
and a mere clown [rustic] was not much more likely to be happy with
them, than they could have been with him. They either had no relations,
on whom they would have been permitted to quarter themselves, or
they thought such a state of dependence but a more specious kind of
beggary. Yet living in an age and country in which well-educated
women not born to fortunes are peculiarly forlorn; with no habits of
exertion, nor even of a rigid frugality; they soon found that, being
thus unable to work, and ashamed to beg, they had no prospect but that
of pining to death in helpless and hopeless penury . . .

At a loss what else to do, they took a farm; and, without ceasing to be
gentlewomen, commenced farmers. This farm they carried on for many
years, much to their credit and advantage; and, as far as example goes,
not less to the advantage of the neighbourhood. To this day the marks of
their good husbandry are to be seen in the village of Rottington.

How it is to be accounted for . . . the fact is indisputable, that those
who have been most distinguished for their endeavours to promote
improvements in agriculture, have but rarely been popular characters.
This was the hard fate of the Spencers; who, instead of gratitude, long
experienced little else than discourtesies and opposition in their neighbourhood. The more active of them was called *Captain Sally*, and her
sister, her *Man Mary*. With the Gentry around them, this was not the
case; by these they were visited and respected as they deserved to be;

and not seldom, in one and the same day, they have divided their hours in helping to fill the dungcart and receiving company of the highest rank and distinction. And it was hard to say, which of these offices they performed with most intelligence and grace, for they even handled the dung-fork with an air of elegance.

To many of their poorer relations they were not only kind but useful. Towards the close of their lives, which happened 14 or 15 years ago, even the most perverse of their neighbours saw their error; and though they continued not to court popularity, they at length became popular; and when they died, they were very sincerely regretted.

SIR F. M. EDEN (from a 'biographical sketch obligingly communicated by a friend'), *State of the Poor* (1797), vol. I, pp. 626–7 (note).

(c) FIGURES IN WILLIAM MARSHALL'S LANDSCAPE

As a reporter on the condition of the rural population, William Marshall (1745–1818) is to be preferred even over the much better known Arthur Young. Where Young saw fit to fill pages with accounts of his visits to the great country houses, Marshall interspersed his descriptions of farming practice with pleasantly informative little sketches of life and character.

Born in a village near Pickering in the North Riding of Yorkshire, he was, as he himself put it, 'born a farmer and could trace his blood through the veins of agriculturists for upwards of 400 years', but 'from the age of 15 was wandering in the ways of commerce in a distant climate', i.e. the West Indies. But after fourteen years he had a violent illness, and returned to England, and in 1774 became manager of a farm of 300 acres near Croydon in Surrey. Six years later he became agent for the Norfolk estates of Sir Harbord Harbord, and then from 1776 so arranged his affairs that he spent the winters in London and the summers in travelling up and down the country, filling notebooks with material which was embodied in due course in his chief publication, the *General Survey from personal experience, observation and inquiry, of the Rural Economy of England*, published in twelve volumes between 1787 and 1798.

Marshall was not only a capable practical farmer and clear writer, but something of a philologist, making a careful note of 'provincialisms' in local speech which he printed as appendixes.

In 1808 he removed from London to his native vale of Cleveland, where he busied himself with managing his own estate and in efforts to establish a College of Agriculture at Pickering.

I

Farming Folk in the Vale of London

The farmers (the higher class excepted) are as homely, in their dress and manners, as those of the more recluse parts of the kingdom, and are far less enlightened and intelligent than those of many parts of it. The reason is, they live chiefly among themselves, as a distinct com-

5. Young woman churning butter.

W. H. Pyne, The Costume of Great Britain

munity, retaining much of the character, probably, of husbandmen of former times, and holding their prejudices as fast, or at this time perhaps faster, than those of the most distant provinces.

The work people of the Vale wear the same marks of rusticity as their employers. The children of farm labourers and other poor working people in the neighbourhood of London rank among the most illiterate of their class in the Island. Few of them (unless of late years, through the establishment of Sunday schools) are taught even to read. A want of free schools is a probable cause of the low state of ignorance in which this class are found, in the southern provinces, comparatively with the same class in the northern.

It is to be observed, however, that a considerable portion of the work people, particularly men, employed in the District are not natives of the country but are collected from all parts of the kingdom. Having been compelled, by crimes or follies, to leave their own countries, they press towards the centre of depravity; or perhaps enter it, and are afterwards vomited from its infectious maw, and thrown, as a grievous pest, upon the surrounding country; or, at best, as a necessary evil, to supply the place of deserving natives, who find work and better wages in the warehouses and workshops of trade and manufacture in town, than husbandry can afford them.

w. MARSHALL, *Agriculture in the Southern Counties* (1799), vol. I, pp. 17–27.

2

The Smithfield Drover

June 13, 1782. This afternoon went to see the Smithfield drover pay off his 'masters' at his chamber at the Angel, at Waltham. The room was full of 'graziers', who had sent up bullocks last week, and were come today to receive their accounts and money.

What a trust! A man, perhaps not worth a hundred pounds, brings down twelve or fifteen hundred, or perhaps two thousand pounds, to be distributed among twenty or thirty persons, who have no other security than his honesty for their money – nay, even the servant of this man is entrusted with the same charge, the master going one week, the man the other. And so it has been for a century past; and I do not learn that one breach has been committed.

The business was conducted with great ease, regularity, and dispatch.

He had each man's account, and a pair of saddle-bags with the money and bills, lying upon the table; and the farmers, in their turn, took their seat at his elbow. Having examined the salesman's account; received their money; drunk a glass or two of liquor; and thrown down sixpence towards the reckoning, they severally returned into the market.

There was only one long face in the company. This was a farmer who had sent up three bullocks, for which he had twenty-four pounds bade at Waltham fair; whereas the salesman's account from Smithfield, notwithstanding the goodness of this week's market, was only twenty-two pounds.

W. MARSHALL, *Rural Economy of Norfolk* (1795), vol. 2, p. 267.

3

The Miller's Bargain

Feb. 28, 1782. About two months ago I took a sample of wheat to North Walsham market, with an intent to make myself acquainted with the business of the corn markets of this country. North Walsham is an afternoon market; corn all sold by sample; some in the market-place, but chiefly at the inns.

Having made my election of a miller, and finding that he 'quartered' at the Bear, I went to his room (he was not in till nearly six) and shewed him my sample; namely, about two handfulls, put in a piece of brown paper; which, agreeable to the fashion of the country, was gathered up in the hand, and tied with a string, in the manner of a pounce-bag.

He asked the price; I told him the best he gave that day; he said a guinea was the highest; I had previously understood that a guinea was 'the top of the market', and sold it to him at that price. He asked how much there was of it; I told him about fifteen coombs. He marked the name, the quantity, and the price, upon the bulge of the paper, and the business was done. His room was set round with farmers, who, the conversation being audible, were witnesses to the bargain.

W. MARSHALL, *Rural Economy of Norfolk* (1795), vol. 2, p. 141.

4

Norfolk Farm Labourers

There is an alertness in the servants and labourers of Norfolk which I have not observed in any other district. That 'custom is second nature' is verified every hour.

The Norfolk husbandman while a boy is accustomed to run by the side of the horses while they trot with the harrows. When he becomes a plowman, he is accustomed to step out at the rate of three or four miles an hour; and, if he drive an empty team, he either does it standing in his carriage, with a sprightliness of air and with a seeming pride and satisfaction, or runs by the side of his horses while they are bowling away at full trot. Thus both his body and his mind become active; and be he go to mow, reap, or other employment, his habit of activity accompanies him – and is obvious even in his air, his manners, and his gait.

A Kentish plowman, on the contrary, accustomed from his infancy to walk, whether at harrow, plow, or cart, about a mile-and-a-half or two miles an hour, preserves the same sluggish step, even in his holidays; and is the same slow, dull, heavy animal in everything he does.

That the Norfolk farm-labourers despatch more work than those of other countries is an undoubted fact, and in this way, I think, it may be fully accounted for.

W. MARSHALL, *Rural Economy of Norfolk* (1795), vol. 2, pp. 177–8.

5

A Norfolk Farmer's Hospitality

The farmers of Norfolk are strongly marked by a liberality of thinking, and in consequence an openness in their manner of conversation. Many of them have been, and some still are rich; this has led them to mix in a greater or a less degree with what is called the world. . . . The lower class however are the same plain men which farmers in general are, living in a great measure with their servants. Another class live in the kitchen with their servants, but eat at a separate table; while the upper class have their 'keeping' rooms and other commodious apartments.

As an instance of the *complacency* and *good breeding* (I do not mean *complaisance* or *politeness*) of the superior class of Norfolk farmer I will relate the circumstances of deportment which occurred to myself at a farm-house at which I slept accidentally.

Our host having given strict orders, and some personal attention, respecting our horses, the company were led into a spacious kitchen, characterised by cleanliness and a cheerful fire. A decent upper servant presented herself. Supper was ordered; and a bottle of wine, in a neat fashionable decanter set upon the table. A smart, but not extravagant, supper soon made its appearance. The housekeeper waited in an adjoining room and a maid-servant at the table, with a degree of propriety and decorum frequently unseen in the houses of those who call themselves gentlemen.

A trifling incident proved the good sense, if not the good breeding, of our host and his family. Forgetting that I was at the table of a *Norfolk farmer*, I asked for an article of the sideboard which was not at hand. The servant went out of the room as if to fetch it; but the housekeeper came in to make an apology for not happening to have it in the house. She withdrew; the maid-servant returned; while the conversation went on without any notice being taken or any observation being made on the awkwardness of the circumstance.

In the morning, when I returned from a walk, I found, in a decently but not extravagantly furnished parlour, two tables set out; one with tea equipage, the other with napkins, bread and butter, ham, radishes, etc. The housekeeper sat at the former, placed on one side of the room, and made tea, which was brought to us at our table at the other; and this without the least shew of parade or formality.

W. MARSHALL, *Rural Economy of Norfolk* (1795), vol. I, pp. 37–9.

6

Servants at the Hiring

Sept. 27, 1784. This morning rode to 'Polesworth statute': a hiring-place for farm servants; the only one of any note in this part of the country, and probably the largest meeting of the kind in England. Servants come (particularly out of Leicestershire) five and twenty or thirty miles to it, on foot! The number of servants collected together in the 'statute yard' has been estimated at two to three thousand. A number, however, which is the less extraordinary, as Polesworth being the only place, in this district, and this the only day – farm servants, for several miles around, consider themselves as liberated from servitude on this day.

Formerly, much rioting and disturbance took place at this meeting; arising, principally, from gaming tables, which were then allowed, and for want of civil officers to keep the peace. But by the spirited exertions of the present high constable, Mr Laking, these riots have been suppressed and prevented.

The principal nuisance at present arises from groups of *balladsingers*, disseminating sentiments of dissipation, on minds which ought to be trained to industry and frugality. A ballad goes a long way towards forming the morals of rustics; and if, instead of the trash which is everywhere, at present, dealt out at these meetings, songs in praise of conjugal happiness, and country life, were substituted, fortunate might be the effects.

w. MARSHALL, *Rural Economy of the Midland Counties* 2nd edn (1796), vol. 2, p. 247.

7

She Made the First 'Stilton'

Leicestershire is celebrated for its 'cream cheese', generally known by the name of *Stilton cheese*. This species of cheese may be said to be a modern produce of the Midland district. Mrs Paulet of Wimondham, in the Melton quarter of Leicestershire, the first maker, is still living.

Mrs Paulet being a relation or an acquaintance of the well-known Cooper Thornhill, who kept the Bell Inn at Stilton (in Huntingdonshire, on the great north road from London to Edinburgh) furnished his house with cream cheese; which, being of a singularly fine quality, was coveted by his customers; and, through the assistance of Mrs Paulet, his customers were gratified, at the expense of half a crown a pound, with cream cheese of a superior quality, but of what country was not publicly known; hence it obtained, of course, the name of Stilton cheese. At length, however, the place of produce was discovered, and the art of producing it learnt, by other dairywomen of the neighbourhood. Dalby first took the lead, but it is now made in almost every village in that quarter of Leicestershire, as well as in the neighbouring villages of Rutlandshire. Many tons are made every year. The sale is no longer confined to Stilton; every innkeeper within fifteen or twenty miles of

133

the district of manufacture is a dealer in Stilton cheese. The price, at present, ten pence a pound, to the maker; and a shilling to the consumer, who takes it at the maker's weight.

w. MARSHALL, *Rural Economy of the Midland Counties* (1796), vol. 1, pp. 320-2.

8

Mighty Drinkers of the Cider Country

Farm labourers [in the Vale of Gloucester] are sufficiently numerous; they are noticeable as being simple, inoffensive, unintelligent, and apparently slow. Their wages are very low, *in money*, being only 1s a day. But *in drink* shamefully exorbitant. Six quarts a day, the common allowance; frequently two gallons; sometimes nine or ten quarts; or an unlimited quantity.

In a cider year, the extravagance of this absurd custom (which prevails throughout the cider counties) is not perceived. But now (1788) after a succession of bad fruit years, it is no wonder the farmers complain of being beggared by malt and hops! They are not, however, entitled to pity. The fault – the crime – is their own. The origin of the evil, I fear, rests with themselves.

In a fruit year, cider is of little value. It is no uncommon circumstance to send out a general invitation, into the highways and hedges, in order to empty the casks which were filled last year, that they may be refilled this. A habit of drinking is not easily corrected. Nor is an art learnt in youth readily forgotten. Men and masters are equally adept in the art of drinking. The tales which are told of them are incredible. Some two or three I recollect. But, although I have no reason to doubt the authorities I had them from, I wish not to believe them. I hope they are not true.

Drinking a gallon-bottle-full, at a draught, is said to be no uncommon feat: a mere boyish trick, which will not bear to be bragged of. But to drain a two-gallon-bottle, without taking it from the lips, as a labourer of the vale is said to have done, by way of being even with master, who had paid him short in *money* – is spoken of as an exploit, which carried the art of draining a wooden bottle to its full pitch.

Two gallons of cider, however, are not a stomach-full. Another man of the vale undertook, for a trifling wager, to drink twenty pints, one immediately after another. He got down nineteen (as the story is gravely told), but these filling the cask to the bung, the twentieth could not of course get admittance.

But the quantity drank, in this extempore way, by the men, is trifling compared with that which their masters will swallow at a sitting. Four well-seasoned yeomen (some of them well known in this vale), having raised their courage with the juice of the apple, resolved to have a fresh hogshead tapped; and, setting foot to foot, emptied it at one sitting.

w. MARSHALL, *Rural Economy of Gloucestershire* (1796), vol. I, pp. 51–3.

9

Hop Picking in Kent

The season of hop picking usually commences in the month of September. The workpeople [are] collected from various quarters. The country itself furnishes a great number, as it is the custom for women, of almost every degree, to assist at the hop picking. The town of Maidstone is nearly deserted in the height of the season. Tradesmen's daughters, even of the higher classes, and those of farmers and yeomen of the first rank and best education, are seen busy at the hop bins. Beside the people of the neighbourhood, numbers flock from the populous towns of Kent, and many from the metropolis; also from Wales, hop picking being the last of the summer works of these itinerants.

A few days before the picking begins, the lanes and village greens swarm with these strolling pickers; men, women, children, and infants, living as much in a state of nature as the American Indians, or the savages of the southern hemisphere; plundering the country of whatever they can easily lay their hands upon, as fruit, potatoes, and more valuable articles.

During the picking, these strollers, and strangers in general, sleep in barns and out-buildings; or in huts, or cabins, built in long ranges for this purpose; or in any hole or by-corner they an creep into. I looked into a human dwelling of the latter cast. It was the ruins of a lime kiln, which had been covered with a roof of hopbines, through which rose the flue of a chimney. Three staves, set up triangle-wise, bestrode the hearth, over which was suspended, from the tops of the staves, a short hazel rod, with two natural hooks – to hang the pot higher or lower. Some large stones round the hearth as seats, and a well-bronzed tobacco pipe in the chimney corner, composed the rest of the furniture.

In West Kent hops are picked into 'bins', namely, cloths, or broad shallow bags hung in square frames, supported by four legs. In the field the workpeople are separated into classes. The *steward* sees to the setting out of the ground, and to the measuring, and keeping the accounts of each picker's earnings, and generally, to the conduct of the whole. The *binmen* draw the poles [from out the ground] and place them over the bins. The *pickers* are divided into 'bins', generally of six to eight each, and three or more bins make a 'set', who work together on the same lot.

In picking, the workpeople stand by the side of the bins, or sit on the frames, between the loaded poles; dropping the hops, as they are separated from the vines, into the bin cloths; beginning at the top of the pole and moving it upward, as it is cleared; two pickers being generally employed on the same pole, one on either side. When finished they throw the poles, with the cleared vines, behind them, into heaps; the binmen continuing to replace them with loaded poles.

The picking is invariably done by measure, by what is called the 'bushel', but in fact by the basket of eleven gallons: the price being regulated by the fullness of the crop and other circumstances, and settled at so many bushels or baskets to the shilling. In 1790 the prevailing price was 'eight for a shilling', or three-halfpence a basket, for hops that produced a middling crop, as ten or twelve hundredweights an acre. For fuller crops, 'twelve for a shilling', or a penny a bushel, is a common price. Of such crops, an expert hand will pick twenty bushels or upwards a day. The earnings of pickers rising from seven to twelve shillings a week.

Hop picking continues for some weeks. The numerous throngs of workpeople, with the attendant swarms of children, which everywhere meet the eye, is peculiarly striking. Whole families, indeed the whole country, may be said to live in the fields, during the busy season of hopping. The country itself, as the picking advances, takes a broken, ragged appearance, disgusting the eye that is set to beautiful objects. But those who stroll through it, and view it in detail, find much that gratifies: and the good humour and garrulity, which is heard in every garden, add to the pleasure.

The hop picking is a sort of jubilee; during which a licence of speech, and relaxation of manners, are authorized by custom; anything may be said, and many things done, which would not pass uncensured at another season.

What strikes a stranger the most, as being himself concerned, is the homage with which he is received, on joining one of those licenced groups. The fairest, or the forwardest, of the female pickers, having selected the finest bunch of hops in her view, approaches him with

9. Industry and Idleness: (*above*) The fellow 'prentices at their looms; (*below*) The industrious 'prentice a favourite, and entrusted by his master.

10. Industry and Idleness: (*above*) The industrious 'prentice out of his time and married to his master's daughter; (*below*) The idle 'prentice in a garret with a prostitute

11. Industry and Idleness: (*above*) The idle 'prentice betrayed by a prostitute; (*below*) The industrious 'prentice alderman of London. The idle one impeached before him by his accomplice

12. Industry and Idleness: The idle 'prentice executed at Tyburn

great respect – and 'wipes his shoes' – or rather touches them with it, and then offers it to him.

Whatever might be the origin of this singular custom, its modern intention is too evident to be mistaken by those who attract its notice. It is that of collecting silver: which either goes towards the hop supper, that is always given on the evening of the last day of picking; or is expended in fulfilling another custom of the hop harvest. This may be termed the *decoration of the hats*. A few days before the picking is completed by any particular planter the company of pickers belonging to such individual, decorate a hat, at their joint expence, with a handker-chief of gaudy hue, and with ribbons and gilded ornaments. This is the hat of the head binman. Another is adorned with ribbons only. This is the carter's. These hats are exposed to public view before the day of finishing, are displayed at the hop supper, and afterwards worn in public; each company endeavouring to outvie the other in finery.

w. MARSHALL, *Rural Economy of the Southern Counties*
(1798) vol. I, pp 242-60

10

Handsome Young Wenches

If ever I employ women in harvest it must be from a scarcity of men; and it must be from real necessity, if I employ more than two. Two women, after the first or second day, will do as much work as half a dozen. By this time their stores of scandal being reciprocally com-municated, they begin to work for amusement.

If it be necessary, or convenient, to employ a number of both men and women, it is but common good management to keep them separate; with this exception – employ 'one man, among women; and one woman, among men'. – A crusty, conceited old fellow will check the gossiping of the women; and I have seen a handsome young wench, raking after, animate more than a gallon of ale. Two are dangerous; they breed contention, and rather hinder than forward the business of the day.

w. MARSHALL, *Agriculture in the Southern Counties* (1799), vol. I,
pp. 352–3.

II

Farm Labour in the West Country

[In West Devonshire] no inconsiderable share of farm labour is done by farmers themselves, their wives, sons and daughters. On the larger farms, however, workpeople of different descriptions are employed.

1. The *labourers* of the district are below par; many of them drunken, idle fellows, and not a few of them may be said to be honestly dishonest; declaring, without reserve, that a poor man cannot bring up a family on six shillings a week and honesty. In addition, however, to these low wages, it is pretty common for farmers to let their constant labourers have corn, at a fixed price, and endeavour to give them piece work. Nevertheless, the wages of the district, seeing the great rise in the price of living, appears to me to be too low, and what the farmers save in the expense of labour they probably lose by pillage and in the poor's rate.

2. *Servants* The most remarkable circumstance in the economy of farm servants in this part of the Island is that of there being no fixed time or place for hiring them; a circumstance which, I believe, prevails throughout the West of England. They are hired either for the year, the half year, or the week; the last a very unusual method of retaining house or indoor farm servants.

When a servant is out of place, he makes enquiries among his acquaintances, and goes round to the farm houses, to offer himself. The practice ... is certainly more convenient to the farmer, and it is less degrading to the servants, than the practice of exposing themselves for hire in a public market; though it may not be so speedy and certain a way of getting a place.

The wages of servants, as those of labourers, are low, compared with those of most other Districts. The yearly wages of men run from six to eight pounds; of women three pounds or three guineas.

3. *Apprentices* It is a common practice throughout Devonshire, and I believe the West of England, to put out the children of paupers, boys more particularly, at the age of seven or eight years, to farmers and others; and to bind them as apprentices until they be twenty-one.

This is an easy and ready way of disposing of the children of paupers, and is fortunate for the children thus disposed of, as enuring them to labour and industry and providing them with better sustenance than they would expect to receive from their parents. To the farmers, too, such children might, one would think, be made highly valuable in their concerns and in the end would become very profitable. The contrary, however, is generally the case – an unfortunate and indeed lamentable circumstance which arises in great measure, I apprehend, from improper treatment.

Instead of treating them as adopted children, or as relations, or as a superior order of servants, whose love and esteem they are desirous of gaining, for their mutual happiness, during the long term of their intimate connexion, as well as to secure their services at a time when they become the more valuable, [the masters] treat them, at least in the early stage of servitude, as the inferiors of yearly or weekly servants; and they are frequently subjected, I fear, to a state of the most abject drudgery. . . . The ordinary consequence is, no sooner are they capable of supporting themselves than they desert their servitude, and the provincial papers are filled with advertisements for 'runaway 'prentices'.

W. MARSHALL, *Rural Economy of the West of England* (1796), vol. I, pp. 107–12.

(d) LAMENT FOR THE OLD-TIME SQUIRE

When I was a young man ... another character was the country 'squire; I mean the little independent gentleman of three hundred pounds per annum, who commonly appeared in a plain drab or plush coat, large silver buttons, jockey cap, and rarely without boots. His travels never exceeded the distance of the county town, and that only at assize and sessions time, or to attend an election. Once a week he commonly dined at the next market town, with the attorneys and justices. This man went to church regularly, settled the parochial disputes between the parish officers at the vestry, and afterwards adjourned to the neighbouring ale-house, where he usually got drunk for the good of his country.

He never played cards but at Christmas, when a family-pack was produced from the mantel-piece. He was commonly followed by a couple of greyhounds and a pointer, and announced his arrival at a neighbour's house by smacking his whip, or giving the view-halloo. His drink was generally ale, except on Christmas, the fifth of November, or some other gala days, when he would make a bowl of strong brandy punch garnished with a toast and nutmeg. A journey to London was, by one of these men, reckoned as great an undertaking as is at present a voyage to the East Indies, and undertaken with scarce less precaution and preparation.

The mansion of one of these 'Squires was of plaster striped with timber or of red brick, large casemented bow windows, a porch with seats in it, and over it a study; the eaves of the house well inhabited by swallows, and the court set round with hollyhocks. Near the gate was a horse-block, for the conveniency of mounting.

The hall was furnished with flitches of bacon, and the mantelpiece with guns and fishing-rods of various dimensions, accompanied by the broad sword, partizan and dagger, borne by his ancestor in the Civil Wars. The vacant spaces were occupied by stags'-horns. Against the wall was posted King Charles's Golden Rules, Vincent Wing's Alman-

ack, and a portrait of the Duke of Marlborough; in his window lay
Baker's *Chronicle*, Fox's *Book of Martyrs*, Glanvil *On Apparitions*,
Quincey's *Dispensatory*, the *Complete Justice*, and a book of Farriery.

In the corner, by the fireside, stood a large wooden two-armed chair
with a cushion; and within the chimney corner were a couple of seats.
Here, at Christmas, he entertained his tenants assembled round a
glowing fire made of the roots of trees and other great logs, and told and
heard the traditionary tales of the village respecting ghosts and witches,
till fear made them afraid to move. In the mean time the jorum of ale
was in continual circulation.

The best parlour, which was never opened but on particular occasions, was furnished with Turk-worked chairs and hung round with
portraits of his ancestors; the men in the character of shepherds, with
their crooks, dressed in full suits and huge full-bottomed perukes;
others in complete armour or buff coats, playing on the base viol or
the lute; the females likewise as shepherdesses, with the lamb and
crook, all habited in high heads and flowing robes.

Alas! these men are no more; the luxury of the times has obliged
them to quit the country and become the humble dependants on great
men, to solicit a place or commission to live in London, to rack their
tenants and draw their rents before due. The venerable mansion is
suffered to tumble down, or is partly upheld as a farmhouse . . .

FRANCIS GROSE, *Olio* (The Grumbler, Essay 11) (1796), pp. 40–44.

CHAPTER 7

UP AND DOWN THE ENGLISH ROADS

'Good roads, canals, and navigable rivers', wrote Adam Smith in *The Wealth of Nations* (Bk. I, Ch. 10, Pt. 2) 'are the greatest of all improvements.' Of the three, roads throughout the eighteenth century and up to the coming of the railways, were by far the most important means of social and commercial communication.

For most of the information concerning the state of the roads in Adam Smith's time we are indebted to two authors who were also great travellers. The first is Daniel Defoe, whose *Tour thro' the Whole Island of Great Britain* was first published in 1724–7 and reflects the condition of affairs in the early part of the century, but was kept up to date in successive editions for the next fifty years or so; and the other is Arthur Young, whose *Tours* in the southern counties, the north, and the east of England, appeared between 1768 and 1771.

Of the two, Defoe gives what is by far the more favourable picture. Thus, the 'few Observations' quoted below from the 1742 edition of the *Tour* are almost ecstatic in their praise. Specially commended are the turnpike roads that were constructed by trusts formed by public-spirited landowners and profit-seeking entrepreneurs under acts of parliament that empowered them to recoup their expenditure out of officially approved tolls.

These turnpikes were undoubtedly a great improvement, but until well past the middle of the century there were not many of them; and even where they existed, there were often big gaps of unimproved trackways between the lengths that had been turnpiked. None of the great main roads of the country was the responsibility of a single turnpike trust.

Nor were the turnpikes anything like so popular as a reading of Defoe might lead one to believe. Thus Adam Smith states that 'it is not more than fifty years ago that some of the counties in the neighbourhood of London petitioned the parliament against the extension of the turnpike roads into the remoter counties', because they feared that these 'remoter counties' would be able to sell their grass and corn cheaper in the London market than they could.

The chief vehicle used for the carriage of goods along the roads was the great broad-wheeled waggon which (so Adam Smith says) when 'attended by two men and drawn by eight horses, in about six weeks

6. A broad-wheeled waggon such as Adam Smith describes.

W. H. Pyne, The Costume of Great Britain

time carries and brings back between London and Edinburgh near four ton weight of goods'. Note the 'broad-wheeled'. For years there was much argument about the respective merits of broad and narrow wheels, until it became generally agreed that the former were preferable, since they did not cut up the road surface so much, and furthermore, left a track just wide enough to accommodate a gentleman on horseback.

Writing a generation or so after Defoe, Arthur Young gives a far less favourable picture: no passages in his *Tours* are better known than those in which he uses such terms as 'detestable', 'infernal', or 'execrable'. Towards the end of the century things seem to have been much better, so that the Christmas-card pictures of coaches speeding along well-kept roads is not altogether fanciful. All the same, as late as 1798 we find John Middleton writing in the most scathing terms of the state of the roads in Middlesex within a few miles of the metropolis.

I

'A few Observations upon the Roads
... of the United Kingdom'

The soil of all the midland part of England, even from sea to sea, is of a deep stiff clay or marly earth, and it carries a breadth of near fifty miles at least, in some places much more. Nor is it possible to go from London to any part of Britain, north, without crossing this clayey dirty part ...

This natural difficulty of the soil through all the midland country, where the carriage at the same time was so prodigious and made some of the highways in a manner impassable, necessarily brought the country to apply to Parliament; and the consequence has been that turnpikes or toll-bars have been set up on the several great roads of England, beginning at London, and proceeding through almost all those dirty deep roads, in the midland counties especially; at which turnpikes all carriages, droves of cattle, and travellers on horseback are obliged to pay an easy toll, which bears no comparison with the benefit reaped thereby; and it is well worth recording for the honour of the present age that this work has been begun, and is in an extraordinary manner carried on, and perhaps may in a great measure be completed within our memory, as to the worst and most dangerous roads in the kingdom. And this is a work of so much general good, that certainly no public edifice, almshouse, hospital, or nobleman's palace, can be of equal value to the country with this, nor at the same time more an honour and ornament to it.

The benefit of these turnpikes appears now to be so great, and the people of all places begin to be so sensible of it, that it is incredible what effect it has already had upon trade in the counties where the roads are completely finished; even the carriage of goods is abated, in some places 6d per hundredweight, in others 12d; which is abundantly more advantage to commerce than the charge paid amounts to; and yet at the same time the expence is paid by the carriers too, who make the abatement, so that the benefit in abating the rate of carriage is wholly and simply the tradesmens, not the carriers.

Yet the advantage is evident to the latter also another way, for they can bring more weight with the same number of horses, nor are their horses so hardworked and fatigued with their labour as they were before; in which one particular it is acknowledged by the carriers, they perform their work with more ease, and the masters are at less expence.

The advantage is also inexpressible to all other kinds of travelling, such as the safety and ease to gentlemen journeying up to London on all occasions, whether to the [Law] Term, to Parliament, to Court, or on any other necessary occasion. Also the riding-post, as well for the ordinary carrying of the mails as for gentlemen when their occasions require speed, is made extremely easy, safe and pleasant by this alteration of the roads.

The safety of travelling . . . is the more to be insisted on, because the Commissioners for these repairs of the highways do daily order bridges to be repaired and enlarged, and new ones built, where they find occasion; which not only serve to carry the water off where it otherwise often spreads and lies, as it were, dammed up upon the road and spoils the way, but where it rises sometimes by sudden rains to a dangerous height; for it is to be observed, that there is more hazard, and more lives lost, in passing or attempting to pass little brooks and streams, which are swelled by sudden showers of rain and where passengers expect no stoppage, than in passing great rivers, where the danger is known and therefore more carefully avoided.

In many of these places the Commissioners have not only built large and substantial bridges but have set up sluices to stop and open channels to carry off the waters, where they used to swell into the highway; and I have been told, years ago, that the several Commissioners in the respective districts had then built between 300 and 400 new bridges where there were none before, or where the former were small and insufficient to carry the traveller safe over the waters. Many of these are within a few miles of London, especially, for example, on the great road from London to Edgeworth, from London to Enfield, from London to St Albans, from London to Croydon, etc.

Besides the benefits accruing from this laudable method we may add the conveniency to those who bring fat cattle, especially sheep, to London in the winter from the remoter counties of Leicester and Lincoln where they are bred; for before, the country graziers were obliged to sell their stocks off in September and October when the roads began to get bad, and when they generally sell cheap; and the butchers and farmers near London used to engross them and keep them till December and January and then sell them, though not an ounce fatter than before, for an advanced price, to the citizens of London; whereas now the roads are in a way to be made everywhere passable, the City will be served with mutton almost as cheap in the winter as in the summer, or the profit of the advance will be to the country graziers who are the original breeders and take all the pains.

This is evidenced to a demonstration in the counties where the roads are already repaired, from whence they bring their fat cattle, and particularly their mutton, in droves, from sixty, seventy, or eighty miles, without fatiguing, harassing, or sinking the flesh of the creatures, even in the depth of winter.

I might give examples of other branches of inland commerce which are and still will be further altered for the better by this repairing the roads, and particularly that of carrying cheese; a species of provision so considerable that nothing, except that of live cattle, can exceed it. This is chiefly made in Cheshire, Gloucestershire, and Warwickshire and the parts adjacent, from whence the nation used to be very meanly supplied, by reason of the great distance of the country where the cheese is made from those where it is chiefly expended.

I could also enlarge upon the convenience that accrues to the trade in fresh fish from the sea coasts to the inner parts of the kingdom, whither, when the ways are bad, they cannot carry them sweet. This of course must greatly increase the consumption of fish in its season, and employ a considerable number of horses and men, as well as increase the shipping by that consumption.

By this I do not only mean the carrying of herrings and mackerel to London, as is practised on the coasts of Sussex and Kent in particular, and bringing salmon from the remote rivers of Severn and Trent, but the carrying of herrings, mackerel, sprats in their season, and whitings and flat fish at other times from the coasts of Yarmouth, Swole, Ipswich, Colchester, Malden, etc., and supplying all the inland counties with them sweet and good, even as far as Northampton and Coventry, etc.

I might give examples where the herrings, which are not the best fish to keep, used, even before these reparations were set on foot, to be carried to those towns, and up to Warwick, Birmingham, Tamworth and Stafford; and though they frequently stunk before they got thither, yet the people were so eager for them that they bought them up at a dear rate; whereas when the roads are everywhere good, they will come in less time, by at least two days in six of what they used to do, and 100 times the quantity will be consumed.

These and many others are the advantages to our inland commerce which we may have room to hope for upon the general repair of the roads. Nor are the laudable undertakings which have of late years been set on foot for rendering many of the inland rivers of this kingdom navigable a less profitable improvement to the public, many of which have been completed and others are completing according to Acts of Parliament already passed for that purpose. And hardly a Session passes but Bills are still continued to be brought in for making others navigable.

All which must greatly tend, with the repairing of the public roads as above, to increase the Trade of this Nation.

DANIEL DEFOE, *Tour* (1742), vol. 3, pp. 248–54.

2

'Infernal, Execrable, Detestable'

Preston to Wigan. Turnpike. I know not, in the whole range of language, terms sufficiently expressive to describe this infernal road. To look over a map, and perceive that it is a principal one, not only to some towns but even whole counties, one would naturally conclude it to be at least decent; but let me most seriously caution all travellers, who may accidentally purpose to travel this terrible country, to avoid it as they would the devil; for a thousand to one but they break their necks or their limbs by overthrows or breaking down. They will here meet with ruts which I actually measured four feet deep, and floating with mud only from a wet summer; what therefore must it be after a winter? The only mending it in places receives, is the tumbling in of some loose stones, which serve no other purpose but jolting a carriage in the most intolerable manner. These are not merely opinions but facts, for I actually passed three carts broken down in these eighteen miles of execrable memory.

To Warrington Turnpike. This is a paved road, and most infamously bad. Any person would imagine the boobies of the country had made it with a view to immediate destruction, for the breadth is only sufficient for one carriage; consequently it is cut at once into ruts; and you will easily conceive what a break-down dislocating road ruts cut through a pavement must be. The pretence of wanting materials is but a mere pretence, for I remarked several quarries of rock, sufficient to make miles of excellent road.

To Liverpool Turnpike. This road is mostly a pavement; the first part of which is such as I have just described, though scarcely so bad. But towards Liverpool is of a good breadth, and as good as an indifferent pavement can be.

To Altringham Turnpike. If possible this execrable road is worse than that from Preston. It is a heavy land, which cuts into such prodigious ruts that a carriage moves with great danger. These sands turn to floods of mud in any season the least wet.

To Manchester Turnpike. Part of it the same as the last; the rest a paved causeway, and done in so execrable a manner, that it is cut into continual holes. For it is made so narrow, that only one carriage can move at a time, and that consequently in a line of ruts.

From Dunholm to Knutsford Turnpike. It is impossible to describe these infernal roads in terms adequate to their deserts. Part of these six miles I think are worse than any of the preceding.

To Newcastle Turnpike. This, in general, is a paved causeway, as narrow as can be conceived, and cut into perpetual holes, some of them two feet deep measured on the level; a more dreadful road cannot be imagined; and wherever the country is the least sandy, the pavement is discontinued, and the ruts and holes most execrable. I was forced to hire two men at one place to support my chaise from overthrowing, in turning out for a cart of goods overthrown and almost buried. Let me persuade all travellers to avoid this terrible country, which must either dislocate their bones with broken pavements, or bury them in muddy sand.

To Burslem Turnpike. Deep muddy ruts in clay.

[Here you must let me pause; for these execrable roads continuing no further, I must in general advise all who travel on any business but absolute necessity, to avoid any journey further north than Newcastle. All between that place and Preston is a country one would suppose devoid of all those improvements and embellishments which the riches and spirit of modern times have occasioned in other parts. . . . I would advise all travellers to consider this country as sea, and as soon think of driving into the ocean as venturing into such detestable roads.

A. YOUNG, *Northern Tour* (1770), vol. IV, pp. 580–5.

3

The Worst Road of All?

Of all the cursed roads that ever disgraced this kingdom, in the very ages of barbarism, none ever equalled that from Billericay to the *King's Head* at Tilbury.

It is for nearly 12 miles so narrow, that a mouse cannot pass by any carriage; I saw a fellow creep under his waggon to assist me to lift, if possible, my chaise over a hedge. The ruts are of an incredible depth. The trees every where over-grow the road, so that it is totally impervious to the sun, except at a few places. And to add to all the infamous circumstances which concur to plague a traveller, I must not forget the eternally meeting with chalk-waggons; themselves frequently stuck fast, till a collection of them are in the same situaton, and twenty or thirty horses may be tacked to each, to draw them out one by one.

A. YOUNG, *Southern Tour* (1768), p. 27

4

A Descent of Turnpikes

The turnpike from Salisbury to four miles the other side of Rumsey, towards Winchester, is, without exception, the finest I ever saw. The trustees of that road highly deserve all the praise that can be given by every one who travels it, for their excellent management; to management the goodness of that road must be owing, for fine as their materials are, yet I have in other roads met with as fine; but never with any that were so firmly united, and kept so totally free from loose stones, rutts and water: and when I add water, let me observe, that it is not by that vile custom of cutting grips for it to run off, to the dislocation of one's bones in crossing them, and to the utter destruction of all common beauty resulting from levelness; but by rendering the surface so immoveably firm, that carriages make no holes for it to settle in; and having every where a gentle fall, it runs immediately off.

To conclude the whole, it is every where broad enough for three carriages to pass each other; and lying in straight lines, with an even edge of grass the whole way, it has more the appearance of an elegant gravel walk than of an highway.

Next to this uncommon road, the great north one to Barnet, I think, must be ranked. Then the Kentish one; and the others to Chelmsford and Uxbridge succeed. Next I rank the 18 miles of finished road, from Cowbridge in Glamorganshire, to six miles this side of Cardiff. As to all the rest, it is a prostitution of language to call them turnpikes; I rank them nearly in the same class with the dark lanes from Billericay to Tilbury fort.

A. YOUNG *Southern Tour*, pp. 248–9.

5

Muddy Middlesex

The turnpike roads in Middlesex bear evident marks of their vicinity to a great city. Scattered villas and genteel houses, in the manner of a continued and rather elegant village, are erected on one or both sides of the roads, for three, five, or seven miles out of London. The foot-paths are thronged with passengers, and the carriage-ways with horses, carts, waggons, chaises, and gentlemen's carriages of every description.

This county is intersected by the three most frequented turnpike roads in the kingdom, namely, the great western road, the great north road, and the eastern, or Harwich road; as also by many others of less note.

Most of the parish highways in the county are superior to any other of equal extent that I have ever seen. They are hard and clean in every sort of weather; so much so, that gentlemen may ride along them, even directly after rain, and scarcely receive a splash.

The turnpike roads, on the contary, are generally very bad; although at the toll-gates of this county there is collected a very large sum of money, probably not less than £30,000 a year, which is uselessly expended in sinking wells, erecting pumps, building carts, and hiring horses and men, to keep the dust down by watering, instead of more wisely scraping it off. By the folly of this practice, the roads are kept many inches deep in mud. The mud indeed is so very deep all the winter, and so fluid after rain, as to render it unsafe to meet horses, owing to their feet throwing the mud not only over an horseman's clothes but also into his eyes.

The road from Tyburn through Uxbridge is supposed to have more broad-wheeled waggons pass over it than any other in the county. During the whole of the winter 1797-8 there was but one passable track on this road, and that was less than six feet wide, and was eight inches deep in fluid mud. All the rest of the road was from a foot to eighteen inches deep in adhesive mud. This track was thronged with waggons (many of them drawn by ten horses, and most of them having broad wheels, even to sixteen inches wide) and farmers' six-inch-wheel carts, which occupied almost the whole of this confined space. It was therefore with great difficulty, and some danger, that horsemen and light carriages could pass.

The road from Hyde-park-corner through Brentford and Hounslow is equally deep in filth. Notwithstanding His Majesty travels this road several times every week, there are not any exertions made towards keeping it clean in winter.

JOHN MIDDLETON, View of the Agriculture of Middlesex (1798),
pp. 393–7.

6

Some Inns at which Arthur Young Stayed

Good roads, and convenient accommodation for travellers, are necessary not only to agriculture and manufactures, but to the fine arts; even to literature, and every embellishment of life; the possession of them implies a state of prosperity and elegance. It is of consequence to know, that in the remotest parts of the kingdom a traveller will meet a reception in most respects different from what he will find in foreign countries; a decent bed; clean sheets; plenty of fuel; wholesome provisions; and generally a civil landlord. As to the prices at some of the following places, I add them as a matter of curiosity; to show, that the north yet continues, beyond all comparison, cheaper than the south, in most of the points in which an inn can indicate it.

Stevenage. Swan. Very good and very civil.

Dunstable. Bull. Very good. Mutton steaks 1s, duck 2s, bread 2d a head.

St Neot's. Cross Keys. Exceeding civil.

Kimbolton. White Lion. Shabby.

Stamford. George. Exceeding good and reasonable; but wretched waiting.

Grantham. George. Very good, uncommonly civil, and very reasonable.

Newark. Saracen's Head. Disagreeable and dear.

Bawtry. Crown. Middling, but cheap. Here we first found dinners charged 1s a head, and nothing for bread and beer.

Rotherham. Crown. Very disagreeable and dirty, but very cheap. Hashed venison, potted mackerel, cold ham, tarts, cheese, and a melon, at 1s a head.

Sheffield. Angel. Very good, exceedingly civil, and cheap.

Leeds. Old King's Arms. Dirty and disagreeable. Veal cutlets, tarts, and cheese for supper, at 8d a head, without malt liquor being charged.

Scarborough. New Inn. Very cheap, but very dirty. Cold ham, chicken, lobster, tarts, anchovies, and cheese, 1s 4d. Coffee or tea, 6d a head.

151

Castle Howard. New Inn. An excellent house, but dear, and a saucy landlady.

Carlisle. Bush. Good. A broiled chicken, with mushroom sauce, a plover, plate of sturgeon, tarts, mince-pies, and jellies, 1s 6d a head.

Kendal. King's Arms. A good house, very civil, and remarkably cheap. A brace of woodcocks, veal cutlets, and cheese, 1s a head, dinner. A boiled fowl and sauce, a roast partridge, potted charr, cold ham, tarts, and three or four sorts of sweetmeats, 8d a head; three people supped. Another supper: cold ham, tarts, potted charr, anchovies, butter and cheese, 6d a head. Tea or coffee 6d a head.

Preston. Black Bull. Indifferent and dear; bad bed chambers, and beds.

Liverpool. Talbot. Cheap; a very bad house.

Manchester. Bull's Head. Mr Budworth is a most sensible intelligent person, and gives travellers the best information relative to the Duke of Bridgwater's navigation.

Oxford. Angel. Very dirty, and not obliging.

Maidenhead Bridge. Good. Very dear. For supper, a stewed carp of about a pound and a half 4s, a duck 2s 6d, a minced pie 9d.

A. YOUNG, Northern Tour (1770), vol. 4, pp. 586–93.

★   ★   ★

King's Lynn. Duke's Head. Exceeding civil and reasonable.

Bury St Edmund's. Angel. Very civil and reasonable.

Braintree. Horn. Very clean and civil.

Chelmsford. Black Boy. Clean, but dear.

Tilbury. King's Head. Very civil, and very reasonable.

Barnet. Red-Lyon. Good and reasonable.

Wycomb. Antelope. Exceeding good, civil, and not unreasonable.

Oxford. Angel. Good.

North-Leach. King's Head. Very bad and very dear.

Gloucester. King's Head. Very good, civil, and reasonable.

Cardiff. White-Lyon. Bad.

   do   Angel. Worse.

Bristol. White-Lyon. Good, but very dear.

Devises. Bear. Exceedingly good, and remarkably civil.

Salisbury. Three-Lyons. Good, but very dear.

Rumsey. Bear. Good.

Winchester. George. Dirty and dear, but very civil.

Wanstead. Eagle. Good.

   do   Bush. Impertinent and dirty.

A. YOUNG, Southern Tour (1768), pp. 282–3.

7

Hogarth's 'Country Inn Yard'

(Plate 16)
The scene is a country inn yard, probably at Chelmsford, at the time passengers are getting into a stage-coach and an election procession is passing in the background. The vulgar roar of our landlady is no less apparent than the grave, insinuating, imposing countenance of mine host, who solemnly protests that a bill he is presenting to an old gentleman in a cocked hat is extremely moderate. An ancient lady, getting into the coach, is, from her breadth, a very inconvenient companion in such a vehicle; but to atone for her rotundity, an old maid of a spare appearance and in a most grotesque habit is advancing towards the steps.

A portly gentleman, with a sword and cane in one hand, is deaf to the entreaties of a poor little deformed postilion, who solicits his customary fee. The old woman smoking her short pipe in the basket, pays very little attention to what is passing round her. Two passengers on the roof of the coach afford a good specimen of French and English manners: Ben Block, of the *Centurion*, surveys the subject of *La Grande Monarque* with ineffable contempt.

In the window are a very curious pair, one of them blowing a French horn and the other endeavouring to smoke away a little sickness which he feels from the fumes of his last night's punch. Beneath them a traveller is taking a tender farewell of the chambermaid. The background is crowded with citizens who have chaired a figure intended to represent Child, Lord Castlemain, who engaged in a violent contest for the county of Essex. The horn-book, bib, and rattle are evidently displayed as cunningly allusive to his name.

JOHN IRELAND, *Hogarth Illustrated*, vol. I, pp. 282–5.

CHAPTER 8

'THE LABOURING POOR'

Readers of *The Wealth of Nations* can hardly fail to notice how many are the passages in which Adam Smith displays a deep practical interest in the welfare of that class of society whom he designates sometimes as 'those who live by wages', sometimes as 'the great body of the people', but more generally, adopting a phrase which had been in circulation since the emergence of a large wage-earning class in Tudor times, as 'the labouring poor'.

In his philosophy, they were deserving of far better treatment than that which was generally accorded them. He thought that their wages should be sufficient to provide a 'plentiful subsistence' and not just enough to keep body and soul together until they had produced the next generation of toilers. He thought it ridiculous to maintain that 'men in general should work better when they are ill-fed than when they are well-fed, when they are disheartened than when they are in good spirits, when they are frequently sick than when they are generally in good health'. He thought that the labourer should be encouraged with 'the comfortable hope of bettering his condition, and of ending his days perhaps in ease and plenty'.

All this is summed up in one of the book's really basic passages. 'No society can surely be flourishing and happy, of which the far greater part of the members are poor and miserable. It is but equity, besides, that they who feed, clothe, and lodge the whole body of the people, should have such a share of the produce of their own labour as to be themselves tolerably well fed, clothed, and lodged.'

Shaming though it be to have to confess it, Adam Smith was virtually alone in thinking in this way. Almost without exception, the contemporary writers on economic matters wrote about the 'labouring poor' with disdainful unconcern, adopting an attitude hardly less harsh than what they showed towards the 'idle poor', by which term they meant those who for one reason or another had dropped out from the army of labour and existed as 'paupers' on the cold charity of the Poor Law.

To take but one example. Arthur Young can hardly be accused of being exceptionally hardhearted, and yet in his *Eastern Tour* we find this paragraph. 'If you talk of the interests of trade and manufacture, every one but an idiot knows, that the lower classes must be kept poor, or they will never be industrious.'

This was written some years before the publication of *The Wealth of Nations*. In his later years, Arthur Young adopted a much kindlier attitude towards his poorer neighbours, and for that Adam Smith may be allowed perhaps some of the credit. But there is no 'perhaps' in claiming that the two authors whose works have been drawn upon for the 'documents' composing this chapter had not only read Adam Smith but taken to heart much of what they had read.

'The only one of Adam Smith's disciples during the eighteenth century to produce any work of importance.' Such is the rather grudging tribute paid by Karl Marx in *Capital* to Sir Frederick Morton Eden, author of the book generally referred to as *The State of the Poor*. The tribute is in fact very well deserved, since Eden accumulated and arranged in order a vast number of facts about the condition of the poorer classes of Britain as the eighteenth century was drawing towards its close.

Nothing in the scanty details of his life goes far to explain his long-sustained interest in the 'lower orders'. He himself belonged to the landed gentry section of the governing class. Born in 1766, he was the eldest son of Sir Robert Eden, Bart, of West Auckland, in the county of Durham, and he succeeded to the baronetcy on his father's death. An uncle was William Eden, whose political services to William Pitt the Younger when Prime Minister were rewarded with the barony of Auckland. He went to Christ Church, Oxford, where he graduated in 1787; married a Miss Smith; and went into business in the City. He became one of the founders of the Globe Insurance Company, and it was in the company's London office that he died suddenly in 1809. He was buried at Ealing.

To this biographical paragraph the most important thing about him remains to be added – his authorship of *The State of the Poor*. This was published in three big quarto volumes in 1797; and such is the book's importance and enduring interest it is only right and proper that, for once at least, its title should be given in full:

'*THE STATE OF THE POOR: or, An History of the Labouring Classes in England, from the Conquest to the Present Period; in which are particularly considered, Their Domestic Economy, with respect to Diet, Dress, Fuel, and Habitation; and the Various Plans which, from time to time, have been proposed, and adopted, for the Relief of the Poor: together with Parochial Reports relative to the Administration of Work-houses, and Houses of Industry; the State of Friendly Societies, and other Public Institutions in several Agricultural, Commerical, and Manufacturing Districts. With a Large Appendix; containing A Comparative and Chronological Table of the Prices of Labour, of Provisions and of other Commodities; an Account of the Poor in Scotland; and many original documents on subjects of National Importance.*

In some 'prefatory remarks' Eden explains that it was the difficulties experienced by the labouring classes, from the high price of grain and of provisions in general, as well as of clothing and fuel, in the years 1794 and 1795, that induced him, 'from motives both of benevolence and personal curiosity', to investigate their condition in various parts of the kingdom. At first he intended to concern himself only with the 'actual poor', by which term he seems to mean those who were in receipt of parish assistance, i.e. paupers; hence the great detail with which he describes the poorhouses and workhouses set up in numerous towns and villages for their reception. But as he progressed in his inquiries he came to the conclusion that it would be more satisfactory if he extended them to include 'accurate details' of the 'Labouring part of the community', i.e. those working for weekly wages, and their dependants.

The chapter likely to be of most interest to the present-day reader is the one which carries the heading, 'Of the Diet, Dress, Fuel, and Habitation, of the Labouring Poor'. In point of fact, this is almost entirely concerned with diet and dress, little being said about fuel and practically nothing about habitation. Furthermore, Eden's knowledge seems to have been derived mainly from the northern parts of the country, and his 'labourers' are almost exclusively farm-labourers, next to no mention being made of the town artisans and mechanics whom in accordance with the then usual terminology, he terms 'manufacturers'. But against this objection it may be pointed out that by far the greater proportion of the labouring population of those days was employed on the land. It is from this chapter that most of the following 'documents' are drawn.

I

The Diet of the Labouring Poor

There seems to be just reason to conclude that the miseries of the labouring poor arise, less from the scantiness of their income (however much the philanthropist might wish it to be increased) than from their own improvidence and unthriftiness; since it is the fact that in many parts of the kingdom, where the earnings of industry are moderate, the condition of the labourers is more comfortable than in other districts where wages are exorbitant.

It must strike everyone who has at all investigated the subject of diet that there is not only a remarkable difference in the proportion of earnings appropriated to the purchase of subsistence by labourers in the North and South of England, but that their mode of preparing their food is no less dissimilar.

In the South of England, the poorest labourers are habituated to the unvarying meal of dry bread and cheese from week's end to week's end; and in those families whose finances do not allow them the indulgence of malt liquor, the deleterious produce of China constitutes their most usual and general beverage. If a labourer is rich enough to afford himself meat once a week, he commonly adopts the simplest of all culinary preparations, that of roasting it; or, if he lives near a baker's, of baking it; and if he boils his meat, he never thinks of forming it into a soup, that would be not only as wholesome and as nourishing, but, certainly, more palatable than a plain boiled joint.

In the North of England, and in Scotland and Wales, on the contrary, the poorest labourers can, and actually do, regale themselves with a variety of dishes that are wholly unknown to the Southern inhabitants of this island . . .

To begin with one of the simplest articles of diet, 'the healsome porritch, chief of Scotia's food' (Burns' *Cotter's Saturday Night*), *hasty-pudding*. It is made of oat-meal, water, and salt, in the following manner: To a quart of water, whilst it is boiling in an open pot, a small quantity of salt is added, and 13 ounces of oat-meal are dropped into it, by little and little, whilst boiling, and stirred about with a stick or a spoon. It is boiled in this manner for two or three minutes, when it becomes pretty thick; and is then taken out of the pot, or pan, for use. Over-boiling makes it tough and clammy. The quantity of oat-meal put into a quart of water is varied, according to the consistency which is required. The above, however, is the most usual proportion; and is sufficient for a meal for two labourers. Hasty-pudding is eaten with a little milk or beer poured upon it; or with a little cold butter put into the middle; or with a little treacle. This dish is extremely nutritious, and is much liked by those who have been accustomed to it. A good meal for one person, supposing the price of oats to be 20s the quarter, will not exceed 1d.

Crowdie is not so generally used as hasty-pudding; it is, however, a very common dish in the North among labourers of all descriptions, but particularly miners, as it is soon made ready, and without much trouble. The process is extremely simple; and consists in pouring boiling water over oat-meal and stirring it a little. It is eaten with milk or butter. There is another sort of crowdie made, by pouring boiling broth on oatmeal: after the dish is stirred about, a piece of fat is taken from the broth and put on the crowdie, instead of butter or milk.

This dish is very common in Scotland, and is accounted a very great luxury by labourers. It is a never-failing dinner with all ranks of people on Shrove Tuesday (as pancakes are in England), and was probably first introduced on that day while the Roman Catholic religion prevailed, to strengthen them against the Lenten Fast; it being accounted the most substantial dish known in that country. On this day there is always put into the bason or porringer, out of which the unmarried folks are to eat, a ring, the finding of which, by fair means, is supposed to be ominous of the finder's being first married.

This latter kind of crowdie is that which is most in use in the North of England; where the greatest advantage and richest treat expected from a small piece of corned beef (which there are few so low or poor as not to indulge themselves with for a Sunday's dinner), is its supplying sufficient stores of savoury skimmings for crowdies.

Frumenty, or *barley-milk*, as made in the North, is barley with the husks taken off (which was formerly done in a kind of large stone mortar, called a knocking-stane, but is now performed in a mill constructed for the purpose), boiled in water near two hours, and afterwards mixed with skimmed milk; sometimes a little sugar is added: it is generally eaten in Cumberland with barley bread.

Barley is also dressed by the peasants in Scotland, and in the North of England, for broth, or barley-milk, by being moistened with water and then beaten with a long wooden mallet, rounded at the end, in a stone mortar. This is called *knocked-bear*, to distinguish it from the pearl barley, which is dressed in the mill.

In the Northern counties *oat-meal* is made in the following manner: the oats are first dried in a kiln; after which the husks are taken off by an operation of the mill called skilling (or shelling); the oats are then cleansed from the dust by another machine, and afterwards ground in the barley-mill, and the meal sifted through a sieve. The farmers usually make from 15 to 40 bushels of oats into meal at a time, according to the number of their family; but enough to serve them from three to six months.

The refuse which remains after the meal has been sifted, and is similar to the bran of wheat, consists chiefly of husks and is called seeds: it is used for *sowens* or *flummery*, which is made in the following manner: the seeds are put into water, where they remain from one to three days; they are then wrung, or strained, out again; and this process is repeated a second and a third time, in different vessels of water. By this contrivance all the mealy particles of the seeds are extracted. The water is then mixed together; and when it has stood about six hours, the clear water is poured off and fresh water is added. When the sediment which is thus obtained is to be used, it must be stirred up, and water put to it till it will just tinge a wooden dish with a whitish colour; it is then put into a pot and boiled, seldom less than half an hour, and often a whole hour. Care must be taken to stir it all the time that it remains over the fire; and it is added, from long tradition, that the mess must always be stirred one way. It is afterwards put into basons, where it acquires a considerable degree of solidity, and becomes perfectly smooth, and very like what in England is called bla-mange. It is eaten with milk; and is an extremely cheap, wholesome, and even delicious dish for supper. This article of subsistence is only used occasionally in the North of England; but in many parts of Scotland, particularly on the North-east coast, it constitutes the invariable dinner of the labourer.

Pease-kail is made by boiling pease till they are soft; the water is then poured over them, and milk is added. Sometimes pease are put into broth, and boiled down into a sort of soup. Neither of these dishes, however, are very generally used, nor much to be commended.

SIR F. M. EDEN, *State of the Poor* (1797), vol. I, pp. 496–501.

2

Potatoes in a Variety of Uses

Potatoes are not only particularly good in the North of England, but used in various ways. They are sometimes roasted or boiled, and eaten with butter, as in the South; but are more commonly boiled (sometimes with the skin on, and sometimes with it taken off), chopped into small pieces, and eaten with butter (either cold or melted), or bacon fried. Potatoes are likewise generally used in the North with roast or boiled meat in the same manner as in the South of England; but when eaten with roast meat, they are commonly first put into the dripping-pan. But the principal way in which this useful root is dressed in the North by labourers' families is by being peeled, or rather scraped, raw; chopped, and boiled together with a small quantity of meat cut into very small pieces. The whole of this mixture is then formed into a hash, with pepper, salt, onions, etc., and forms a cheap and nutritive dish; which being common also in ships, is by sailors called *lobscouse*.

No vegetable is, or ever was, applied to such a variety of uses in the North of England as the potatoe: it is a constant standing dish, at every meal, breakfast excepted, at the tables of the Rich, as well as the Poor: and it is generally supposed that they are produced in much greater perfection in Lancashire, and districts near Lancashire, than in other parts of England. This, however, I conceive is a mistake. I have indeed eat potatoes there, which, when brought to the table, and touched with a fork, fell into powder, like some of the fungus tribe. Potatoes, however, from the same field or garden, when sent up to London, appear to be quite a different production: the outside is generally too much done, and is either sodden or watery; whilst the centre of the potatoe remains as hard as it was when taken out of the ground . . .

The very general use which is now made of potatoes in these kingdoms, as food for man, is a convincing proof that the prejudices of a nation, with regard to diet, however deeply rooted, are by no means unconquerable. Within the present century, this useful vegetable production seems to have been considered as food only fit for the poorest class in the community; but it seems probable, from the following instances [given in a report of the Board of Agriculture concerning the culture and use of potatoes] of the progress which various districts have made in the cultivation of this valuable root, that, in the course of a few years, the consumption of potatoes in this kingdom will be almost as general and universal as that of corn.

In the central Highlands of Scotland, potatoes are become the principal food of the people, and are considered as the greatest blessing that modern times have bestowed on the country: they have probably more than once saved it from the miseries of famine. It would be difficult to calculate how much the introduction of potatoes into the Hebrides has improved the arable land, and bettered the condition of the poorer inhabitants. It is of all others the most valuable root in Perthshire. In Banff, had it not been in general use in 1783 it is probable that many of the inhabitants would have perished for want of food. It is a common practice in Devonshire to make bread of potatoes mixed with flour. In Cardiganshire, potatoes, with barley-bread, form the chief sustenance of the poor. It is no uncommon thing in Somersetshire for a family, consisting of father, mother, and five or six children, to consume twenty sacks per year, 240 lbs the sack, or 20 lbs per head per week, allowing twelve weeks' cessation from this food. Indeed the children nearly subsist on it, and the deprivation thereof would bring the whole family to the parish.'

State of the Poor, vol. 1, pp. 501–6.

3

Oat-meal and Good Looks

There are many different sorts of bread used in the North of England ... In Lancashire and the West Riding of Yorkshire a sort of oat-bread is called *riddle-bread*. It is mostly eaten with tea; and, for this purpose, is preferred to wheaten bread. A native of Cumberland told me that the oat-bread which he ate in Lancashire (and which I presume was this sour riddle-bread), was extremely disagreeable to his taste; he was astonished that any person could like it; and added, that though he had been in different parts of the kingdom, he had never eat any bread he liked so well as the Cumberland barley-bread. On the other hand, the Lancashire people, being accustomed to oat-bread, are equally averse to that made from barley. Such are the powerful effects of custom!

The very healthy appearance of those inhabitants of Lancashire who subsist principally on oaten-bread invalidates the following observations of Adam Smith respecting this article of diet. He says,

'In some parts of Lancashire, it is pretended that bread of oatmeal is a heartier food for labouring people than wheaten bread', and says he has frequently heard 'the same doctrine held in Scotland'. He adds, 'I am, however, somewhat doubtful of it. The common people of Scotland, who are fed with oatmeal, are in general neither so strong nor so handsome as the same rank of people in England, who are fed with wheaten bread. They neither work so well, nor look so well; and as there is not the same difference between the people of fashion in the two countries, experience would seem to show, that the food of the common people in Scotland is not so suitable to the human constitution as that of their neighbours of the same rank in England.'

These remarks do not appear to me to be warranted by fact: handsomer and more muscular men are not reared in any part of the British dominions, than in those countries where the oatmeal diet is predominant. The 33rd Regiment, which goes by the name of the *Haver-cake Lads*, and which is usually recruited in those parts of the West Riding of Yorkshire, where oat-bread is in common use, has been often remarked, as well as the Lancashire regiments, to be composed of some of the finest looking soldiers in his Majesty's service. It likewise deserves notice, that oat-bread, as well as potatoes, constitutes a very considerable portion of the diet of the labouring classes in Ireland, from whom we draw those whom Adam Smith considers as perhaps the strongest men in the British dominions – the chairmen, porters, and coal-heavers in the metropolis.

I should rather ascribe the good looks of the labouring classes in England, to superior cleanliness, and a difference of climate. The filth and smoke in which a cotter's family in Scotland are enveloped when at home, and the parching winds to which they are exposed when abroad, contribute, no doubt, to render the appearance of the Highland pea-santry (though they are, perhaps, as stout and as muscular as their Southern neighbours) less ruddy and blooming than that exhibited by the natives of more favoured regions. Uncleanliness in dress is like-wise no less unfavourable to good looks.

State of the Poor, vol. i, pp. 513–14.

4

Drink More Milk!

It is not to be expected that milk should ever form a considerable part of the diet of labourers in the South of England until the practice of keeping cows becomes more general among cottagers than it is at present. In many parts of the island, however, considerable difficulties will occur in attempting to introduce this custom. In the vicinity of large towns, the value of grass land is much too high to enable labourers to rent it to advantage; and in other districts where there is hardly any thing but arable land, and the maintenance of a cow depends on straw, turnips, cabbages, or puchased hay, the system of cow-keeping is much too operose for a labourer to engage in.

I am, however, persuaded, that even in London, where milk is extremely dear (now 3½d the quart), poor householders might occa-sionally use it to considerable advantage. A small quantity of it, judi-ciously applied, would render many dishes tender and delicate, which, from their toughness, and the drought which they occasion, are not only unpalatable but expensive. A labouring man, in the metropolis, who thinks he cannot afford milk and therefore obliges his family to drink their tea in a very crude state, by way of economy, buys himself half a pound of fat bacon (at 10d or 1s the pound) for dinner. This creates such a thirst, that he is fain to allay it with no inconsiderable quantity of porter.

State of the Poor, vol. i, pp. 531–2.

5

'Washy Stuff!'

With regard to broths and soups composed of barley-meal or oat-meal and potatoes, the aversion to them in many parts of the South is almost insuperable. I have known instances during the last winter, when the Poor were extremely distressed by the high price of provisions, of their rejecting soup which was served at a Gentleman's table. Their common outcry was: 'this is washy stuff, that affords no nourishment: we will not be fed on meal, and chopped potatoes, like hogs!'

Even in their employers, ancient prejudices are in general so deeply rooted, that they are persuaded that a diet, which chiefly consists of liquids, will not enable their labourers to perform their work; or (to use an homely phrase) that it will not stick to their ribs like plain dry wheaten bread.

I readily admit that a diet consisting entirely of liquids would neither gratify the palate nor enable the body to support any violent fatigue. There is, however, a medium between food entirely liquid and entirely solid. And, after all, I am persuaded, that the South-country labourer, notwithstanding his conviction of the necessity of substantial diet, takes more liquids into his stomach than the Cumberland or the Yorkshire-man. Exclusive of beer (when he can afford it) and spirits, the quantity of water (which, with tea, forms a deleterious beverage that is seldom qualified with milk or sugar), poured down the throats of a labourer's family is astonishing. Any person who will give himself the trouble of stepping into the cottages of Middlesex and Surrey at meal-times, will find that, in poor families, tea is not only the usual beverage in the morning and evening, but is generally drank in large quantities even at dinner.

State of the Poor, vol. I, pp. 533–5.

6

The Labourer's Daily Pint

Purchased liquor is an article of expenditure particularly prevalent in the Southern counties. There is hardly a labouring man, of any account whatever, who does not think it necessary to indulge himself, every day, in a certain quantity of malt liquor; and if taxed with drinking too much, he thinks it a sufficient, and by no means, an unbecoming apology for himself, to allege that, excepting on a Saturday evening, or occasions of festivity, he rarely allows himself more than a pint, or at most a pot, of beer a day. In cyder countries, the peasantry are equally liberal to themselves in the use of that beverage.

This is not the case in the North; where, besides the pure limpid stream, the general drink of the labouring classes is either whey or milk, or rather milk and water; or, at best, very meagre small beer. And though drinking to excess is said to be a Northern vice, as being indeed most natural to the cold regions of the North; and it is by no means pretended that a Northern peasant is not as prone to brutalise himself by drunkenness as any other; they have not yet become habituated to consider any strong drink as a necessary of life. It is reserved as an indulgence for extraordinary festivals; for a horse-race; a merry-making; or a market-day; and resorted to, not merely for *shallow draughts*, but with the avowed purpose of *drinking deep*. And as these occasions are not of very frequent recurrence, the expense of them is consequently very inferior to that which is incurred by those who, besides such occasions as these, allow themselves a daily portion of beer.

State of the Poor, vol. 1, pp. 542–3.

7

The Dress of the Labouring Poor

In the midland and southern counties of England the labourer, in general, purchases a very considerable portion, if not the whole, of his clothes from the shopkeeper. In the vicinity of the metropolis, working people seldom buy new clothes; they content themselves with a cast-off coat, which may be usually purhased for about 5s, and secondhand waist-coats and breeches. Their wives seldom make up any article of dress, except making and mending clothes for the children.

In the north, on the contrary, almost every article of dress worn by farmers, mechanics, and labourers, is manufactured at home, shoes and hats excepted – that is, the linen thread is spun from the lint, and the yarn from the wool, and sent to the weaver's and dyers', so that almost every family has its web of linen cloth annually, and often one of woollen also, which is either dyed for coats or made into flannel, etc. Sometimes black and white wool are mixed, and the cloth which is made from them receives no dye.

Although broad cloth, purchased in the shops, begins now to be worn by opulent farmers, and others, on Sundays, yet there are many respectable persons, at this day, who never wore a bought pair of stockings, coat, nor waistcoat, in their lives; and, within these past twenty years, a coat bought at a shop was considered as a mark of extravagance and pride, if the buyer was not possessed of an independent fortune. There are, however, many labourers so poor, that they cannot even afford to purchase the raw material necessary to spin thread or yarn at home, as it is some time before a home manufacture can be rendered fit for use.

It is generally acknowledged that articles of clothing can be purchased in the shops at a much lower price than those who make them at home can afford to sell them for; but that, in the wearing, those manufactured by private families are very superior both in warmth and durability.

State of the Poor, vol. 1, pp. 554–5.

8

Cumbrian Clothing

In Cumberland, the usual price of a hat worn by labourers is about 2s 6d; a coat purchased (four yards) costs about 2s 6d a yard; a waistcoat takes a yard and a half; a pair of leather breeches costs 3s 6d; labourers sometimes wear breeches of flannel or coloured cloth. A tailor charges 5s for making a whole suit.

A linen shirt takes 3¼ yards at 17d a yard; this is strong and wears well. About 11 oz of wool at 8d the lb will make a pair of stockings. They are almost invariably spun and knit at home.

Women's dress generally consists of a black stuff hat, of the price of 1s 8d; a linen bed-gown (stamped with blue), mostly of the home manufacture – this usually costs in the shops about 5s 6d; a cotton or linen neck-cloth, price about 1s 6d; two petticoats of flannel, the upper one dyed blue, value of the two about 11s 6d; coarse woollen stockings, home manufacture, value about 1s 8d; linen shift, home manufacture, 2½ yards, at 1s 5d the yard. Women generally wear stays, or rather boddice, of various prices. Their gowns are sometimes made of woollen stuff, 6 yards at 1s 6d the yard. The women generally wear black silk hats and gowns on Sundays and holidays.

State of the Poor, vol. 1, pp. 556–7.

9

Price List of 'Ready-mades'

———

The following are the prices of clothes as sold in a slop-shop [shop for ready-made clothing] in the neighbourhood of London:

	s	d
Men –		
A good foul-weather coat (will last very well two years)	13	0
A common waistcoat	6	6
A pair of stout breeches (one year)	3	9
Stockings, the pair	1	10
A dowlas [coarse linen] shirt	4	6
A pair of strong shoes	7	0
A hat (will last three years)	2	6
Women –		
A common stuff gown	6	6
Linsey-woolsey petticoat	4	6
A shift [chemise]	3	8
A pair of shoes	3	9
Coarse apron	1	0
Check apron	2	0
A pair of stockings	1	6
A hat, the cheapest sort (will last two years)	1	8
Coloured neck-handkerchief	1	0
A common cap		10
Cheapest kind of cloak (will last two years)	4	6
Pair of stays (will last six years)	6	0

State of the Poor, vol. 1, pp. 557–8.

10

Labourers' Wives

Few writers on . . . political economy have adverted to the circumstances and situation of a class of our people who form, perhaps, the most essential link in social order and domestic happiness: I mean the *wives* of labourers.

If the right, which every labourer possesses, of disposing of the produce of his labour, is the great incentive to industry; is it either unfair or unreasonable to presume, that the incapacity which married women labour under, of acquiring property, is one of the principal causes why they contribute so little to the fund which is to maintain a family?

In the greatest part of England, the acquisition of the necessaries of life, required by a labourer's family, rests entirely on the husband. If he falls sick, and is not a member of a Friendly Society, his wife and children must inevitably be supported by the parish. There is no other resource; for, to whatever cause it is to be ascribed, the wife, even in such an exigency, can do nothing.

I do not mean to contend, that, either with a view to national profit, or individual independence, it is desirable that the female part of a labourer's family should perform the toilsome duties of porters and ploughmen, as is the case in Liège and Switzerland, and even in some parts of Scotland; or that they should employ those hours which they can spare from the management of domestic concerns, in a sedentary and unwholesome manufacture, as is the case with the lace-makers in Buckinghamshire and Northamptonshire. The labours of the field, it is said, are adverse to child-bearing; and this is one of the reasons which I have heard assigned for the infecundity of the negroes in the West-Indies. I am not physiologist enough to say, how far this opinion is, or is not, well founded: but I own, I suspect it to have been advanced on but slight grounds. There are, however, various occupations which the wife of a peasant or artificer would, it is probable, be often inclined to pursue, were she only allowed to have a voice as to the disposal of her earnings.

As the Law now stands, the moment she acquires them, they become the absolute property of her husband; so that it is not to be wondered at, that she conceives she has fulfilled her duty in attending to the children; and that he, conscious that the support of the family depends on his exertions, should so often become imperious and tyrannical.

(It is a not very uncommon article of information in the news-paper, that a labourer has exchanged wives with his neighbour, or carried his bedfellow to market with a halter about her neck, and sold her for the moderate price of five shillings.)

The instances are not few, where a stupid, drunken, and idle man, has an intelligent and industrious wife, with perhaps both the opportunity and the ability to earn enough to feed her children, but who yet is deterred from working, from a thorough conviction that her mate would, too probably, strip her of every farthing which she had not the ingenuity to conceal.

There is, perhaps, no better mode of ascertaining what degree of comfort is enjoyed by a labourer's family, than by learning what portion of his weekly earnings he commits to his wife's disposal. It makes a very material difference whether he or she holds the purse-strings. . . . For one extravagant mother, I am persuaded, there are at least twenty improvident fathers.

State of the Poor, vol. I, pp. 624–9.

As his name implies, Revd. David Davies (1741–1819) was a Welsh-man. He was born at Machynlleth, in Montgomeryshire, and studied at Jesus College, Oxford, a college which then and for long afterwards was possessed of an exclusively Welsh connection. There he graduated B.A. in 1778; he took his M.A. in 1785, and in 1800 was awarded a doctorate in Divinity.

On leaving Oxford, he was ordained in the Church of England, and from 1782 until his death was rector of the little village of Barkham, near Wokingham, in Berkshire. As such he is described on the title-page of the book for which he is very justly remembered: *The Case of Labourers in Husbandry stated and considered*, that was published at Bath and London in 1795.

In this he tells us very little about himself, but that little is altogether to his credit. Clearly, he was a country parson who took a very fatherly interest in his flock, but in this (fortunately) he was not alone. What distinguishes him is his practical concern for the conditions under which his parishioners were required to live, his sympathetic understanding of their difficulties, his 'apology' for their alleged defects, and his sensible proposals for the improvement of their lot. Then as a compiler of 'family budgets' he was one of the pioneers in this important and rewarding department of social science.

I

The Distressed Condition of Labouring Families

In every nation the welfare and contentment of the lower denomina-tions of people are objects of great importance, and deserving continual attention. For the bulk of every nation consists of such as must earn their daily bread by daily labour. It is to the patient industry of these that the higher ranks are every where indebted for most of their enjoyments. It is chiefly on these that every nation depends for its population, strength, and security. All reasonable persons will therefore acknowledge the equity of ensuring to them at least the necessary means of subsistence.

But of all the denominations of people in a state, *the labourers in husbandry* are by far the most valuable. For these are the men, who, being constantly employed in the cultivation of the earth, provide the staff of life for the whole nation. And it is the wives of these men, who rear those hardy broods of children, which, besides supplying the country with the hands it wants, fill up the voids which death is continually making in camps and cities. And since they have thus a peculiar title to public regard, one might expect to see them everywhere comfortably accommodated. Yet even in this kingdom, distinguished as it is for humanity and political wisdom, they have been for some time past suffering peculiar hardships.

In visiting the labouring families of my parish, as my duty led me, I could not but observe with concern their mean and distressed condition. I found them in general but indifferently fed; badly clothed; some children without shoes and stockings; very few put to school; and most families in debt to little shopkeepers. In short, there was scarcely any appearance of comfort about their dwellings, except that the children looked tolerably healthy. Yet I could not impute the wretchedness I saw either to sloth or to wastefulness. For I knew that the farmers were careful that the men should not want employment; and had they been given to drinking, I am sure I should have heard enough of it. And I commonly found the women, when not working in the fields, well occupied at home; seldom indeed earning money, but baking their bread, washing and mending their garments, and rocking the cradle.

These poor people, in assigning the cause of their misery, agreed in ascribing it to the high prices of the necessaries of life. 'Every thing (they say) is so dear, that we can hardly live.' In order to assure myself, whether this was really the case, I enquired into the particulars of their earnings and expences; and wrote the same down at the time, just as I received them from each family respectively, guarding as well as I could against error and deception. . . . These accounts of the earnings and expenses of labouring families, in my own parish, were collected about Easter 1787, when affairs relating to the poor were under the consideration of the Parliament and the public. From what loose information I could then gather near home, I saw sufficient reason to believe that they presented but too faithful a view of the general distress

7. Welsh peasant women washing clothes in a mountain stream.
W. H. Pyne, The Costume of Great Britain

of such families throughout this and the neighbouring counties. And the vast increase of the poor-rate, at that time everywhere a subject of complaint, rendered it very probable that the same misery had overspread the kingdom.

REVD. D. DAVIES, *Labourers in Husbandry* (1795), pp. 1–7.

2

Expenses and Earnings of Six Labouring Families

(Parish of Barkham in the county of Berks, taken at Easter 1787)
No. 1 A man and his wife, and five children, the eldest eight years of age and the youngest an infant. The man receives the common weekly wages of 7s eight months in the year, and by task work the remaining

four months about 1s weekly more. The wife's common work is to bake bread for the family, to wash and mend ragged clothes, and to look after the children; but at beansetting, haymaking, and harvest she earns as comes one week with another about 6d.

Weekly Expenses:	s	d
Flour, 7½ gallons at 10d per gallon	6	3
Yeast, to make into bread, 2½d, and salt, 1½d		4
Bacon, 1 lb boiled two or three times with greens:		
the pot liquor, with bread and potatoes, makes a mess		
for the children		8
Tea, 1 oz, 2d; sugar, ¾ lb, 6d; ½ lb butter or lard, 4d	1	0
Soap, ¼ lb at 9d		2¼
Candles, ¼ lb one week with another, at 9d		3
Thread, thrum, and worsted, for mending apparel, etc.		3
Deficiency of Earnings, 5¼d	8	11¼

No. 2 A woman, whose husband is run away, and six children; the eldest, a boy of 16 years of age, earns 2s 6d a week; the next a boy of 13, earns, but not constantly, 1s 6d a week; four of the children too young to earn anything. This family has received from the parish, during four years, a weekly pension of 5s; lives in the parish-house rent free; and is supplied with some fuel and some clothing, at the parish expense.

Weekly Expenses	s	d
Flour, for bread, 6 gallons	5	0
do, ½ gal for puddings and thickening the children's		
messes		5
Yeast, 2d; salt, 1½d		3½
Bacon, 2 lb at 8d (with sometimes a sheep's head)	1	4
Tea, 1½ oz, 4d; sugar, ½ lb, 4d; butter, ½ lb, 4d	1	0
Soap, 2½d; candles, 3d; thread, worsted, etc., 3d		8½
	8	9

Weekly earnings with parish allowance, 9s; weekly expenses 8s 9d. _Surplus of earnings 3d weekly._

No. 3 A man, his wife, and four small children, the eldest under six years of age, the youngest an infant. The husband, if he has constant health and employment, earns on an average 8s; the wife does not earn above 6d.

Weekly Expenses	*s*	*d*
Flour	5	0
Yeast, 2d; salt, 1½d; soap, 2¼d; candles, 3d; thread, &c, 3d		11¾
Bacon, 1 lb, 8d; butter, ½ lb, 4d; sugar, ¾ lb, 6d; tea, 1 oz, 2d	1	8
Surplus of Earnings 10¼d	7	7¾

No. 4 A man, his wife, and three small children, the eldest not quite five years old, the youngest an infant. The man's business is to follow a farmer's team, for which he has 8s a week throughout the year. He has besides, either his diet in his employer's house 6 weeks in harvest, or instead of it 18s; which is per week, 4d. The wife earns at a medium about 8d a week. Total earnings, 9s.

Weekly Expenses	*s*	*d*
Flour, 3 gallons at 10d	2	6
Yeast, 1d; salt, 1½d		2½
Bacon: the farmer of whom they rent their dwelling, lets them have a fatted hog, weight about 14 score (on condition of their not keeping any pigs or poultry) at 1s per score under the market-price: this at 6s 6d per score (1787) comes to £4 11s, and as it lasts the family the whole year, it is per week exactly	1	9
Cheese, about 28 lb per year at 4½d per lb: 10s per annum		2½
Tea, 2¼d; sugar, 8d; butter, 4d	1	2¼
The wife, having an infant at the breast, and fancying *very* small beer better than mere water, brews a peck of malt once a month, which costs 1s 4d – hops ¼ lb 4d – this is per week		5
Soap, 3d; candles, 3d; thread and worsted, 2d.		8
Surplus of Earnings, 2s 0¾d	6	11¼

No. 5 A man, his wife, and three young children, the eldest six years of age and the youngest an infant. The man has, summer and winter, the common pay, 7s; and he has also a mess of milk for breakfast, and small beer, worth at least 1s more. The woman earns, as she believes, by washing and needle-work, by breeding poultry, and at harvest-work when she has no child to nurse, 1s. Total of earnings, 9s.

Weekly Expenses	s	d
Flour, say 4½ gallons per week	3	9
Yeast and salt		3
Meat: bought a pig and fatted it; price of the pig 10s 6d; cost 6d a week for 42 weeks before fatting, £1 1s; was fatted with one sack of beans 15s, one cask of pease 16s, and 5 bushels of ground barley 25s, total £4 7s 6d. When killed, it was estimated to weigh about 14 score pounds; it cost, therefore, 6s 4d per score. This, with a few sheeps' head and shins of beef will last all the year, and is per week	1	8
Beer: they seldom brew but against a christening	—	
Tea, sugar, butter	1	0
Soap, starch, candles, worsted, on an average	1	0
Surplus of Earnings, 1s 4d	7	8

No. 6 A man, his wife, and two young children, the eldest seven years of age, the youngest four. The man earns, one week with another, if constantly employed, 8s. The woman earns on an average not more than 6d. Total earnings, 8s 6d.

Weekly Expenses	s	d
Flour, 5 gallons	4	2
Yeast and salt		3
Bacon, 1½ lb at 8d	1	0
Tea, 1 oz, 2d; sugar, ½ lb, 4d; butter, ½ lb, 4d		10
Soap, ¼ lb, 2¼d; candles, 3; worsted, 3d.		8¼
Surplus of Earnings, 1s 6¾d	6	11¼

Note on Women's Earnings

If any one should think that the women's earnings are stated too low in these accounts, he will be convinced that they are not, on considering that these women commonly begin the world with an infant, and are mere nurses for ten or twelve years after marriage, being always either with child, or having a child at the breast; consequently incapable of doing much other work beside the necessary business of their families, such as baking, washing, and the like. In winter they earn next to nothing, few of them having in their youth learnt to knit and spin; and if in summer they are able to go to harvest work, they must pay some person a shilling a week out of their earnings for looking after their children. It is probable therefore that from 6d to 9d a week is as much as labourers' wives in general, hereabout, earn on an average the year through.

Annual Outgoings

The expenses already set down are only the weekly outgoings, exclusive of house-rent, fuel, clothing, lying-in, sickness, and burials; these being best allowed for by the year, may be called annual outgoings, and are as under:

Rent of a cottage, or part of an old farm-house, with a small £ s d piece of garden ground, for a family, is from two pounds to two guineas; say   2 0 0

Fuel This is turf cut from the common, and when bought costs 12s per family; but as the man can cut in a week nearly enough to serve his family all the year, and the farmers (if the distance be not great) will give the carriage for the ashes, let this be charged at a little more than one week's wages   10 0

Clothing

1. The man's. Wear of a suit per annum, 5s; wear of a working jacket and breeches, 4s; two shirts, 8s; one pair of stout shoes nailed, 7s; two pair of stockings 4s; hat, handkerchief, &c. 2s. Sum, £1 10s.

2. The wife's. Wear of gown and petticoats, 4s; one shift, 3s 6d; one pair of strong shoes, 4s; one pair of stockings, 1s 6d; two aprons, 3s; handkerchiefs, caps, &c, 4s. Sum, £1.

3. The children's. Their clothing is (usually) partly made up of the parents' old clothes, partly bought at second-hand. What is bought (supposing three children to a family) cannot well be reckoned at less than £1; where there are more than three children, 7s may be added, and where there are fewer, 7s may be deducted, for each; let the whole be estimated at   3 10 0

(Note Very few poor people can afford to lay out this sum in clothes, but they should be enabled to do it; some cottagers breed a few fowls, with which they buy what sheets and blankets they want; but those who live in old farm-houses are seldom allowed (to use their own words) to keep a pig or a chick.)

Lying-in The child's linen, 3 or 4s; the midwife's fee, 5s; a bottle of gin or brandy always had upon this occasion, 2s; attendance of a nurse for a few days, and her diet, at least

5s; half a bushel of malt brewed, and hops, 3s; to the
minister for churching, 1s; – call the sum £1 and suppose
this to happen but once in two years: this per annum   10   0
Casualties (1) in sickness there is the physick to be paid for,
and the loss of time to be allowed for; (2) burials: poor
people having many children, sometimes lose one. For both
these together it seems moderate to allow per annum   10   0

                    Sum of these annual outgoings   7   0   0

This sum being divided by 52, gives us 2s 8¼d per week. If therefore
any one desires to know the *whole* weekly expenses of a family (consisting of a man and his wife with three children) in order to compare
it with the whole of their weekly earnings, he must add 2s 8¼d to the
current weekly expense of the family. Where there are more than three
children, twopence more must be added for each; and where there are
fewer, twopence must be deducted, the reason for which may be seen
under the article Clothing above.

Notes
Few poor families can afford themselves more than 1 lb of meat weekly.
Price of the half-peck loaf of household wheaten bread, 11½d.
Price of the gallon of flour, 10d.
The tea used per family is from 1 to 1½ oz per week, at 2d per oz.
Soft sugar, ½ lb at 7d to 8d per lb.
Salt butter, or lard, ½ lb at 7½d to 8d per lb.
Milk. Suckling is here so profitable (to furnish veal for London) that
     the poor can seldom either buy or beg milk.
Malt is so dear that they seldom brew any small beer, except against a
     lying-in or a christening.
Soap. To eke out soap, they burn green fern, and knead the ashes into
     balls, with which they make a lye for washing.
               Labourers in Husbandry, pp. 8–19.

3

'An Apology of the Poor'

Poor people are often censured for want of frugality and economy in
the management of their earnings. In particular, they are accused of

extravagance in eating wheaten bread; of being over-nice in neglecting as they do the use of potatoes; and of a luxurious excess in drinking tea. It may be proper to see what force there is in these charges.

First, it is asked, Why should our labouring people eat wheaten bread? Were they content, as the poor people of this country were formerly, and as the poor of other countries are still, with bread of an inferior quality, they might then spare money for other purposes, and live with more comfort than they usually do.

It is wonderful how readily even men of sense give into this censure, neither considering the different circumstances of different countries at the same time, nor the different circumstances of the same country at different times. They assume that the condition of the working people of this kingdom is the same now, in all *other* respects, as it was formerly; which is by no means the case.

If the working people of other countries are content with bread made of rye, barley, or oats, have they not milk, cheese, butter, fruits, or fish, to eat with that coarser bread? And was not this the case of our own people formerly, when these grains were the common productions of our land, and when scarcely wheat enough was grown for the use of the nobility and principal gentry? Flesh-meat, butter, and cheese, were then at such moderate prices, compared with the present prices, that poor people could afford to use them in common. And with a competent quantity of these articles, a coarser kind of bread might very well satisfy the common people of any country.

Time, which changes all things, has gradually changed the circumstances of this kingdom. Our lands have been so much improved, that wheat is as common now as rye and barley were formerly. A sufficient quantity of wheat is now annually produced for the consumption of, probably, three-fourths of our people. In the corn counties it is chiefly on the crop of wheat that the farmer relies for the ability to pay his rent. And if the labouring people, of whom the mass of every nation consists, were to cease to eat it when produced, how, let me ask, would the farmer then dispose of his corn? And how could he pay his landlord the high rent now demanded of him?

But this is not all. The prices of meat, butter, and cheese, are so much increased, in consequence of the increase of riches, luxury, and taxes, that working people can now scarcely afford to use them in the smallest quantities. So that they depend almost entirely upon the bread they eat for strength to perform their daily labour. That bread should therefore be of a good kind. But it is certain that wheaten bread contains much more nourishment than barley bread; and it is probable that the difference in this respect is such as to compensate for the difference of price . . .

It appears then that the economy of eating inferior bread is, in the present state of things, at least very questionable. But, were it otherwise, a change in this respect is scarcely practicable. The corn business is now carried on in a systematical way, from which the dealers will not depart. Formerly the labourer could have corn of different kinds mixed in any proportion, in exchange for his labour, even more readily than he could get money. His wife carried it to the mill, had it ground and dressed, and then brought it home, and baked it for the family. There was no intermediate person except the miller, between the farmer and the consumer, to receive a profit. But now it is out of the course of business for the farmer to retail corn by the bushel to this or that poor man; except in some particular places, as a matter of favour, to his own labourers. The great farmer deals in a wholesale way with the miller; the miller with the mealman; and the mealman with the shopkeeper, of which last the poor man buys his flour by the bushel. For neither the miller, nor the mealman, will sell the labourer a less quantity than a sack of flour under the retail price at shops: and the poor man's pocket will seldom allow of his buying a whole sack at once . . .

Upon the whole, labouring people, having neither meat, nor cheese, nor milk, nor beer, in sufficient quantities, eat good bread where every body else eats it. You say, they cannot afford to do this; and you blame their extravagance. But can you, who blame them, give a reason, why they, whose hands have tilled the ground, and sown and reaped the grain, are not as well entitled to eat good bread, as manufacturers? or, as the servants of gentlemen's families? or, as the paupers in houses of industry and parochial work-houses? or as the felons in your gaols?

Use of Potatoes

2dly. It is sometimes said that poor people neglect too much the use of potatoes; as potatoes would not only save bread, but, by helping to keep a pig, give them more meat than they can now afford themselves.

Though the potatoe is an excellent root, deserving to be brought into general use, yet it seems not likely that the use of it should ever be general in this country. The use of wheat, spreading with improvements in husbandry, will probably supersede it in many places where it is now in request. The potatoe has the advantage in cheapness only: wheat is superior in all other respects. Besides, there are two other circumstances which forbid the common people in the richer countries from cultivating potatoes as much as they might otherwise be inclined to do.

1st. The want of sufficient garden ground. This appears truly strange in a country where a third part of the land at least lies waste; and where, if every poor family were allowed as much of this waste land as they could, when not otherwise employed, cultivate with the spade and the pick-axe, it would be undoubtedly a great public benefit. Yet such is the fact.

In consequence of the law of settlements, it has been, and is, the policy of parishes (in order to ease the rates and check their increase, and also to render the labourers entirely dependent on their employers) to destroy cottages, some of which had ground about them. And this destruction has been greatly promoted by the system of engrossing farms. For the engrossing farmer, occupying sometimes half a dozen farms, converts all the farm-houses, except that in which his own family resides, into dwellings for the poor. After taking such part of the garden belonging to each house as he chooses, for his own use, he divides the rest, as he had before divided the house, into several portions, allotting to each of his under-tenants about a quarter of a rood of ground, with perhaps an apple-tree or two. The occupier of this scanty bit of ground, desiring some variety in his food (and variety is known to be wholesome), instead of planting the whole in potatoes, produces from it a little of many things: beans, pease, cabbages, onions, and some potatoes too. He works at it early and late to make it yield him something constantly. And it is hard to say what better use he can possibly put it to.

But, 2dly, If the labouring man has ground enough, as is here and there the case, the want of milk is another impediment to the use of potatoes. Wheaten bread may be eaten alone with pleasure; but potatoes require either meat or milk to make them go down: you cannot make many hearty meals of them with salt and water only. Poor people indeed give them to their children in the greasy water in which they have boiled their greens and their morsel of bacon: and, blessed be God! children will thrive, if they have but enough of any thing. As to meat, we know very well how little of that they are obliged to content themselves with.

Butter-milk is the thing, if they could get it. In Wales and Ireland (and in some parts of England too) potatoes and butter-milk make one meal a day in most families almost all the year. But taking England in general, butter-milk is too little regarded as an article of diet. The method of churning in the southern counties makes it only fit for swine. Where the method of churning is such as to produce it sweet and good, there a poor family may always either beg or buy a jug of butter-milk; and there too we find potatoes in use. But the use of potatoes must be very limited, where milk cannot be cheaply procured . . .

Tea-drinking
3dly. The topic on which the declaimers against the extravagance of the poor display their eloquence with most success, is *tea-drinking*.

Why should such people, it is asked, indulge in a luxury which is only proper for their betters; and not rather content themselves with milk, which is in every form wholesome and nourishing?

Were it true that poor people could every where procure so excellent an article as milk, there would be then just reason to reproach them for giving the preference to the miserable infusion of which they are so fond. But it is not so. Wherever the poor can get milk, do they not gladly use it? And where they cannot get it, would they not gladly exchange their tea for it? The truth is, that very few labouring people can afford to purchase a cow, for a cow would cost the earnings of almost half a year. But, were they able to purchase one, where could they find pasture for her? The commons are so covered with the rich farmer's herds and flocks, that the poor man's cow would soon be starved there. And the little ground about their cottages is barely sufficient for garden stuff. They cannot therefore produce milk for themselves. And as to buying milk, it is not to be had in many places for love or money. In such places as are within reach of the capital and other great towns (and the influence of these now extends a vast way) the farmers find the most profitable use of a cow to be *suckling*, in order to supply the markets with veal. Besides, there are thousands of parishes, which, since little farms have been swallowed up in greater, do not support so many cows as they did by fifty and sixty in a parish. And thus the poor are very much at a loss for due supplies of milk.

Is there any thing else that they can substitute for milk? Time was when *small beer* was reckoned one of the necessaries of life, even in poor families; and it seems to have been designed by Providence for the common drink of the people of this country, being deemed a preservative against some of its worst diseases. Were the poor able to afford them-selves this wholesome beverage, it would well enough compensate for the scarcity of milk. But, on account of the dearness of malt, which is, most unfortunately for them, a principal subject of taxation, small beer has been these many years beyond their ability to use in common.

Under these circumstances, the dearness of malt, and the difficulty of procuring milk, the only thing remaining for them to moisten their bread with, was *tea*. This was their last resource. Tea (with bread) furnishes one meal for a whole family every day, at no greater expense than about one shilling a week at an average ...

Still you exclaim, *Tea is a luxury*. If you mean fine hyson tea, sweet-ened with refined sugar, and softened with cream, I readily admit it to be so. But *this* is not the tea of the poor. Spring water, just coloured with a few leaves of the lowest-priced tea, and sweetened with the brownest sugar, is the luxury for which you reproach them. To this they have recourse from mere necessity; and were they now to be deprived of this, they would be immediately reduced to bread and water. Tea-drinking is not the cause, but the consequence, of the distresses of the poor ...

In fine, this charge of mismanagement made against labouring people, seems to rest upon no solid ground. For a long time past their condition has been going from bad to worse continually. Small indeed is the portion of wordly comforts now left them. Instead therefore of grudging them so small an enjoyment as a morsel of good bread with their miserable tea; instead of attempting to shew how it may yet be possible for them to live *worse* than they do; it well becomes the wisdom of the present age to devise means how they may be better accommodated. Give to some the ability to keep a cow; and then all will have milk. Give to all the ability to drink small beer at home; and then few will frequent ale-houses. He that can procure for them these two benefits, nay, he that can procure for them *one* of these two, will receive the blessing of the grateful poor, and deserve the applause of all good men.

Labourers in Husbandry, pp. 31–40.

4

Ale-houses and Poachers

Ale-houses have undoubtedly brought many families to want, infamy, and ruin. As the improvidence of the people encourages these houses, so do these houses encourage that improvidence. Ale-houses would not be so common as they are, if the keepers of them did not find their account in the improvidence of the people: nor would the people be so improvident as they are, if ale-houses did not every where tempt them to drown their senses, and waste their time and money in them.

But the loss of sense, time, and money is not the worst consequence of frequenting these places. There is good reason to believe, that the prevailing corruption of morals in the common people has been very much owing to what is heard, seen, and practised in them. It is in these houses that men, by falling into bad company, get the evil habits of idleness, blasphemy, and drunkenness; which prepare them for the worst crimes. The love of strong drink acquired here drives numbers upon unlawful ways of making money: among which, from the high request that *game* is held in, and from the little risk attending the trade, *poaching* is very generally followed.

To be a clever poacher is deemed a reputable accomplishment in the country; and therefore parents take care to instruct their children betimes in this art, which brings them on gradually and regularly to pilfering and stealing. For poachers, in prowling about at night, if they miss of game, properly so called, are sometimes suspected of seizing on their neighbours poultry, and such other things as they can find a vent for. By following these works of darkness, the loss of sleep and excessive drinking in time ruin their health. They get agues and other disorders, which disqualify them from either working or poaching, and then they and their families come on the parish.

Labourers in Husbandry, pp. 59–60.

5

Welsh Farm Labourers

Account of Two Labouring Families in the Parishes of Llanfawr and Llangeil, Merionethshire, North Wales, in 1788

Family No. 1: a man, his wife, and four children, the eldest ten years old.
Family No. 2: a man, his wife, and six children, the eldest nine years old.

It is presumed that the two families above specified are sufficient to give a general idea of the labouring poor. Those that cannot, or will not work, are supported by parish relief, and by begging, which is an old-established trade, to which men, women, and children devote themselves without the least degree of shame. One reason to which we may attribute so much begging in this and the neighbouring counties is the want of profitable manufactories. The knitting of coarse woollen stockings chiefly employs boys, girls, and grown persons of both sexes, in the inland parts of Merionethshire.

That it is an unprofitable manufacture is evident, as they knit, walking, talking, begging, without hardly ever looking at their work; and though they exhibit an instance of unexampled industry, yet they are obliged to beg to make up the deficiencies of their earnings.

Earnings

No. 1 The man earns per week at a medium 6s 6d; the woman 9d; the children 3d

No. 2 The man earns per week at a medium 6s; the woman 1s; the children 1s

Amount per annum: No. 1, £19 10s; No. 2, £20 16s

Expenses	No. 1 (£sd)	No. 2 (£sd)
per week: meal of barley or oats, butter, sugar, salt, milk, potatoes, soap, tallow, &c.	7 6½	7 11½
Amount per annum	19 12 2	20 13 10
add: clothes, rent, fuel, and other extras per annum	4 10 0	5 0 0
Total expenses per annum	24 2 2	25 13 10
Total earnings per annum	19 10 0	20 16 0
Deficiencies of earnings	4 12 2	4 17 10

Notes

Rent of a cottage and garden, from 15s to 25s per annum. Fuel, dear in this country, consisting chiefly of turf and peat, the ashes estimated at a small value, say 25s. Clothing is often manufactured by poor families for their own use, with the wool which they beg at shearing time; some few articles, such as shoes, they buy, which we shall estimate at 26s. Lying-in, etc., as in the Barkham account, £1 15s.

Average price of a bushel of oatmeal, of which the poor make bread, 5s. The above quantity will serve a family of six or seven persons for a week. In general, tea is not drunk by poor families in Wales, except in the towns where milk is scarce. To eke out soap, they use chamber-lye [urine]. Butter is bought at an average for 6½d a pound all the year round.

Parish rates in this county are from 3s 6d to 4s. Widows and their families receive some parish relief, but are chiefly supported by begging from door to door. The dole which they receive is oatmeal.

Labourers in Husbandry, pp. 190–1.

6

Aberdeenshire Peasants

The Peasantry in Aberdeenshire may be ranked in three classes, viz. 1st Cottars, or merely day-labourers. 2ndly. Tradesmen, being sub-tenants. 3rdly. The very poorest, being old men or widows, whose children (if they had any) are gone to service, have families of their own, gone to trades, or have left the country.

Class First Rent a house, a cottage, a cabbage garden, and two or three acres of land from the farmer.

		£	s	d
He ploughs their land, brings home their peats (fuel); for this, they pay him in cash at a medium of 10s per acre of the ground		I	IO	O
The man gives his work in harvest, receiving two meals a day, and one firlot of meal (32 lbs) for harvest supper home to his family; his harvest wages being valued at		I	O	O
He gives three days work at casting the farmer's peats, and forming his sheep or cattle folds at 8d.			2	O
Annual clothing to self, wife, and children		I	O	O
He buys two bolls of meal (256 lbs) more than the produce of his land, at 12s.		I	4	O
He uses salt 5s; fish 4s; soap, starch, blue, hardly any, say Is.			IO	O
In lyings-in, burials, or other incidents		I	O	O
Lamp-oil 4s; rushes dipt in it for candles 0; tea, sugar, butchers' meat, none; treacle or molasses when sick, Is.			5	O
Total Expenses		6	II	O

	£	s	d
Suppose him to have five children under eight years, which, as the mothers nurse at least twelve months, is the hardest case possible, deducting the work above given to his master, and the time employed on his own ground, he may hire himself in the year 120 days at 8d.	4	O	O
He rears a calf yearly, which at the year old is worth from 20s to 25s.	I	I	O
The eldest child attends the youngest, while the mother earns at spinning 6d per week	I	6	O
Two or three hens will produce in eggs and chicken		4	O

In the long winter evenings, the husband cobbles shoes, mends the family clothes, and attends the children while the wife spins. Some husbands spin or knit stockings, make horse or oxen harness of stript and dried rushes, &c. for sale

Total earnings 6 11 0

The produce of their garden and lands, and cow, give them what more meal they want above the two bolls already mentioned, with milk, potatoes, turnips, greens, and ale at Christmas; butchers' meat none.

If by sickness, loss of cow or calf, or other accidents, they are reduced to poverty and real want, the Kirk Session and private charity support them during that time only; or if their loss and want be too much for the ordinary session charities, the minister intimates a collection to be made for them only next Sunday at church.

The same person, after his eldest child, whether boy or girl, is eight years old, begins to hold up his head; the boy keeps cattle or sheep, the girl spins linen yarn, and earns 6d per week, some more. As the other children advance he becomes still more independent. When all boys, many of them learn to spin or knit stockings at a very early age.

Class Second Tradesmen, who have like houses, gardens, and grounds for the like rent and services – the only difference is, his employing his own time at his trade, which is generally more profitable, and enables him to live better. In case of sickness or misfortune, he is relieved and supported as the other.

Class Third Have a hut, near a peat-moss, from a farmer, for which they pay him 12d to 20d a year, and what is called a rick (smoak) hen to the landlord, for the privilege of taking fuel of peats from the moss. While able, they beg through the parish and neighbourhood, and often live more comfortably than the first class. When through age or infirmity they cannot go out to beg, they are poorly off, if they have not laid up any thing in their begging days (but this many of them do), being only supported by private charity or the Kirk Session, whose highest charity allowance is 1s per week.

This is the truest state of our Country Peasantry. I meddle not with Towns, where tea and gin are introduced among the meanest – their wages are higher, and constant employment more certain – but gin debauches the morals of both sexes, and they are in general much less comfortable than the Country Peasants.

'General State of the Expences and Earnings of the Peasantry in the North Part of Aberdeenshire', transmitted by DR FINDLAY, of Fraserburgh, January 1789, *Labourers in Husbandry*, pp. 192–4.

CHAPTER 9

THE CHANGING FACE OF
BRITISH INDUSTRY

(a) ARTHUR YOUNG AMONG THE NORTHERN MANUFACTURERS

When Arthur Young went on his famous 'Tours' in the late 1760s he was principally concerned with what was going on in agriculture. But at the same time he also kept an eye open for anything interesting in the way of manufacturing developments in the places he visited. Thus it came about that he was among the very first to remark on those changes which, a hundred years later, a brilliant young Oxford don named Arnold Toynbee was to designate as 'the Industrial Revolution'.

The term would have surprised him. 'Revolution' was not at all the word he would have chosen to describe what he saw in the industrial centres of the northern counties, any more than he would have deemed it applicable to the developments in agriculture which had started somewhat earlier. What he observed were *changes*, plenty of them, but these were the outcome of other changes which had been going on for a very long time.

Not that the nomenclature is of much importance. What *are* of lasting interest are Young's accounts of those townships in which the spirit of industry was being increasingly manifested. The impressions he carried away with him and subsequently published are characterised by a thrusting energy, a breezy confidence, a bustling enterprise.

This was in the dawn of the revolution. Water power was still the main source of energy, and a really big water wheel was something to marvel at; canals were the last word in transport improvements. The steam-engine and the railway were things of the future, and as yet hardly dreamed of. But factories were dotting the landscape, and the smoke of countless chimneys was threatening to obscure the sky.

I

Kendal's Many Manufactures

Kendal is a well built and well paved town, pleasantly situated in the midst of beautiful country. It is famous for several manufactories, the chief of which is that of knit stockings, employing near five thousand hands by computation. They reckon one hundred and twenty wool-combers, each employing five spinners, and each spinner four or five knitters; if four, the amount is two thousand four hundred. This is the full work, supposing them all to be industrious; but the number is probably much greater.

They make five hundred and fifty dozen a week the year round, or twenty-eight thousand six hundred dozen annually. The price per pair is from 22d to 4s, some boys' at 10d. If we suppose the average 3s, or 36s a dozen, the amount is £51,480.

The wool they use is chiefly Leicestershire, Warwickshire, and Durham; they generally mix Leicestershire and Durham together. The price 8d, 9d, and 10d per lb. They send all the manufactures to London by land carriage, which is said to be the longest, for broad wheel waggons, of any stage in England.

The earnings of the manufacturers are as follows, per week: The combers, 10s 6d. The spinners, women, 3s; children of ten or twelve years, 2s. The knitters, 2s 6d; children of ten or twelve years, 2s. All the work-people have constant employment if they please.

The making of cottons is likewise a considerable manufacture in this town. They are called Kendal cottons, chiefly for exportation, or sailors' jackets, about 10d or 1s a yard, made of Westmoreland wool, which is very coarse, selling only at 3d or 4d per lb. This branch employs three or four hundred hands, particularly shearmen, weavers, and spinners. The shearmen earn per week 10s 6d, the weavers (chiefly women) 4s 3d, the spinners 3s 3d. All have constant employment.

Their third branch of manufacture is the linsey woolsey, made chiefly for home consumption, of Westmoreland, Lancashire, and Cumberland wool; the hands are chiefly weavers and spinners. The first earn 9s and 10s a week; the second (women) 4s 6d or 5s. The farmers and labourers spin their own wool, and bring it to market every week. There are about five hundred weavers employed, and from a thousand to thirteen hundred spinners in town and country.

Their fourth manufacture is the tannery, which employs near a hundred hands, who earn from 7s to 7s 6d a week. They have likewise a small manufactory of cards, for carding cloth. Another also of silk. They receive the waste silk from London, boil it in soap, which they call scowering, then it is combed by women (there are about thirty or forty of them), and spun, which article employs about an hundred hands; after this it is doubled and dressed, and sent back again to London . . .

Kendal is a very plentiful and cheap place; fat stubble geese are sold at 1s 4d each. This is so cheap, that a [church] living I heard of is not a very fat one – £4 a year, a pair of *wooden shoes*, and a *goose-gate*. Alas, poor Rector! A goose-gate is the right of keeping a goose on the common. All the poor in this country wear wooden shoes.

A. YOUNG, *A Six Month's Tour through the North of England* (4 vols, 1771), vol. 3, pp. 132–6.

2

Warrington's Workers

At Warrington the manufacture of sail-cloth and sacking are very considerable. The first is spun by women and girls, who earn about 2d a day. It is then bleached, which is done by men, who earn 10s a week; after bleaching it is wound by women, whose earnings are 2s 6d a week; next it is warped by men, who earn 7s a week; and then starched, the earnings 10s 6d a week. The last operation is the weaving, in which the men earn 9s, the women 5s, and boys 3s 6d a week.

The spinners in the sacking branch earn 6s a week, women; then it is wound on bobbins by women and children, whose earnings are 4d a day; then the starchers take it, they earn 6s a week; after which it is wove by men, at 9s a week. The sail-cloth employs about three hundred weavers, and the sacking an hundred and fifty; and they reckon twenty spinners and two or three other hands to every weaver.

The spinners never stand still for want of work; they always have it if they please; but weavers are sometimes idle for want of yarn, which, considering the number of poor within reach (the spinners of the sacking live chiefly in Cheshire), is melancholy to think of.

Here is likewise a small pin manufactory, which employs two or three hundred children, who earn from 1s to 2s a week. Another of shoes for exportation, that employs four or five hundred hands (men), who earn 9s a week.

Vol. 3, pp. 163–5.

3

High Prices at Manchester

The Manchester manufactures are divided into four branches: the Fustian, the Check, the Hat, and the Small Wares. All these are subdivided into many branches, of distinct and separate work . . .

In general, all these branches find, that their best friend is an high price of provisions. I was particular in my inquiries on this head, and found the sentiment universal.

The manufacturers themselves, as well as their families, are in such times better clothed, better fed, happier, and in easier circumstances, than when prices are low, for at such times they never worked six days in a week, numbers not five, nor even four; the idle time spent at alehouses, or at receptacles of low diversion; the remainder of their time of little value; for it is a known fact, that a man who sticks to his loom regularly, will perform his work much better, and do more of it, than any one who idles away half his time, and especially in drunkenness.

The master manufacturers of Manchester wish that prices might always be high enough to enforce a general industry; to keep the hands employed six days for a week's work; as they find that even one idle day, in the chance of its being a drunken one, damages all the other five, or, rather, the work of them.

But at the same time, they are sensible, that provisions may be too high, and that the poor may suffer in spite of the utmost industry; the line of separation is too delicate to attempt the drawing, but it is well known by every master manufacturer at Manchester, that the workmen who are industrious, rather more so than the common run of their brethren, have never been in want in the highest of the late high prices.

Vol. 1, pp. 187–94.

4

Rotherham's Iron Works

Rotherham is famous for its iron works, of which it contains one very large one belonging to Mr Walker, and one or two smaller. Near the town are two collieries, out of which the iron ore is dug, as well as the coals to work it with; these collieries and works employ together near 500 hands.

The ore is here worked into metal and then into bar iron, and the bars sent to Sheffield to be worked, and to all parts of the country. This is one branch of their business. Another is the foundry, in which they run the ore into metal, pigs, and then cast it into all sorts of boilers, pans, ploughshares, etc.

The forgemen work by weight, and earn from 8s to 20s a week, but 12s or 14s the average; the foundry men are paid by the week, from 7s to 10s. No boys are employed younger than 14, such from 3s to 4s a week. In the collieries, the men earn from 7s to 9s a week.

There are few women employed; and only in piling old bits of scrap iron (which are brought to Rotherham by way of Hull from Holland, London, etc.) into the form of small pyramids, upon round pieces of stone, after which they are set into the furnace till they become of a malleable heat, and are then worked over again.

Vol. 1, pp. 115–16.

5

'Immense Earnings' at Sheffield

Sheffield contains about 30,000 inhabitants, the chief of which are employed in the manufacture of hard-ware.

In the plated work some hundreds of hands are employed; the men's pay extends from 9s a week to £60 a year. In works of curiosity, it must be supposed that dexterous hands are paid very great wages. Girls earn 4s 6d and 5s a week; some even to 9s. No men are employed that earn less than 9s. Their day's work, including the hours of cessation, is thirteen.

In the cutlery branch there are several subdivisions, such as razor, scissar, lancets, flems, etc. Among these the grinders make the greatest earnings; 18s, 19s, and 20s a week are common among them. But this height of wages is owing in a great measure to the danger of the employ-ment, for the grindstones turn with such amazing velocity, that by the mere force of motion they now and then fly in pieces, and kill the men at work on them.

These accidents used to be more common than they are at present; but of late years they have invented a method of chaining down an iron over the stone on which the men work in such a manner that in case of the above mentioned accidents, the pieces of stone can only fly forwards, and not upwards; and yet the men by the force of the breaking have been thrown back in a surprising manner, and their hands struck off by shivers of the stone.

The mechanism of these grinding wheels is very curious. Many grindstones are turned by a set of wheels which all receive their motion from one water-wheel, increasing in velocity from the first movement to the last; in the finishing wheels it is so great, that the eye cannot perceive the least motion.

In the other branches of the cutlery, workmen earn from 1s 6d and 2s to 10s 6d a day. The first are common wages, and the last easily earned by the polishers of the razors. Surprising wages for any manual performances!

I would advise you in case you take this place in your way to the more northerly parts ... to view the tilting mill, which is a blacksmith's immense hammer in constant motion on an anvil, worked by water-wheels. The force of this mechanism is so great that you cannot lay your hand upon a gate at three perches distance, without feeling a strong trembling motion, which is communicated to all the earth around.

Upon the whole, the manufacturers of Sheffield make immense earnings. There are men employed in more laborious works, that do not earn above 6s or 7s a week, but their number is very small; in general they get from 9s to 20s a week; and the women and children are all employed in various branches, and earn very good wages, much more than by spinning wool in any part of the kingdom.

Vol. 1, pp. 122–6.

6

'Waste of Strength' at Newcastle?

———

Newcastle is supposed to contain forty thousand souls, and to employ of its own, five hundred sail of ships, four hundred of which are colliers.

The people employed in the coal-mines are prodigiously numerous, amounting to many thousands; the earnings of the men are from 1s to 4s a day, and their firing. The coal waggon roads, from the pits to the water, are great works, carried over all sorts of inequalities of ground, so far as the distance of nine or ten miles. The tracks of the wheels are marked with pieces of timber let into the road for the wheels to run on, by which means one horse is enabled to draw, and that with ease, fifty or sixty bushels of coal . . .

About five miles from Newcastle are the iron works, late Crawley's [Crowley's] supposed to be among the greatest manufactories of the kind in Europe. Several hundred hands are employed in it, insomuch that £20,000 a year is paid in wages. They earn from 1s to 2s 6d a day, and some of the foremen so high as £200 a year. The quantity of iron they work up is very great, employing three ships to the Baltic that each make ten voyages yearly and bring seventy tons at a time. They use a good deal of American iron, which is as good as any Swedish, and for some purposes much better. They manufacture anchors as high as seventy hundredweight, carriages of cannon, hoes, spades, axes, hooks, chains, etc. In general their greatest work is for exportation, and are employed very considerably by the East India company; they have of late had a prodigious artillery demand from that company.

As to the machines for accelerating several operations in the manufacture, the copper rollers for squeezing bars into hoops, and the scissors for cutting bars of iron – the turning cranes for moving anchors into and out of the fire – the beating hammer, lifted by the cogs of a wheel; these are machines of manifest utility, simple in their construction, and all moved by water. But I cannot conceive the necessity of their executing so much of the remaining work by manual labour. I observed eight stout fellows hammering an anchor in spots which might evidently be struck by a hammer, or hammers, moved by water upon a vast anvil, the anchor to be moved with the utmost ease and quickness, to vary the seat of the strokes. It is idle to object the difficulty of raising such a machine; there are no impossibilities in mechanics. An anchor of twenty tons may, undoubtedly, be managed with as much ease as a pin. In other works besides the anchor-making I thought I observed a waste of strength.

Vol. 3, pp. 6–11.

John Aikin (1747–1822) was the son of Revd John Aikin, D.D., a minister among the Presbyterians who became a Unitarian. He was born in Kibworth in Leicestershire, but was early taken to Warrington, some sixteen miles from Manchester, where his father was largely instrumental in the establishment of the Academy, an institution for the education of the sons of Dissenters. He was educated at the Academy, apprenticed to a surgeon-apothecary, and studied medicine at Edinburgh University, after which for some ten years he was a tutor on the staff of the Warrington Academy. Then, having qualified M.D. at Leyden University, in Holland, he set up in practice at Yarmouth. Here at the time of the French revolution his liberal ideas on religion and politics brought him into disfavour, and he removed in 1792 to London, where again he practised as a physician until incapacitated by a stroke. But he was able to continue with those literary activities that had engaged him since he was a youth (sometimes in conjunction with his sister Mrs Barbauld, a minor poetess), and in particular his *General Biography* in ten volumes which occupied him for nearly twenty years. He is best remembered, however, for his splendid quarto, *A Description of the Country from thirty to forty Miles round Manchester* (1795), of which he was the responsible editor.

I

Manchester's Rise to Greatness

It is probable that few or no capitals of £5,000 or £4,000 acquired by trade existed here [in Manchester] before 1690. However, towards the latter end of the last century and the beginning of the present, the traders had certainly got money beforehand, and began to build modern brick houses, in place of those of wood and plaster.

For the first thirty years of the present century, the old-established houses confined their trade to the wholesale dealers in London, Bristol, Norwich, Newcastle, and those who frequented Chester fair. The profits were thus divided between the manufacturer, the wholesale and the retail dealer; and those of the manufacturer were probably less per cent upon the business they did, than in the present time. The improvement of their fortunes was chiefly owing to their economy in living, the expense of which was much below the interest of the capital employed.

Apprentices at that time were now and then taken from families which could pay a moderate fee. By an indenture dated 1695 the fee paid appears to have been sixty pounds, the young man serving seven years. But all apprentices were obliged to undergo a vast deal of laborious work, such as turning warping mills, carrying goods on their shoulders through the streets, and the like. An eminent manufacturer in that age used to be in his warehouse before six in the morning, accompanied by his children and apprentices. At seven they all came in to breakfast, which consisted of one large dish of water-pottage, made of oatmeal, water, and a little salt, boiled thick, and poured into a dish. At the side was a pan or bason of milk, and the master and apprentices, each with a wooden spoon in his hand, without loss of time, dipped into the same dish, and thence into the milk pan; and as soon as it was finished they all returned to their work.

In George the First's reign many country gentlemen began to send their sons apprentices to the Manchester manufacturers; but though the little country gentry did not then live in the luxurious manner they have done since, the young men found it so different from home, that they could not brook this treatment, and either got away before their time, or, if they stayed till the expiration of their indentures, they then, for the most part, entered into the army or went to sea. The little attention paid to rendering the evenings of apprentices agreeable at home, where they were considered rather as servants than pupils, drove many of them to taverns, where they acquired habits of drinking that frequently proved injurious in after life. To this, in part, is to be attributed the bad custom of gilling, or drinking white wine as a whet before dinner, to which at one period a number of young men fell a sacrifice.

When the Manchester trade began to extend, the chapmen used to keep gangs of pack-horses, and accompany them to the principal towns with goods in packs, which they opened and sold to shop-keepers, lodging what was unsold in small stores at the inns. The pack-horses brought back sheep's wool, which was bought on the journey, and sold to the makers of worsted yarn at Manchester, or to the clothiers of Rochdale, Saddleworth, and the West Riding of Yorkshire. On the improvement of turnpike roads waggons were set up, and the pack-horses discontinued; and the chapmen only rode out for orders, carrying with them patterns in their bags. It was during the forty years from 1730 to 1770 that trade was greatly pushed by the practice of sending these riders all over the kingdom, to those towns which before had been supplied from the wholesale dealers in the capital places before mentioned. As this was attended not only with more trouble but with much more risk, some of the old traders withdrew from business, or confined themselves to as much as they could do on the old footing, which, by the competition of young adventurers, diminished yearly.

In this period strangers flocked in from various quarters, which introduced a greater proportion of *young* men of some fortune into the town, with a consequent increase of luxury and gaiety. The fees of apprentices becoming an object of profit, a different manner of treating them began to prevail. Somewhat before 1760, a considerable manufacturer allotted a back-parlour with a fire for the use of his apprentices, and gave them tea twice a day. His fees in consequence rose higher than had before been known, from £250 to £300; and he had three or four apprentices at a time. The highest fee known as late as 1769 was £500.

Within the last twenty or thirty years the vast increase of foreign trade has caused many of the Manchester manufacturers to travel abroad, and agents or partners to be fixed for a considerable time on the Continent, as well as foreigners to reside at Manchester. And the town has now in every respect assumed the style and manners of one of the commercial capitals of Europe.

Present State of Manchester

With respect to government, Manchester remains an open town, destitute (probably to its advantage) of a corporation, and unrepresented in parliament. Its municipal officers are a borough-reeve and two constables, elected annually in October at the court leet. The borough reeve is an officer almost peculiar to this place, and who seems formerly to have been the chief magistrate; but at present his proper office is the distribution of certain charities, though in point of rank he is considered as the first man at all public meetings, and takes the chair. The constables are the real executive officers.

Manchester and Salford, in several streets and the market place, bear great marks of antiquity, as there are still standing nearly whole streets of houses built of wood, clay and plaster.

The new streets built within these few years have nearly doubled the size of the town. Most of them are wide and spacious, with excellent and large houses, principally of brick made on the spot; but they have a flight of steps projecting nearly the breadth of the pavement, which makes it very inconvenient for foot passengers. When two people meet one must either go into the horse road or over the flight of steps, which in the night time is particularly dangerous, as the lamps are not always lighted. Very few of the streets are yet flagged, which makes the walking in them, to strangers, very disagreeable. As Manchester may bear comparison with the metropolis itself in the rapidity with which whole streets have been raised, and in its extension on every side towards the surrounding country; so it unfortunately vies with, or exceeds the metropolis in the closeness with which the poor are crowded in offensive, dark, damp, and incommodious habitations, a too fertile source of disease!

At each extremity of Manchester are many excellent houses, very elegantly fitted up, chiefly occupied by the merchants of the town, which may in some measure be considered as their country residences, being from one to two miles from their respective warehouses. Ardwick-green, to the south of the town on the London road, is principally inhabited by the more opulent classes, so as to resemble, though on a small scale, the west end of the city of London.

To conclude our description of Manchester – we may without hesitation pronounce it to be that of the modern trading towns of this kingdom which has obtained the greatest accession of wealth and population; and it is but justice to say, that in no town has opulence been more honourably and respectably enjoyed.

JOHN AIKIN, M.D., *A Description of the Country from thirty to forty miles round Manchester* (1795), pp. 181–206.

2

A Prospect of Liverpool

The harbour of Liverpool is entirely artificial consisting of docks formed within the town, and communicating with the river [Mersey]. No maritime town in Great Britain, perhaps in Europe, can vie with Liverpool in the number and extent of these works, which afford conveniences in loading and unloading of ships superior to those enjoyed by any natural harbours.

Of the docks, there are two kinds, the wet and the dry. The former are so constructed with flood-gates that water is pounded in them to keep the ships afloat in all times of the tide. The latter are the entrances to the others, and partake of the ebb and flow of the river. The wet docks are usually occupied by such ships as go foreign voyages; the dry, by coasting vessels: between these are several graving docks, which admit or exclude the water at pleasure, and are capable or receiving two or three vessels at a time, for the purpose of repairing them.

The docks extend along the river nearly the breadth of the town. In the centre is the Old Dock, running up a considerable way towards the heart of the town. To the west of it lies the Salthouse Dock, and the bason or dry dock, serving as the common entrance to both. These were the first constructed. To the north of these is situated George's Dock, with its dry bason, the next of these works, hollowed and embanked out of the river beach. And to the south are the newest docks, called the King's and Queen's, with one common dry bason at the entrance. The duke of Bridgwater has a small dock of his own between these and the Salthouse dock. The length of quays afforded by all these capacious basons will appear on calculation to be so great as to eclipse all the most famous of the river or shore quays in the different sea-ports.

The vast labour and expense of these works will readily be conceived by one who considers that they must all have been hollowed by hand from the shore, in continual opposition to the tides, which often in an hour destroy the labour of weeks; and that the piers must be made of sufficient height and strength to bear the daily efforts of a sea beating in, and constantly endeavouring to recover its ancient boundaries.

On the sides of the docks are warehouses of uncommon size and strength, far surpassing in those respects the warehouses of London. To their different floors, often ten or eleven in number, goods are craned up with great facility. Government in particular has here a very extensive tobacco warehouse, occupying a large compass of ground. The space round the docks is sufficient to give room for loading and unloading, and all the occupations of the sailors, without interruption of each other, or of the crowds of passengers. Strangers may with ease drive along the quays, and enjoy the busy scene without danger of inconvenience; a pleasure nowhere to be obtained on the river at London, where the close wharfs are absolutely inaccessible except by carts, and by them not to be approached without great obstruction.

On the west side of the North Dock, by the river side, is a pier forming a fine parade, 420 yards in length, and of considerable breadth, which is a favourite walk of the inhabitants and strangers. It commands a noble view of the harbour from the rock point or commencement of the sea to the distance of several miles up the river, and a beautiful landscape on the Cheshire side. Hence all the ships are distinctly seen as they work in and out of the harbour, and enter or quit the docks.

Baths A little northwards of the North Dock, Mr Wright, an eminent shipbuilder of the town, has erected a set of elegant and commodious sea-baths, divided into separate baths and rooms for both sexes, each bath supplied with water from the centre. On the outside are steps for the convenience of swimmers who choose to launch into the open water, and who may frequently be seen plunging among the waves of a boisterous tide.

Being upon the subject of bathing, we shall mention an extraordinary mode of taking this salutary amusement *without baths*, practised upon the beach below the town for some weeks in the height of summer. It is a custom with the lower class of people, of both sexes, for many miles up the country, and even as far as the manufacturing districts to the very extremity of the county, to make an annual visit to Liverpool, for the purpose of washing away (as they seem to suppose) all the collected stains and impurities of the year. Being unable to afford a long stay, or to make use of artificial conveniences, they employ two or three days in strolling along shore, and dabbling in the salt-water for hours at each tide, covering the beach with their promiscuous numbers, and not much embarrassing themselves about appearances. As the practice, however, seems conducive both to health and pleasure, it is not to be wished that rigid notions of delicacy should interfere with this only mode which the poor have of enjoying it.

Supply of provisions, &c Few towns of the size are more plentifully and regularly supplied with provisions of all kinds, brought from a great distance round. The farms in the vicinity are much devoted to the production of milk, the demand for which, in so populous a place, is almost unlimited. The Lancashire coast is not favourable for the establishment of fisheries [but] the Isle of Man furnishes supplies of the cheaper sorts, especially herring. As an article of luxury rather than of provision, turtle may be noticed, which arrives in considerable cargoes with the West India ships, and is no where better dressed or more hospitably bestowed, accompanied with unsparing draughts of beverage made from the excellent rum and limes derived from the same quarter of the world.

Good water is, however, more of a rarity here than could be wished: and a stranger is struck with the water-carts driving through the streets, from which this necessary article is sold at a halfpenny per bucket, a circumstance by no means conducive to cleanliness among the poor, or even those of a middling condition.

Domestic Trades On the whole, Liverpool is less of a manufacturing town than Bristol, nor does it supply so many articles for the use of the

West India islands. It possesses, however, glass houses, salt works, copper works, iron foundries, many houses for the refining of sugar, and a number of public breweries. . . . A population of 51,190 in 1773 is merely a conjectural calculation, and probably too low.

pp. 354–74.

3

Leeds, Centre of the Cloth Manufacture

Though the woollen trade in Yorkshire has properly no one common centre, yet the town of Leeds has latterly been always reckoned, in opulence and population, the principal place of the West Riding; and it bears a high rank among our manufacturing towns.

The mixed cloths in the last century were exposed for sale on the battlements of the bridge over the Aire, and as the manufactory increased, were removed to the large street called Briggate, subject to the inconvenience of bad weather, and of being stored in adjoining cellars from one market day to another. The white cloths were sold in a room. Each of them is now deposited in a separate covered hall, erected for the purpose, where they remain without disturbance till sold.

The mixed cloth hall was erected at the expense of the manufacturers in 1758. It is a quadrangular building, enclosing an open area, and is divided into six covered streets, each of which contains two rows of stands, the freehold property of separate manufacturers. Each stand is twenty-two inches in front, and the whole number is 1,770; but as about twenty individuals are in possession of two stands each, the number of master manufacturers of mixed cloth, proprietors of the hall, must not be estimated at more than 1,750. These have all served a regular apprenticeship to the making of coloured cloth, which is an indispensable condition of their admission into the hall. Another small hall has lately been erected for the accommodation of irregulars, and near 100 stands are already let.

The present white cloth hall was built in 1775. It is a quadrangle like the other, and is divided into five streets, each with a double row of stands, the number of which is 1,210, but there are generally about forty persons who have two stands each. There are supposed to be about 200 mixed, and more than 100 white cloth manufacturers, of an inferior description, who have served a regular apprenticeship, but

13. The Sleeping Congregation

14. Beer Street

15. Gin Lane

16. (*Above*) The Distressed Poet: as he seeks for inspiration, his wife is frightened by the milk-woman's presentation of her unpaid score. (*below*) Country Inn Yard

THE CHANGING FACE OF BRITISH INDUSTRY

having no property in the halls, pay a fixed fee for every piece of cloth they expose for sale.

The whole number of master broad-cloth manufacturers in the West-Riding of Yorkshire is about 3,240. Not a single manufacturer is to be found more than one mile east, or two north, of Leeds; nor are there many in the town of Leeds, and those only in the outskirts.

The white cloth is manufactured chiefly in a tract of country forming an oblique belt across the hills that separate the vale of Calder from the vale of Aire, terminating at Shipley on the Aire, and not coming within less than about six miles of Leeds on the right.

The cloths are sold in their respective halls rough as they come from the fulling mills. They are finished by the merchants, who employ dressers, dyers, &c., for that purpose; these, with drysalters, shop-keepers, and the different kind of handicraftmen common to every town, compose the bulk of the inhabitants of Leeds.

The dispersed state of the manufacturers in villages and single houses over the whole face of the country, is highly favourable to their morals and happiness. They are generally men of small capitals, and often annex a small farm to their other business: great numbers of the rest have a field or two to support a horse and a cow, and are for the most part blessed with the comforts, without the superfluities, of life.

pp. 570–4.

4

Child Labour in the Cotton Mills

The invention and improvements of machines to shorten labour, has had a surprising influence to extend our trade, and also to call in hands from all parts, especially children for the *cotton mills*. It is the wise plan of Providence, that in this life there shall be no good without its attendant inconvenience. There are many which are too obvious in these cotton mills, and similar factories, which counteract that increase of population usually consequent on the improved facility of labour. In these, children of very tender age are employed; many of them collected from the *workhouses* in *London* and *Westminster*, and transported in crowds, as apprentices to masters resident many hundred miles distant, where they serve, unknown, unprotected, and forgotten by those to whose care nature or the laws had consigned them.

These children are usually too long confined to work, in close rooms,

201

often during the whole night; the air they breathe from the oil, &c., employed in the machinery, and other circumstances, is injurious: little regard is paid to their cleanliness, and frequent changes from a warm and dense to a cold and thin atmosphere, are predisposing causes to sickness and disability, and particularly to the epidemic fever which so generally is to be met with in these factories.

It is also much to be questioned, if society does not receive detriment from the *manner* in which children are thus employed during their early years. They are not generally strong to labour, or capable of pursuing any other branch of business, when the term of their apprenticeship expires. The females are wholly uninstructed in sewing, knitting, and other domestic affairs, requisite to make them notable and frugal wives and mothers. This is a very great misfortune to them and to the public, and is fully proved by a comparison of the families of labourers in husbandry, and those of manufacturers in general. In the former we meet with neatness, cleanliness, and comfort; in the latter, with filth, rags, and poverty, although their wages may be nearly double to those of the husbandmen. It must be added, that the want of early religious instruction and example, and the numerous and indiscriminate association in those buildings, are very unfavourable to their future conduct in life.

To mention these grievances, is to point out their remedies; and in *many* factories they have been adopted with true benevolence and much success.

pp. 219–21.

5

The Duke of Bridgewater's Canals

Those magnificent plans which have rendered the name of the Duke of Bridgewater [1736–1803] so celebrated in the history of canal-navigation, commenced in the years 1758 and 1759, when Acts were passed enabling him, first, to carry a canal from Worsley to Salford, and also to Hollinferry on the Irwell; and secondly, to deviate from that course, and carry his canal from Worsley across the river Irwell to Manchester, through the township of Stretford.

Possessing an extensive property at or near Worsley, rich in coals, which could not by land carriage be conveyed so advantageously as those from the pits on the other side of that town, the Duke was naturally led to consider a better mode of conveyance. . . . The original and commanding abilities of his engineer, that wonderful self-instructed genius James Brindley [1716–72] pointed out a mode of effecting his purpose.

This first undertaking was marked with the features of greatness. At its upper extremity in Worsley it buries itself in a hill, which it enters by an arched passage, partly bricked and partly formed by the solid rock, wide enough for the admission of long flat-bottomed boats, which are towed by means of hand-rails on each side. This passage penetrates near three-quarters of a mile before it reaches the first coal-works. . . . In the passage at certain distances air funnels are cut through the rock, issuing perpendicularly at the top of the hill . . .

To this subterraneous canal the coals are brought from the pits within the bowels of the hill in low waggons holding about a ton each, which, as the work is on the descent, are easily pushed or pulled by a man along a railed way to the stage over the canal, whence they are shot into one of the boats. These boats hold seven or eight tons, and several of them being linked together, are easily drawn out by the help of the rail to the mouth of the subterraneous passage, where a large bason is made, serving as a dock. From hence they are sent along the canal to Manchester, in strings drawn by a horse or two mules . . .

The most striking of all the aqueduct works is in this first canal, where it passes over the navigable river Irwell at Barton bridge. The aqueduct begins upwards of 200 yards from the river, which runs in a valley. Over the river itself it is conveyed by a stone bridge of great strength and thickness, consisting of three arches, the centre one 63 feet wide and 38 feet above the surface of the water, admitting the largest barges navigating the Irwell, to go through it with masts and sails standing. The spectator was, therefore, here gratified with the extraordinary sight, never before beheld in this country of one vessel sailing over the top of another . . .

This canal, after passing Barton bridge, was conveyed on the level with great labour and expense, in a circuitous route of nine miles to Castlefield, adjacent to Manchester . . .

When the Duke of Bridgewater undertook this great design, the price of carriage on the river navigation was twelve shillings the ton from Manchester to Liverpool, while that of land carriage was forty shillings the ton. The Duke's charge on his canal was limited to six shillings, and together with this vast superiority in cheapness, it had all the speed and regularity of land carriage.

The articles conveyed by it were likewise much more numerous than those by the river navigation: besides manufactured goods and their raw materials, coals from the Duke's own pits were deposited in yards at various parts of the canal, for the supply of Cheshire; lime, manure,

8. Scout Mill, a cotton mill romantically situated beside the river Tame near Stalybridge; and (*below*) Barton Bridge, where the Bridgewater Canal crosses over the River Irwell.

J. Aitkin, Description of the Country . . . round Manchester

and building materials were carried from place to place; and the markets of Manchester obtained a supply of provisions from districts too remote for the ordinary land carriage.

A branch of useful and profitable carriage hitherto scarcely known in England was also undertaken, which was that of passengers. Boats on the model of the Dutch *treckschuyts*, but more agreeable and capacious, were set up, which at very reasonable rates and with great convenience, carried numbers of persons daily between Manchester and the principal extent of the canal.

pp. 112–16.

[Three generations of Abraham Darby's – father, son, and grandson – played a great part in the development of the English iron industry. Abraham Darby I (1677–1717) son of a farmer near Dudley, started a brass and iron foundry at Bristol and in 1709 leased a furnace at Coalbrookdale, a Shropshire valley with a stream running down into the Severn. Abraham Darby II (1711–63) managed the Coalbrookdale undertaking and invented a method of smelting iron ore by the use of coke. Abraham Darby III (1750–91) carried on the business with marked success, but is best known as the builder of the Iron Bridge across the Severn (referred to in the article by Arthur Young below), the first iron bridge to be constructed anywhere in the world; it was opened in 1779.]

Crossing the ferry, where Mr Darby has undertaken to build a bridge of one arch of 120 feet, of cast iron, I passed to his works up Colebrook Dale. The waggon ways that lead down to the river, instead of wood are laid with cast iron, and those made for the lime stone waggons on the steep hills are so contrived that the loaded waggon winds up the empty one on a different road. Pass his new slitting mills, which are not finished, but the immense wheels 20 feet in diameter of cast iron were there, and appear wonderful. Viewed the furnaces, forges, etc., with the vast bellows that give those roaring blasts, which make the whole edifice horribly sublime.

These works are supposed to be the greatest in England. The whole process is here gone through from the digging of the iron stone to making it into cannons, pipes, cylinders, etc. All the iron used is raised in the neighbouring hills, and the coal dug likewise, which is charred, an invention which must have been of the greatest consequence after the quantity of cord wood in the kingdom declined.

Mr Darby in his own works employs near 1,000 people, including colliers. The colliers earn 20d a day, those who get the limestone 1s 4d, the founderers 8s to 10s 6d a week. Boys of 14 earn 1s a day at drawing coal baskets in the pits. The coal mines are from 20 yards to 120 feet deep.

Colebrook Dale is itself a very romantic spot, it is a winding glen between two immense hills which break into various forms, and all thickly covered with wood, forming the most beautiful sheets of hanging wood. Indeed too beautiful to be much in unison with that variety of horrors art has spread at the bottom; the noise of the forges, mills, etc., with all their vast machinery, the flames bursting from the furnaces with the burning of the coal and the smoke of the lime kilns, are altogether sublime . . .

A. YOUNG, 'A Tour in Shropshire' (1776), *Annals of Agriculture* (1785), vol. 4, p. 168.

(d) CRAWSHAY'S IRON WORKS IN SOUTH WALES

[Richard Crawshay (1739–1810), born at Normanton, near Leeds, was the son of a small yeoman farmer, which he might have become himself if at the age of 16 he had not quarrelled with his father and run away to London. He was twenty days on the way, and on arrival sold his pony, his only asset, for £15. He obtained employment with an ironmonger in Upper Thames Street, and was put in charge of the department selling flat-irons. Here the 'Yorkshire boy' showed himself cute enough to counter the wiles of the London washerwomen, who were reputed to thieve two irons for every one they paid for. Having won his master's confidence, he went on to marry his daughter, and eventually on his retirement succeeded to the business.

Having some capital behind him, he was attracted by reports of iron-trade developments in South Wales. Leaving his son William in charge of the ironmongery store, which continued to provide him with funds, he went to Merthyr and secured the lease of a small works engaged in boring cannon. In 1786 he was enabled to acquire the lease of the Cyfartha works, where with difficulty he manufactured ten tons of bar-iron weekly. But he proceeded to build new furnaces, forges, and rolling-mills, and did a big trade in making cannon for the British armies engaged in the long war with France. In the year before his death he was producing 10,000 tons of iron a year, and his weekly wages bill for the 1,500 men he employed amounted to £2,500. When he died his fortune was estimated at a million and a half.]

Mr Crawshay's iron works at Cyfartha (Merthyr Tydvil) are by now by far the largest in this kingdom, probably indeed the largest in Europe; and in that case, as far as we know, the largest in the world. The machinery is gigantic. The most remarkable piece of mechanism is the great water wheel [built] by Watkin George. Its diameter is fifty feet, and it has the power of fifty horses.

The number of smelting furnaces at Merthyr Tydvil is about sixteen.

Six of these belong to Cyfartha Works; the rest to other gentlemen. Around each of these furnaces are erected forges and rolling mills for converting pig into plate and bar iron.

When the first furnaces and forges were erected [about 1755], there could not exist the slightest glimmering of prescience, that this little obscure Welsh village would, in less than forty years, grow up to be far more populous than any other town in Wales. The population in 1802 was found to be upwards of ten thousand.

The first houses that were built were only very small and simple cottages for furnace-men, forge-men, miners, and such tradesmen as were necessary to construct the required buildings, with the common labourers who were employed to assist them. These cottages were most of them built in scattered confusion, without any order or plan. As the works increased, more cottages were wanted, and were erected in the spaces between those that had been previously built, till they became so connected with each other as to form a certain description of irregular streets, very much on the plan of Crooked Lane in the City of London.

These streets are now many in number, close and confined, having no proper outlet behind the houses. They are consequently very filthy, for the most part, and also doubtless very unhealthy. Some streets, it is to be observed, have within these few years been built, and more are building, on a better plan, on straighter lines, and wider, having decent houses, with commodious outlets, and other necessary attentions to cleanliness and health. In some of the early and rudely connected streets we frequently see the small, miserable houses taken down, and larger and very seemly ones built in their stead.

Shopkeepers, innkeepers, forge-men, some of them at least, and in no inconsiderable numbers, are making comfortable fortunes, and consequently improving their dwellings. Mr Crawshay, however, is more conspicuously qualified to set them an example of industry than elegance. His house is surrounded with fire, flame, smoke, and ashes. The noise of hammers, rolling mills, forges, and bellows, incessantly din and crash upon the ear. Bars and pigs of iron are continually thrown to the hugely accumulating heaps that threaten to close up every avenue of access. It is more humorously than truly said in the neighbourhood, that such scenery is most congenial to the taste, such sounds most lulling to the repose of the owner . . .

The workmen of all descriptions at these immense works are Welshmen. The language is almost entirely Welsh. The number of Englishmen among them is very inconsiderable. But the ill effects which large collections of the lower classes produce upon the state of manners, are here very observable, though by no means to so great an extent as in the manufacturing towns of England. The simplicity, sincerity, and disinterestedness of the peasant is lost in the mercenary cunning and extortion of the mechanic. But a few miles off, you can scarcely prevail with the rustic to accept your gratuity, though he has lost half his day's work by directing you over the mountains; here, you are beset with the demands of importunate hordes upon your purse . . .

The men employed at these works are too much addicted to drinking, but in other respects no great immoralities are to be found among them; far less indeed than might have been expected from the tide of dissoluteness which is usually found to flow in upon a place, from the rapid increase of vulgar population. The principal check to immorality arises from the ironmasters, as the proprietors are called, being magistrates of the county.

BENJAMIN HEATH MALKIN, *The Scenery, Antiquities and Biography of South Wales, from materials collected during two excursions in the year 1803* (1804), pp. 175–80.

Comparing Scotland with England, Adam Smith asserted that England was much the richer, and that Scotland, although she was advancing to greater wealth, was doing so nothing like so fast as England. The demand for labour in Scotland was much lower, as was clear enough from the fact that so many Scotsmen wanted to emigrate and so few English. Wages, too, were lower in Scotland than south of the border: the improvements in agriculture, manufactures, and commerce had begun much earlier in England than in Scotland, and these were bound to improve the demand for labour and give a lift to wages.

But Scotland was catching up. Although in some parts of the Highlands and Western Islands the wages of common labour were 3s a week, practically the same as in the previous century, throughout the Lowlands the most usual wages for common labourers were eightpence a day, and sometimes a shilling about Edinburgh and in the counties bordering on England, and lately there had been a considerable rise in the demand for labour in certain places. One of these places was Carron, whose great iron works are described below in an extract from the *Statistical Account of Scotland.*

This is one of the outstanding publishing enterprises of the eighteenth century, and the man chiefly responsible for it was Sir John Sinclair (1754–1835), a Caithness landowner, who devoted his life to the promotion of agriculture and the general welfare. Finding himself hampered by the lack of authoritative information concerning the country and its people, he framed the plan of a *Statistical Account*, the material for which should be provided by the ministers in every parish in Scotland, which would be collated and edited by himself. This great work was published in twenty-one volumes between 1791 and 1799, and later its contents were summarised and reviewed in an *Analysis of the Statistical Account*. Sinclair was a MP for more than thirty years, and in 1793 was appointed president of the newly formed Board of Agriculture, which he had done much to promote.

The account of Mr Dale's cotton mills at New Lanark is also taken from the *Statistical Account*. David Dale (1739–1806) was the son of humble parents in Ayrshire. As a boy he was apprenticed to a Paisley weaver, and then became some sort of commercial traveller. Having met Richard Arkwright, he joined with him in 1783 in the erection of cotton mills at New Lanark, near the Falls of Clyde, which provided the water power. There he became exceedingly prosperous, and used his wealth in promoting the welfare of his workpeople, young children in particular. He sold his interests in the mills to Robert Owen and his partners in 1799, and Owen married his eldest daughter. He passed his latter years in Glasgow, where he had his own chapel of 'Old Independents'.

John Lettice (1737–1832), the author of the third item below, was an English clergyman, who after serving as chaplain and secretary to the British Embassy at Copenhagen, became rector of Seaford in Sussex. He wrote poetry and did translations, but his chief work was his *Letters on a Tour through various parts of Scotland in 1792*.

I

The Carron Ironworks that Robert Burns Saw

The Carron ironworks are situated on the northern banks of the river Carron; and though they are not in this parish, yet many of the workmen live in it, and as they are not two miles from the town of Falkirk, the shops and markets thereof are generally resorted to by those who are employed in the various operations of that extensive manufacture.

The Carron Company have a charter for employing a capital of £150,000. It is divided into 600 shares, and no person can have a vote in the management unless he be possessed of ten shares.

These works were first projected and established by Dr Roebuck, and Messrs Cadell and Garbet. They were joined by other gentlemen of respectability, and the Company are now in a very flourishing condition. The works are under the immediate direction of Mr Joseph Stainton, who is also a partner. They are supplied with iron-ore from Lancashire and Cumberland, and with ironstone from the county of Fife, etc. They have limestone from Burntisland, etc., and coals from Kinnaird, Carronhall, and Shieldhill. All the materials which are made use of at these works are brought to them by water-carriage, except coals, and these are found in their neighbourhood. At an average, they use 800 tons of coal, 400 tons of ironstone and ore, etc., and 100 tons of limestone per week.

The ironstone is first calcined in an open fire; but the iron-ore needs no preparation in order to be fit for the blast-furnaces. There are five furnaces of this description, which are supplied with strong currents of air from cast-iron cylinders instead of bellows. These cylinders are not only more durable than bellows, but have more power, and produce a better effect. There are also fifteen furnaces which are kept in action by the external air, without the aid of an artificial blast.

At Carron all kinds of cast-iron goods are made in the best manner. A short kind of cannon called the Carronade was invented there. Bar iron is also made, and in accomplishing this business the following method is pursued. The pig iron is melted in a finery, where coke is used; while hot, it is beaten out into plates about an inch in thickness. These plates are afterwards broken into pieces about two inches square. They are then scoured in an iron cylinder, which is connected with the water-wheel, and when they are properly prepared by this operation, they are put into pots, made of fire-clay, and in an air-furnace are brought to a welding heat; in this state of preparation they are put under the hammer, and wrought into blooms; the blooms are heated in a hollow fire and then drawn into bars for various uses. In this condition the iron is equal in goodness to that which is imported from Russia.

The machinery is moved by the water of the river Carron, and for a supply in time of drought they have a reservoir to the extent of about 30 acres. But as this precaution is not enough in very dry seasons, they have moreover an engine for throwing back the water that it may be used again; this engine raises 4 tons every stroke, and makes about 7 strokes in a minute.

If we take into account, along with the people who are directly employed in the manufacture at Carron, those also who are engaged in the mines and pits, together with those who carry materials to the works, we may estimate the whole as two thousand people.

Robert Burns's Visits
Nobody is admitted to view the works on Sundays, except those who are properly recommended, or known to be worthy of attention, Mr Burns, the Ayrshire poet, not knowing or not attending to this regulation, made an attempt to be admitted (in 1787), without discovering who he was, but was refused by the porter. Upon returning to the inn at Carron [Stirling] he wrote the following lines upon a pane of glass in a window of the parlour into which he was shown:

We came na' here to view your warks
   In hopes to be mair wise,
But only, lest we gang to hell,
   It might be na surprise.
But when we tirl'd [rattled] at your door,
   Your porter dought na hear us;
So may, should we to hell's yetts [gates] come,
   Your billy Satan fail us.

A few weeks later Robert Burns paid a second visit to Carron Foundry, when he was given a very favourable reception. As he toured the works, he beheld in their tremendous furnaces and broiling labours a resemblance to the cavern of the Cyclops.

REVD. JAMES WILSON, Minister of the Parish of Falkirk, *Statistical Account of Scotland* (1797), vol. 19, pp. 93–6.

2

Mr Dale's Mills at New Lanark

New Lanark, where the cotton mills are situated, is about a short mile from Lanark. It is entirely the creation of the enterprising and well known Mr David Dale.

In 1784 Mr Dale feued [leased] the site of the mills and village, with some few acres of ground adjoining. This spot of ground was at that period almost a mere morass, situated in a hollow den, and of difficult access. Its only recommendation was the very powerful current of water that the Clude could be made to afford it; in other respects, the distance from Glasgow and the badness of the roads were rather unfavourable.

The first mill was begun in April 1785, and a subterraneous passage of near 100 yards in length was also formed through a rocky hill for the purpose of an aqueduct to it. In summer 1788 a second one was built ... and the proprietor has since erected other two, all of which are meant to be driven by one and the same aqueduct. In March 1786 the spinning commenced, and the manufactory has been in a constant progressive state of advancement.

In March 1791, from an accurate account then taken, it appears that there were 981 persons employed at the mills, whereas there are now (November 1793) 1,334 (men 145; women 217; boys 376; girls 419; masons, carpenters, labourers, employed in erecting buildings, and mechanics 177).

With regard to the health of the workpeople, it is sufficient to say that of all the children provided with meat and clothing by the proprietor amounting this and last year to 275, and for seven years back never fewer than 80, only five have died during the period of 7 years. In mentioning so extraordinary a fact, it may be expected that something should be said of their diet and treatment.

The *diet* consists of oatmeal porridge, with milk in summer or sowens, i.e. oat-meal flummery, with milk in winter twice a day, as much as they can take, barley broth for dinner made with good fresh beef every day; and as much beef is boiled as will allow 7 oz English a-piece each day to one half of the children, the other half get cheese and bread after their broth, so that they dine alternately upon cheese and butchermeat, with barley bread or potatoes; and now and then in the proper season they have a dinner of herrings and potatoes.

They, as well as the others, begin work at six in the morning, are allowed half an hour for breakfast, an hour for dinner, and quit work at 7 at night; after which they attend the school at the expense of the proprietor till 9. They sleep in well-aired rooms, three in a bed; and proper care is taken to remove those under any disease to separate apartments . . .

Great attention is paid to the morals of the children and others at these mills. Large manufactories have sometimes been considered in another light, but Mr Dale and all concerned must have the voice of the public to the contrary. Marriages have greatly increased in the parish since their erection, as the benefits arising from a family are obvious. Indeed the anxiety of the proprietor to have proper teachers and instructors for children will ever redound to his honour . . .

Families from any quarter possessed of a good moral character, and having children fit for work, above nine years of age, are received – supplied with a house at a moderate rent, and the woman and children provided with work. The children, both those fit for work and those who are too young for it, have the privilege of attending the school gratis, the former in the evening, the latter during the day. Three professed teachers are paid by Mr Dale for this purpose, and also seven assistants who attend in the evenings, one of whom teaches writing. There is also a Sunday school at which all the masters and assistants attend.

Before leaving this article of cotton mills I cannot help noticing a circumstance peculiar to such manufactures, which may afford a useful hint to poor widows with families. In most other manufactures, a woman who has a family, and becomes a widow, is generally in a most helpless situation. Here the case is very different, for the greater number of children a woman has, she lives so much the more comfortably;

and upon such account alone, she is often a tempting object for a second husband. Indeed, at cotton mills, it often happens, that young children support their aged parents by their industry.

The people [of Lanark] are, in general, industrious though not remarkably so. They are naturally generous, hospitable, and fond of strangers, which induces them sometimes to make free with the bottle, but drunkenness, among the better class of inhabitants, is of late rather unusual. Upon the whole, they are a decent, orderly people, and crimes are seldomer committed here than in any other parish of equal population. In short, they are generally honest, decent, religious, and strict in their attendance at divine worship.

WILLIAM LOCKHART OF BARONALD, *Statistical Account of Scotland* (1795), vol. 15 (Lanark), pp. 34–42.

3

Lively Doings at Rothesay's Cotton Mill

The flourishing state of Rothesay has not solely arisen from its herring-fishery and its commerce. The establishment of cotton-mills has contributed to it in a degree highly worth consideration. Individuals of the lower class, able to work, need never remain unemployed; and in fact, there is scarcely an idle person in the place.

This is the first station in Scotland where a cotton-mill was projected. The first mill was erected about eleven years ago, and the second is very nearly finished. The great water-wheel of the latter is 24 feet in diameter, and the breadth of its periphery not less than six. This wheel is really a grand object; and its dark colour, approaching to black, combined with its magnitude and prodigious power, when in motion, impresses a sublime idea. This vast body in its rotation communicates movement to a horizontal beam, resembling the mast of a first-rate man of war, and an hundred feet in length. Round this are fixed a great number of vertical wheels, which turn as many horizontal ones; and these again are connected with others, ranged above them, through four or five stories of the new edifice, alternately vertical and horizontal. The effect procured by this whole combination of wheels is the ceaseless whirling of many thousand spindles, and the regular movement of all that machinery by which cotton is carded, spun, twisted, and every operation performed, till it is prepared for the loom.

Five hundred persons, many of them children, are at present engaged in the mill, first erected; and the second, we were told, will soon require that number to be doubled. These thousand persons, with the assistance of this powerful machinery, are able, it is supposed, to perform the work of twenty thousand, without it. After reflecting on the vast sum of effects here produced by one of the mechanical powers, we were naturally led to contemplate the invention itself, as one of the most laudable exertions of practical science. And it was highly pleasing to observe such a number of little hands, made early useful, in the application and removal of the materials to and from this grand machine. Nor did it add little to the satisfaction with which we had contemplated the scene, to have witnessed the appearance of health and cheerfulness in the generality of persons engaged in it.

Night was now coming on, and we retired to our inn, which we had left two hours before in perfect order and tranquillity. But we had scarcely re-entered and sat down to an early supper, meaning to retire soon to bed, when we suddenly heard a great deal of running up and down; the voices of men and women, in all the adjoining rooms, some talking, others singing and whistling. Presently, struck up a merry strain of music in a room directly beneath us. Dancing succeeded. The whole house shook: our table, our seats, our very plates and spoons, responsively partook the general movement, as we ourselves did a few minutes afterwards. For as soon as we found that all thoughts of sleep must be deferred for a season, we descended in haste in order to see the company and the ball.

Having squeezed with some effort through the crowd of the passage and the doorway, many a bonny lad and lassie did we see; who, having finished their day at the cotton-works, were very nimbly, and not ungracefully, performing the lively evolutions of the Scottish reel. The dance, and the music, were national, and merited the attention of the stranger. To give you, however, any precise ideas of the nature of the steps, with all the crossing, shuffling, springing, and frisking of the dancers; or to describe their setting-to, their figuring in and out and turning about; their clapping of hands and snapping of fingers, would be impossible.

There was something of all this, and more, in the dance; every man had his partner, and the number of couples, in each reel, seemed indefinite. The music, and the dance, began very temperately, in a kind of *adagio* movement. Each couple glided gently along, for two or three rounds; the motion increased by degrees, till it became brisker and more lively; at length wonderfully rapid; and concluded like the German valse, by each pair joining hands and whirling round with a velocity continually accelerated, till the parties, growing giddy, began to reel and ended the dance, but when unable either to move or even to stand any longer.

I should not have omitted to mention that a certain rapturous yelp, which every now and then escapes the male dancers in the height of their glee, seems to give new spirit to their movements.

Considerable credit was due to that address and circumspection of the swains, by which they avoided trampling upon the naked feet of the nymphs, whilst most vigorously footing it very near to them in shoes of a very massive sole.

After a short pause the dance was renewed, and an agreeable young woman invited us to partake in it. As it was impossible not to have sympathised in the animation of the scene I know not that any thing but our ignorance of the steps and the figures prevented our accepting the challenge. Our excuse allowed us, however, to remain spectators, till the assembly broke up and departed, according to their custom, at eleven o'clock.

J. LETTICE, BD, *Letters on a Tour through various parts of Scotland, in the year 1792* (1794), pp. 134–42.

CHAPTER 10

THE SCOTLAND THAT
ADAM SMITH KNEW

(a) KIRKCALDY

Adam Smith seems to have known only three places in Scotland really well. The first of these was, of course, Kirkcaldy (in old records the name may be found spelled Kirkaldy or Kirkaldie, but the pronunciation has always been *Kirkawdy*), which was not only his birthplace but where he spent his youth and in which for a large part of his life he had his home. It was in a house in the High Street that he wrote *The Wealth of Nations*.

The one feature that seems to have impressed every visitor to the place was its length, and for good reason it was commonly spoken of as the 'lang toun'. Thus Andrew Fairservice in Sir Walter Scott's *Rob Roy* (the principal action in which may be dated to 1715) proudly informs his young English companion that Kirkcaldy, one of the 'mony royal boroughs yoked on end to end like ropes of ingans' (onions) along the coast of Fife, 'is langer than any town in England'.

A few years earlier Daniel Defoe, being in Scotland on some matter of government business, one day rode down Kirkcaldy's main street and noted how long it was. By no great stretch of the imagination we may see him calling on Mr Adam Smith, Senior, at the Custom House and obtaining from him some of those local details which in due course he included in the account that is reproduced as our first 'document'. This is taken from the first edition of the justly celebrated *Tour thro' the whole Island of Great Britain*, the only edition published in Defoe's lifetime. It may be remarked that on the title-page the book is said to be by 'A Gentleman': Defoe's name was not given until the 7th edition, of 1769.

Nail-making
Among other things that caught Defoe's attention was that 'convenient yard' at the east end of the town where ships were built and repaired. This was something that the people of Kirkcaldy had been engaged in for generations. They are said, indeed, to have been the first to use

iron nails for the purpose, manufactured locally, instead of the wooden dowels that had been customary hitherto. Iron scrap was imported from the Continent in exchange for coal and salt, and the nails found a ready sale not only in Kirkcaldy but among the builders of the New Town at Edinburgh and in the Glasgow shipyards.

Although there were no naileries in Kirkcaldy itself, there were several in the immediate neighbourhood; and there is no reason to question the tradition reported by Alexander Campbell in his *Journey from Edinburgh through Parts of North Britain* (1802) that it was at 'the manufactory of iron nails at Path-head' that 'the frequent contemplation of the dexterity with which the nailers performed their tasks suggested to the late celebrated author of *The Wealth of Nations* the vast advantages that result from the division of labour, in turning to account the industry and ingenuity of individuals, the fundamental proposition of his admirable speculation'.

Very likely, too, that 'village in Scotland' mentioned by Adam Smith, 'where, I am told, it is not uncommon for a workman to carry nails instead of money to the baker's shop or the ale house' may be located at Pathhead, only a short walk from Kirkcaldy.

Scottish serfdom

Yet other features jotted down by Defoe were the coal-pits and salt-pans, and yet he did not realise that the men and women employed in these particularly dirty and arduous occupations were serfs. Nor, for that matter, did Adam Smith, for in his account of serfdom as still existing in some of the countries of Europe, he omitted Scotland from his list. Some of those visitors who came fresh to Scotland did, however, notice it, and were duly shocked. Thus Thomas Pennant, the indefatigable Welsh traveller who toured parts of Scotland in 1769 and 1772, denounced 'this disgrace' as a 'remnant of slavery'.

It may be noted that the hope expressed in Pennant's final paragraph was fulfilled, for in 1775 and 1799 acts of parliament gave the poor salters and colliers their legal freedom. And yet, so far from accepting this as a blessing, there were some of their number who looked upon it as just a dodge on the part of their masters to avoid having to make the small payment that was customary when one of their women gave birth to an addition to their livestock.

For our concluding picture of Kirkcaldy just before the century's close we have recourse to the *Statistical Account* for which Sir John Sinclair was mainly responsible.

I

Daniel Defoe's Description

Kirkcaldy is a larger, more populous, and better-built town than any on this coast. Its situation is in length, in one street running along the shore, from east to west, for a long mile, and very well built, the streets clean and well paved; there are some small by-streets or lanes, and it has some considerable merchants in it, I mean in the true sense of the word Merchant.

There are also several good ships belonging to the town. Also as Fife is a good corn country, here are some that deal very largely in corn, and export great quantities both in England and Holland. Here are great quantities of linen shipped off for England; and as these ships return freighted either from England or Holland, they bring all needful supplies of foreign goods; so that the traders in Kirkcaldy have really a very considerable traffick both at home and abroad.

There are several coal-pits here, not only in the neighbourhood but even close to the very sea, at the west end of the town, and where, one would think, the tide should make it impossible to work them. At the east end of the town is a convenient yard for building and repairing of ships, and farther east than that several salt-pans for the boiling and making of salt.

DANIEL DEFOE, *A Tour thro' the Whole Island of Great Britain* (1727), vol. 3, pt. 2, pp. 139–40.

2

'Remnant of slavery'

Adjoining Pathhead, a place of check-weavers and nailers, is Kirkaldie, a long town, containing sixteen hundred inhabitants. This, like most other towns of Fife, depends on the coal and salt trade.

There is one class of men on this coast, and I believe in most of the coal counties of North Britain [Scotland], from whom all power of migration is taken, be their inclinations for it ever so strong. In this very island is, to this day, to be found a remnant of slavery paralleled

9. In Skye, Western Islands of Scotland. A woman and girl (left) are grinding corn in a quern; while (right) ten girls are performing the 'luagh' or 'walking the cloth', whereby it is cleansed and finished, 'a substitute for the fulling-mill'. This they do with their hands and bare feet in turn, singing as they go, until 'the fury of the song arrives at such a pitch that you would imagine a troop of female demoniacs to have been assembled'.

T. Pennant, *A Tour in Scotland and Voyage to the Hebrides* (1772)

only in Poland and Russia: thousands of our fellow subjects are at this time the property of their landlords, appurtenances to their estates, and transferable with them to any purchasers.

Multitudes of colliers and salters are in this situation, who are bound to the spot for their lives; and even strangers who come to settle there are bound by the same cruel custom, unless they previously stipulate to the contrary. Should the poor people remove to another place on a temporary cessation of the works, they are liable to be recalled at will, and constrained to return on severe penalties.

This, originally founded on vassalage, might have been continued to check the wandering spirit of the nation, and to preserve a body of people together, of whose loss the whole public might otherwise feel the most fatal effects.

(This disgrace, I believe, is now under consideration of parliament, and will, I hope, be removed.)

THOMAS PENNANT, *A Tour in Scotland and Voyage to the Hebrides,* 2nd edn (1776), pp. 202–4.

3

Place and People in 1790

The town of Kirkaldy is situated at the foot of a bank on the sea-shore. It is properly but one street, with a few lanes of small extent opening on each side of it. The principal part of the street appears to have been originally wider than it is now. At present the street is narrow, in some places inconveniently so; winding and irregular, deformed by the frequent projection of contiguous houses and stairs, and as the traveller daily feels, wretchedly paved. The houses are in general mean, awkwardly placed with their ends to the streets, and constructed without any regard for order or uniformity.

The only public buildings worthy of notice are the town-house and the church. The town-house stands near the middle of the town, and contains the hall in which the magistrates and council assemble for conducting the general business of the burgh. Over the town-house is the prison, with separate apartments for debtors and criminals, and under it is the guard-house, the meal market, and the public weigh-house. The whole forms a plain building of hewn stone, ornamented with a tower and a spire. The tower contains the town-clock and bell, and serves as the repository of the archives of the burgh. The church stands on the top of the bank which rises immediately behind the town. It is a large unshapely pile that seems to have been reared at different times to suit the growing population of the parish.

The public school is under the care of two masters, who teach in separate rooms. The first master teaches Latin, French, arithmetic, book-keeping, etc.; the second, English and history. The first master has a salary of £20 yearly, which with the school fees, etc., makes his living about £60.

On one side of the town the sea is separated from it by a beach of firm and level sand on which the inhabitants have always, excepting at the height of the tide, a safe and agreeable walk, and by which the traveller may generally avoid the uneasy jolting of a long and rugged pavement. As the sand continues firm and smooth, and the ground shelves gradually for a great way into the sea, this place is peculiarly favourable for sea-baths, for which purpose there has been for some years an increasing resort to it during the months of summer and harvest.

The inhabitants are in general healthy, and many of them attain a good old age. The most prevalent disease is the chronic rheumatism. On the 1st day of January 1790 there were in the town 646 families, containing 2,607 souls.

Manners and Customs

Among the upper classes the style of living is genteel but not luxurious or expensive. Allowing for the diversity of circumstances, all classes dress well, and are generally civil in their manners and decent in their external deportment. The great body of the people are industrious and sober, but 31 houses and 19 shops licensed to sell retail spirits – a number that is in the proportion of 1 to 13 of all the families in the place – furnish room to suppose that from this part of the public character there must be exceptions. Strong drink appears to have been long a considerable article in the consumption of Kirkaldy. Far down in the present century it was the practice, even among citizens of some character, to take a regular *whet* in the forenoon, and most commonly to spend the evening in the public-house.

The Statistical Account of Scotland (1796), Parish of Kirkaldy, Co. Fife, by REVD. MR THOMAS FLEMING, vol. 18, pp. 1–61.

(b) GLASGOW

If Adam Smith had not passed some of the best years of his life in Glasgow he might never have written *The Wealth of Nations*.

When he went there in 1737 he was a schoolboy, and he was not much more when after three years he left to go to Oxford. But the thirteen years from 1751 to 1763 when he held a professorship at the college, or university, were the making of him. He had returned to Glasgow to teach, but the teacher became the taught.

Soon after his arrival he began to mix with the business men of the place, and he was on particularly good terms with Andrew Cochrane who is described in *Humphry Clinker* as 'one of the sages of this kingdom'. He joined Cochrane's Political Economy Club, the first of its kind to be established anywhere. The information he gathered in his numerous contacts helped to enliven his lectures, and in due course was incorporated in the pages of his great book.

The first of the 'documents' given below comes from the second (1738) edition of the *Tour thro' the Whole Island of Great Britain* that was originally written by Daniel Defoe, and was reprinted with but slight alteration. It shows a city on the upward curve of progress, a people full of energy and enterprise, which continues to be the impression given in *Humphry Clinker*, which describes the place as it was in 1765. In between we have the highly informative account of life at Glasgow College, written by Revd Dr Alexander Carlyle (1722–1805), a distinguished minister of the Church of Scotland who numbered Adam Smith, David Hume, and Tobias Smollett among his friends.

I

'A Very Fine City'

Glasgow is a very fine city. The four principal streets are the fairest for breadth and the finest built that I have ever seen in one city together. The houses are all of stone, and generally equal and uniform in height, as well as in front. The lower stories for the most part stand on vast square Dorick columns, with arches which open into the shops, adding to the strength as well as beauty of the building. In a word, 'tis one of the cleanliest, most beautiful, and best built cities in Britain.

It stands on the side of a hill, sloping to the river; only that part next the river, for near one third part of the city, is flat, which is, by this means, exposed to the water upon any extraordinary flood.

Where the streets meet, the crossing makes a spacious market-place, as you may easily imagine, since the streets are so large of themselves. As you come down the hill from the North Gate to this place, the Tolbooth and Guildhall make the north-west angle, or right-hand corner of the street, which is now rebuilding in a very magnificent manner. Here the Town Council sit, and the Magistrates try such causes as come within their cognizance, and do all their other public business.

On the left hand of the same street is the University, the building of which is the best of its kind in Scotland. It was founded by Bishop Turnbull in the year 1454, but has been much enlarged since, and the fabrick almost all new built. It is lofty and spacious, all of free-stone, and consists of two large squares, or courts, in which are very handsome lodgings for the professors and scholars. Here is a Principal, with Regents and Professors in every science, as there is at Edinburgh. The Scholars wear red gowns, and the Masters of Arts and Professors wear black gowns, with a large cape of velvet to distinguish them.

In the higher part of the town stands the great church, formerly cathedral and metropolitical, and dedicated to the memory of St Mungo, who was bishop here about the year 560. It is a magnificent and stately edifice, and surprises the beholders with its stupendous bigness and the art of the workman. The several rows of pillars, and the exceeding high spire on a square tower in the middle of the cross shows a wonderful piece of architecture. It is now, like St Giles's at Edinburgh, divided into several preaching-places . . .

Glasgow is a City of Business, and has the face of foreign as well as domestic trade; nay, I may say, 'tis the only city in Scotland, at this time, that apparently increases in both. The Union [with England, in 1707] has, indeed, answered its end to them more than to any other part of the Kingdom, their trade being new formed by it; for as the Union opened the door to the Scots into our American colonies, the Glasgow merchants presently embraced the opportunity, and though, at its first concerting, the Rabble of this city made the most formidable attempt to prevent it, yet afterwards they knew better, when they found the great increase of their trade by it; for they now send near fifty sail of ships every year to Virginia, New England, and other English colonies in America . . .

The share they have in the herring-fishery is very considerable; and they cure their herrings so well, and so much better than they are done in any other part of Great Britain, that a Glasgow Herring is esteemed as good as a Dutch one.

The Clyde is not navigable for large ships quite up to the town, but they come to a wharf and quay at Newport-Glasgow, which is within a very little of it, where they deliver their cargoes, and either put them on shore there, or bring them up to the city in lighters. The Custom-House is also here; and their ships are repaired, laid up, and fitted out, either at Greenock or this place, where work is done well, and labour is cheap . . .

Here are two very handsome sugar-baking houses, carried on by skilful persons, with large stocks, and to a very great perfection. I had the curiosity to view one of them, and I think it equal to any I ever saw in London. Here is likewise a large distillery for distilling spirits from the molasses drawn from the sugars.

Here is a manufacture of plaiding, a stuff cross-striped with yellow, red, and other mixtures, for the plaids, or veils, worn by the women in Scotland, which is a habit peculiar to the country. Here is a manufacture of muslins, which is, I believe, the only one of its kind in Britain; these they make so good and fine, that great quantities of them are sent into England, and to the British plantations, where they sell at a good price. They are generally striped, and are very much used for aprons by the ladies, and sometimes as head-clothes by the English women of the meaner sort.

Nor are the Scots without a supply of goods for forming their cargoes to the English colonies, without sending to England for them. . . . They have woollen manufactures of their own, such as Stirling serges, Musselburgh stuffs, Aberdeen stockings, Edinburgh shalloons, blankets, etc. . . . The trade with England being open, they have now all the Manchester, Sheffield, and Birmingham wares, and likewise the cloths . . . and coarse manufactures of the North of England, brought as cheap to them by horse-packs as they are carried to London. They have linen of most kinds, especially diapers and table-linen, damasks, and many other sorts not known in England, and cheaper than there, because made at their own doors. What linens they want from Holland or Hamburgh they import from thence as cheap as the English can do; and for muslins, their own are very acceptable, and cheaper than in England. Gloves they make better and cheaper than in England, for they send great quantities thither.

Another article which is very considerable here is Servants, and these they have in greater plenty and upon better terms than the English, without the scandalous art of kidnapping, wheedling, betraying, and the like; for the poor people offer themselves fast enough, and think it their advantage, as it certainly is, to serve out their times soberly in the foreign plantations, and then become diligent planters themselves; which is a much wiser course than to turn thieves, or worse, and then be transported by force, under a pretence of mercy to save them from the gallows. . . .

DANIEL DEFOE, *A Tour thro' the Whole Island of Great Britain*, 2nd edn. (1738), vol. 3, pp. 258–63.

2

Recollections of a Student at Glasgow College

It must be confessed that at this time [1743] they were far behind in Glasgow, not only in their manner of living but in those accomplishments and that taste that belong to people of opulence, much more to persons of education.

There were only a few families of ancient citizens who pretended to be gentlemen; and a few others, who were recent settlers there, who had obtained wealth and consideration in trade. The rest were shopkeepers and mechanics, or successful pedlars, who occupied large warerooms full of manufactures of all sorts, to furnish a trade to Virginia. It was usual for the sons of merchants to attend the College for one or two years, and a few of them completed their academical education.

In this respect the females were still worse off, for at that period there was neither a teacher of French nor of music in the town. The consequence of this was twofold: first, the young ladies were entirely without accomplishments, and in general had nothing to recommend them but good looks and fine clothes, for their manners were ungainly.

Secondly, the few who were distinguished drew all the young men of sense and taste about them; for, being void of accomplishments, which in some respects make all women equal, they trusted only to their superior understanding and wit, to natural elegance and un-affected manners.

The manner of living, too, at this time, was but coarse and vulgar. Very few of the wealthiest gave dinners to anybody but English riders [commercial travellers], or their own relations at Christmas holidays. There were not half-a-dozen families in town who had men-servants; some of those were kept by the professors who had boarders. There were neither post-chaises nor hackney-coaches in the town, and only three or four sedan-chairs for carrying midwives about in the night, and old ladies to church, or to the dancing assemblies once a fortnight.

The principal merchants, fatigued with the morning's business, took an early dinner with their families at home, and then resorted to the coffeehouse or tavern to read the newspapers, which they generally did in companies of four or five in separate rooms, over a bottle of claret or a bowl of punch. But they never staid supper but always went home by nine o'clock, without company or further amusement. At last an arch fellow from Dublin, a Mr Cockaine, came to be master of the chief coffeehouse, who seduced them gradually to stay supper by placing a few nice cold things at first on the table, as relishers to the wine, till he gradually led them on to bespeak fine hot suppers, and to remain till midnight.

There was an order of women at that time in Glasgow, who, being either young widows not wealthy, or young women unprovided for, were set up in small grocery-shops in various parts of the town, and generally were protected and countenanced by some creditable mer-chant. In their back shops much time and money were consumed; for it being customary then to drink drams and white wine in the forenoon, the tipplers resorted much to those shops, where there were bedrooms; and the patron, with his friends, frequently passed the evening there also, as taverns were not frequented by persons who affected characters of strict decency.

I was admitted a member of two clubs, one entirely literary, which was held in the porter's lodge at the College, and where we criticized books and wrote abridgements of them, with critical essays. The other club met in Mr Dugald's tavern near the Cross, weekly, and admitted a number of young gentlemen who were not intended for the study of theology. Here we drank a little punch after our beefsteaks and pan-cakes, and the expense never exceeded 1s 6d, seldom 1s.

Autobiography of Revd. Dr Alexander Carlyle (first pub. 1860), pp. 72–7.

3

'A Perfect Bee-hive of Industry'

Glasgow is one of the prettiest towns in Europe; and, without all doubt, it is one of the most flourishing in Great Britain. In short, it is a perfect bee-hive in point of industry . . .

The people have a noble spirit of enterprise. Mr Moore, a surgeon, introduced me to all the principal merchants of the place. Here I became acquainted with Mr Cochran, who may be styled one of the sages of this kingdom. He was first magistrate at the time of the last rebellion [the Forty-Five]. I sat as member when he was examined in the House of Commons; upon which occasion Mr Pitt observed he had never heard such a sensible evidence given at that bar.

I was also introduced to Dr John Gordon, a patriot of a truly Roman spirit, who is the father of the linen manufacture in this place, and was the great promoter of the City workhouse, infirmary, and other works of public utility. Had he lived in ancient Rome, he would have been honoured with a statue at the public expense.

I moreover conversed with one Mr Glassford, whom I take to be one of the greatest merchants in Europe. In the last war [Seven Years' War: 1756–63], he is said to have had at one time five and twenty ships, with their cargoes, his own property, and to have traded for above half a million sterling a year.

TOBIAS SMOLLETT, *Humphry Clinker* (1771), letter from Squire Bramble to Dr Lewis, 28 August.

4

Changes in the Ways of Living

For the most part, the people of Glasgow are industrious and still economical. They are in general contented and happy in their situation. They grumble at taxes, and the high price of provisions; and some of the more ambitious wish for some more political consequence than they at present enjoy. As they are getting rich, this desire will increase; yet, notwithstanding, there is at present much difficulty to get proper persons, of the merchant rank, to accept the offices of councillors and magistrates, almost every year furnishing instances of their paying a fine rather than serve.

Riches in Glasgow were formerly the portion of a few merchants. These, from the influence of the manufactures, are now diffusing themselves widely among a great number of manufacturers, mechanics, and artisans. This has made an alteration in the houses, dress, furniture, education and amusements of the people of Glasgow within a few years, which is astonishing to the older inhabitants, and has been followed by a proportional alteration in the manners, customs, and style of living of the inhabitants. And as many of the merchants have of late years been engaging in manufactures and trade, the distance in point of rank and consequence between merchants and tradesmen has now become less conspicuous than it was before the American war.

The strict severity and apparent sanctity of manners formerly remarkable here, have yielded to the opposite extreme. There is now a great deal more industry on six days of the week, and a great deal more dissipation and licentiousness on the seventh. Great crimes were formerly very uncommon; but now robberies, housebreakings, swindling, pickpockets, pilferers, and consequently executions, are become more common. These delinquents, as well as common prostitutes, are often little advanced above childhood; and yet a healthy child of 7 or 8 years, or at most 10 years of age, can now earn a very decent subsistence from some of the numerous manufactories established among us.

Statistical Account of Scotland (1793), vol. 5, pp. 534–5.

5

The Women of Glasgow

I was astonished, in a climate so cold and so humid as that of Glasgow, to see the greater part of the lower class of females, and even many of those in easy circumstances, walking about with their heads and feet bare, their bodies covered only with a jump, and a gown and petticoat of red stuff, which descended to the middle of their legs; and their fine long hair hanging down without any other ornament than a crooked comb to keep back that part which would otherwise fall over their faces. This garb of the females, simple as it may be, is not destitute of grace. As there is nothing to fetter their movements, they display an elegance and agility in their gait so much the more striking, as they are in general tall, well made, and of a charming figure. They have a clear complexion, and very white teeth.

It is not to be inferred, because they walk bare-footed, that they are neglectful of cleanliness; for it appears that they wash frequently, and with equal facility, both their feet and their hands. In a word, the women of Glasgow will be always seen with pleasure by the lovers of simple nature.

B. FAUJAS DE SAINT-FOND, *Travels in England, Scotland, and the Hebrides* (Paris, 1797; English version, 1799), pp. 205-6.

6

'Singular Laundresses'

Having both read and heard much related of the manner of washing their linen at Glasgow, curiosity led me to the mead by the river side. For the poor women here instead of the water coming to them, as in London, are obliged to travel loaded with their linen to the water; where you may daily see great numbers washing, in *their* way; which if seen by some of our London prudes, would incline them to form very unjust and uncharitable ideas of the modesty of these Scottish ladies.

Many of them give a trifle to be accommodated with the use of a large wash-house near the river, where about a hundred may be furnished with every convenience for their purpose. But by far the greatest part make fires, and heat the water in the open air; and as they finish their linen they spread it on the grass to dry, which is the universal mode of drying throughout Scotland.

I had walked to and fro several times, and began to conclude either that the custom of getting into the tubs and treading on the linen, either never had been practised or was come into disuse; but I had not waited more than half an hour when many of them jumped into the tubs, without shoes or stockings, with their shifts and petticoats drawn up far above their knees; and stamped away with great composure in their countenances, and with all their strength, no Scotchman taking the least notice, or even looking towards them, constant habit having rendered the scene perfectly familiar.

On conversing with some gentlemen of Glasgow on this curious subject, they assured me that these singular laundresses (as they appeared to me) were strictly modest women, who only did what others of un-

10. Inside a Weaver's cottage in Islay, Hebrides. 'A set of people worn down with poverty . . . lean and withered, dusky and smoke-dried; their habitations scenes of misery, made of loose stones, without chimneys or doors. . . . But my picture is not of this island only.'

T. Pennant, A Tour in Scotland and Voyage to the Hebrides (1772)

blemished reputation had been accustomed to do for a long series of years; and added, that at any other time a purse of gold would not tempt them to draw the curtain so high.

Memoirs of the Firty-five first years of the Life of James Lackington (7th edition, 1794), pp. 293–5.

When Adam Smith moved to Edinburgh in 1778, on his appointment to the well-paid position of a Commissioner of Customs, he rented Panmure House, a seventeenth-century 'mansion' which had been, years before, Lord Panmure's town house, situated on the north side of the Canongate, with pleasant views across the valley to the Calton hill.

Humphry Clinker contains a good description of Edinburgh in the mid-1760s, but Captain Topham's *Letters from Edinburgh, written in the years 1774 and 1775; containing some Observations on the Diversions, Customs, Manners and Laws of the Scotch Nation* is even more valuable, since it shows us the city in which Adam Smith was shortly to become resident. As will be seen, this is a very sprightly production, and its author, Edward Topham (1751–1820) was as sprightly as his book.

After Eton, Cambridge, and travels on the Continent, Topham made his appearance at Edinburgh in November, 1774, and remained there until the following spring; his book was published in 1776, after his return to London, and perhaps it was on the proceeds that he purchased a commission in the Life Guards (whence he is usually referred to as Captain Topham). He wrote light pieces and plays, and was celebrated as a bright young man about town. For several years he lived with Mrs Mary Wells, a beautiful young actress, and in 1787 started a paper, *The World*, to give her a 'puff' in her stage career. But after five years he disposed of both the lady and the paper, and eventually retired to an estate in Yorkshire.

Smollett's and Topham's accounts have the charm of idiosyncrasy, but they are both based on the experiences of a few months only. Another account lies ready to hand, however, that was the fruit of half a century's active participation in the business, social, and intellectual life of the Scottish capital.

William Creech (1745–1815) was the son of a minister at Newbattle, in Midlothian, and studied at Edinburgh University with a view to entering the medical profession. But he finally resolved to become a bookseller, and apprenticed himself to Kincaid of Edinburgh, where he did so well that by 1773 he was sole partner in the firm, which he proceeded to develop into the leading bookselling and publishing concern in Scotland. He had his shop in the Luckenbooths, close by St Giles's cathedral. Adam Smith was one of his frequent callers, and another was the young Robert Burns, for Creech was the publisher of the first Edinburgh edition of Burns's Poems. From 1811 to 1813 Creech was Lord Provost of Edinburgh.

Not only did Creech encourage young authors, but he was something of an author himself. Over the years he penned a number of bright little pieces and informative essays on a variety of topics which were published in the Edinburgh papers, the *Courant* in particular; but his most enduring production is his *Account of the Manners and Customs in Scotland between 1763 and 1783*, which was originally in the form of two Letters to Sir John Sinclair, editor of the *Statistical Account of Scotland*. This appeared first in a collection of Creech's writings entitled *Fugitive Pieces*, published in 1791, and a little later was reprinted in Sinclair's *Statistical Account*, for which purpose it was extended to the year 1793. An expanded edition of *Fugitive Pieces* was issued in 1815, shortly after Creech's death.

From Sinclair's great work comes the final item – Revd Dr Alexander Carlyle's graphic account of the fishwives and other women who 'carried' to Edinburgh from Inveresk, some five miles along the coast to the east.

I

'A Moderate Kingdom's Capital'

Edinburgh stands upon two hills and the bottom between them; and, with all its defects, may very well pass for the capital of a moderate kingdom.

The palace of Holyrood-House stands on the left, as you enter the Canongate. This is a street continued from hence to the gate called Nether Bow, which is now taken away; so that there is no interruption for a long mile from the bottom to the top of the hill on which the castle stands in a most imperial situation. Considering its fine pavement, its width, and the lofty houses on each side, this would be undoubtedly one of the noblest streets in Europe, if an ugly mass of mean buildings, called the Lucken-Booths, had not thrust itself into the middle of the way.

The city is full of people, and continually resounds with the noise of coaches and other carriages, for luxury as well as commerce. As far as I can perceive, here is no want of provisions. The beef and mutton are as delicate here as in Wales; the sea affords plenty of good fish; the bread is remarkably fine; and the water is excellent, though I'm afraid not in sufficient quantity to answer all the purposes of cleanliness and convenience; articles in which, it must be allowed, our fellow-subjects are a little defective.

The water is brought in leaden pipes from a mountain in the neighbourhood, to a cistern on the Castle-hill, from whence it is distributed to public conduits in different parts of the city. From these it is carried in barrels, on the backs of male and female porters, up two, three, four, five, six, seven, and eight pair of stairs, for the use of particular families.

Every story is a complete house, occupied by a separate family; and the stair being common to them all, is generally left in a very filthy condition; a man must tread with great circumspection to get safe housed with unpolluted shoes.

Nothing can form a greater contrast than the difference betwixt the outside and inside of the door; for the good women of this metropolis are remarkably nice in the ornaments and propriety of their apartments, as if they were resolved to transfer the imputation from the individual to the public.

You are no stranger to their method of discharging all their impurities from their windows, at a certain hour of the night, as the custom is in Spain, Portugal, and some parts of France and Italy – a practice to which I can by no means be reconciled; for notwithstanding all the care that is taken by their scavengers to remove this nuisance every morning by break of day, enough still remains to offend the eyes, as well as other organs of those whom use has not hardened against all delicacy of sensation . . .

All the people of business at Edinburgh, and even the genteel company, may be seen standing in crowds every day, from one to two in the afternoon, in the open street, at a place where formerly stood a market-cross . . . . The company thus assembled are entertained with a variety of tunes, played upon a set of bells, fixed in a steeple hard by. As these bells are well-toned, and the musician, who has a salary from the city, for playing upon them with keys, is no bad performer, the entertainment is really agreeable, and very striking to the ears of a stranger . . .

Edinburgh is a hotbed of genius. I have had the good fortune to be made acquainted with many authors of the first distinction . . . and I have found them all as agreeable in conversation as they are instructive and entertaining in their writings.

The university is supplied with excellent professors in all the sciences; and the medical school, in particular, is famous all over Europe. The students of this art have the best opportunity of learning it to perfection, in all its branches, as there are different courses for the theory of medicine, and the practice of medicine; for anatomy, chemistry, botany, and the *materia medica*, over and above those of mathematics and experimental philosophy; and all these are given by men of distinguished talents. What renders this part of education still more complete, is the advantage of attending the infirmary.

Now we are talking of charities, here are several hospitals, exceedingly well endowed, and maintained under admirable regulations; and these are not only useful, but ornamental to the city. Among these I shall only mention the general workhouse, in which all the poor, not otherwise provided for, are employed, according to their different abilities, with such judgment and effect that there is not a beggar to be seen within the precincts of this metropolis.

Even the kirk of Scotland, so long reproached with fanaticism and canting, abounds at present with ministers celebrated for their learning, and respectable for their moderation. I have heard their sermons with equal astonishment and pleasure.

T. SMOLLETT, *Humphry Clinker* (1771); letters from Squire Bramble to Dr Lewis, dated 18 July and 8 August.

2

Captain Topham's 'Letters'

In this city [Edinburgh] there is no inn that is better than an ale-house, nor any accommodation that is decent, cleanly, or fit to receive a gentleman.

On my arrival, my companion and self, after the fatigue of a long day's journey, were landed at one of these stable-keepers (for they have modesty enough to give themselves no higher denomination) in a part of the town which is called the Pleasance; and on entering the house, we were conducted by a poor devil of a girl without shoes or stockings and with only a single linsey-woolsey petticoat, which just reached half-way to her ankles, into a room where about twenty Scotch drovers had been regaling themselves with whisky and potatoes. You may guess my amazement, when we were informed that this was the best inn in the metropolis - that we could have no beds, unless we had an inclination to sleep together, and in the same room with the company which a stage-coach had that moment discharged!

On inquiry, we discovered that there was a good dame by the Cross who let lodgings to strangers. She was easily found out, and with conciliating complaisance conducted us to our destined apartments, which were six stories high. In the whole we had only two windows, which looked into an alley five foot wide, where the houses were at least ten stories high, and the alley itself was so sombre in the brightest sunshine that it was impossible to see any object distinctly.

CAPT. F. TOPHAM, *Letters from Edinburgh* (1776), pp. 18–20.

Height of Gentility

In the High Street, the ground floors and cellars are in general use of for shops by the tradesmen, who here style themselves Merchants; the better sort of people dwell in fifth and sixth stories. In London such an habitation would not be deemed the most eligible, and many a man in such a situation would not be sorry to descend a little lower.

Some years ago, a Scotch gentleman who went to London for the first time, took the uppermost story of a lodging-house, and was very much surprised to find what he thought the genteelest place in the whole at the lowest price. His friends who came to see him in vain acquainted him with the mistake he was guilty of. '*He ken'd vary weel,*' he said, '*what gentility was, and when he had lived all his life in a sexth story, he was not come to London to live upon the ground*' (pp. 10–11).

Quaint Shop Signs

The merchants here have the horrid custom of painting on the outside of their houses the figure of the commodity which is to be sold within; which makes the oddest appearance you can conceive, for each story, perhaps, from top to bottom, is chequered with ten thousand different forms and colours, so that the whole resembles the stall of a fair, presenting at one view the goods of a variety of shops. They are likewise remarkably fond of glaring colours, as red, yellow, and blue, on which the figures are painted in black.

You would laugh to see a black quartern loaf directly over a black full-trimmed periwig of a professor, with a Cheshire cheese and a rich firkin of butter displayed in black greasiness under stays, petticoats, and child-bed linen (p. 28).

Sunday Observance

Pass thro' Edinburgh during the time of service, and you will not meet with a single creature: the streets are silent and solitary, and you would conclude from the appearance of them, that some epidemical disorder had depopulated the whole city.

But the moment prayers are over, the scene changes: they pour from the churches in multitudes. Even with every care possible, you are driven from one side to another, till your shoulders are almost dislocated; for they are so intently employed with meditating on the good things they have heard, and the enjoyments of another life, that they have no time to look before them. They proceed in one uniform pace, with their large prayer-books under their arms, their eyes fixed steadily on the ground, and wrapped up in their plaid cloaks, regardless of every thing that passes. After having remained some time at home, they again sally out to church, where they continue till five o'clock in the evening.

At this hour all public devotions are over for the day, and they then begin their little schemes of entertainment. The young Girls, who have been melting in devotion for the space of six or seven hours, take walks in the meadows and other places with their Lovers, in order to amuse themselves; and it often happens that this heavenly temper of mind produces effects which are quite the reverse. The older people, whose religion is less enthusiastic, retire to little innocent parties, where the scandal of the town, and the faults of their neighbours, are very piously discussed (pp. 235–6).

Favourite Dishes of the Scotch Nation
I am just come from a dinner, from which I rose up almost famished with hunger, and tantalized to death by the enjoyment of other people, because my friend must needs entertain with dishes in the Scotch taste. As he is a true native of the North, and very zealous for the honour of his country and every thing that relates to it, it was impossible for me not to like a mixture which had received the sanction of the whole kingdom of Scotland. This was a *Hagis*: a dish not more remarkable or more disgusting to the palate than in appearance.

When I first cast my eye on it, I thought it resembled a bullock's paunch, which you often meet in the streets of London in a wheelbarrow; and on a nearer inspection I found it really to be the stomach of a sheep, stuffed till it was as full as a football. An incision being made in the side, the entrails burst forth and presented a display of oatmeal, sheep's liver, and lights.

My politeness got the better of my delicacy, and I was prevailed upon to taste it; but I could go no further, and after a few encomiums on its being tender and savoury, I turned a hungry face towards a large tureen in the middle, which the master of the feast called Cocky-leaky and, with the greatest appearance of luxury and glee in his countenance, extracted from a quantity of broth, in which it had been boiled with leeks, a large cock, which I dare say had been the herald of the morn for many a year. My plate was filled first, and I began upon it. It was so hard and tough that it seemed to require the stomach of an ostrich to digest it; and I could not help thinking that it would have cut a much better figure in a main than on a table, as I would have defied the best warrior cock that ever came victorious from the pit of battle to have produced a breast more impenetrable or a leg better fortified with spurs and sinew. But the Scotchmen devoured it unmercifully, and the ladies enjoyed the broth.

I was next solicited to eat some Sheep's head, which had raised my curiosity for some time to find out what it was; and on being told, I concluded it was the head of a black sheep, and perhaps on that account a rarity. I inquired of my neighbour the manner of [its] dressing; and on account of his close attachment to his plate it was with difficulty I squeezed from him, in half-eaten words, that it was nothing but a plain-boiled, common sheep's head with the skin on, from which the wool had been singed, which was the cause of its dark complexion.

But behold the Solan Goose! To be brief, a part of the breast fell to my share, which was something better than a tern or a sea-gull but had a strong, oily, unpalatable flavour; of a blackish colour, and so very tender, that it gave me the opportunity of putting a bit into the orifice of my stomach, which by this time began to be rapacious for want of something to devour. However, plenty of good Claret and agreeable conversation made up other deficiencies ...

As I am on the subject of eating, I will finish with mentioning three other dishes which are common in this country: Cabbiclow, Barley-broth, and Friars-chicken. The first is cod-fish salted and boiled with parsley and horse-radish. They eat it with egg-sauce, and it is extremely luscious and palatable. Barley-broth is beef stewed with pearl barley and greens; and the other is chicken cut into small pieces and boiled with parsley, cinnamon, and eggs, in strong beef soup (pp. 156–61).

Petticoats aloft!
As Edinburgh is situated on the borders of the sea and surrounded by hills of an immense height, the currents of air are carried down between them with a rapidity and a violence which nothing can resist. It has frequently been known that in the New Town three or four people have scarce been able to shut the door of the house; and it is very common to hear of sedan chairs being overturned. It seems almost a necessary compliment here, to wait upon a lady the next morning, to hope she got safe home. In many visits which I have made since I came here, two people have been obliged to go on each side of a chair, to keep it

even while other two have carried it, and sometimes even this pre-caution has not been sufficient.

Not many days ago an officer whom I have the honour of being acquainted with, a man of six feet high and, one would imagine, by no means calculated to become the sport of winds, was, however, in follow-ing another gentleman out of the Castle, lifted up by their violence from the ground, carried over his companion's head, and thrown at some distance on the stones. This is a literal fact.

The chief scene where these winds exert their influence is the New Bridge, which by being thrown over a long valley open at both ends and particularly from being balustraded on each side, admits the wind in the most charming manner imaginable; and you receive it with the same force you would do were it conveyed to you through a pair of bellows.

It is far from unentertaining for a man to pass over this bridge on a tempestuous day. In walking over it this morning I had the pleasure of adjusting a lady's petticoats which had blown almost entirely over her head, and which prevented her disengaging herself from the situation she was in; but in charity to her distresses, I concealed her charms from public view.

One poor gentleman, who was rather too much engaged with the novelty of the objects before him, unfortunately forgot his own hat and wig, which were lifted up by an unpremeditated puff, and carried entirely away (pp. 272–75).

'Cadie!'

All day long and most of the night, a certain number of the set of men called Cadies stand, waiting for employment, at the Cross in the High-street. To tell you what these people do is impossible, for there is nothing almost which they do not do.

They know everything and everybody. The moment a stranger comes into Edinburgh they know it; how long he is to stay, whither he is going, where he comes from and what he is. Whatever person you may want, they know immediately where he is to be found.

Whether you stand in need of a *valet de place*, a pimp, a thief-catcher, or a bully, your best resource is to the fraternity of Cadies. Whoever has occasion for them has only to pronounce the word 'Cadie' and they fly from all parts to answer the summons (pp. 87, 359).

3

William Creech's 'Then – and Now'

Edinburgh in 1763 was almost entirely confined within the city walls. The suburbs were of small extent. To the north, there was no bridge; and (till of late) the New Town, with all its elegant and magnificent buildings, squares, rows, courts, etc., extending upwards of a mile in length and near half a mile in breadth, did not exist.

It may with truth be said, that there is not now in Europe a more beautiful terrace than Prince's Street, nor a more elegant street than George Street. The views from Queen Street, to the north, exhibit a scene of grandeur and beauty unparalleled in any city.

It is a moderate calculation to say, that three millions sterling have been expended on buildings and public improvements in and about the city of Edinburgh since 1763, the environs of which cannot be surpassed in views of the sublime, the picturesque, and the beautiful.

In 1763 people of quality and fashion lived in houses which in 1783 were inhabited by tradesmen, or by people in humble and ordinary life.

Wonders of Coach Travel
In 1763, there were two stage-coaches, with three horses, a coachman, and postilion to each coach, which went to the port of Leith (a mile and a half distant) every hour from eight in the morning till eight at night, and consumed a full hour upon the road. There were no other stage-coaches in Scotland except one, which set out once a month for London, and it was from twelve to sixteen days upon the journey.

In 1783 there were five or six stage-coaches to Leith every half-hour, which ran it in fifteen minutes. There are now stage-coaches, flies and diligences, to every considerable town in Scotland, and to many of them two, three, four, and five. To London there were no less than sixty stage-coaches monthly, or fifteen every week, and they reached the capital in four days. And in 1786 two of these stage-coaches (which set out daily) reached London in sixty hours, by the same road that required twelve or sixteen days by the established coach in 1763.

A person may now set out on Sunday afternoon, after divine service, from Edinburgh to London; may stay a whole day in London, and be again in Edinburgh on Saturday at six in the morning! The distance from Edinburgh to London is 400 miles. Forty years ago it was common for people to make their will before setting out on a London journey.

In 1763, the hackney-coaches in Edinburgh were few in number, and perhaps the worst of the kind in Britain. In 1783 the number was more than tripled, and they were the handsomest carriages, and had the best horses, for the purpose, of any, without exception, in Europe.

Hotel Accommodation

In 1763 a stranger coming to Edinburgh was obliged to put up at a dirty uncomfortable inn, or to remove to private lodgings. There was no such place as an hotel; the word, indeed, was not known, or was only intelligible to persons acquainted with the French. In 1783, a stranger might have been accommodated, not only comfortably but most elegantly, at many public hotels; and the person who, in 1763, was obliged to put up with an accommodation little better than that of a waggoner or carrier, may now be lodged like a prince, and command every luxury of life.

Dining and Wining

In 1763, people of fashion dined at two o'clock, or a little after it; business was attended to in the afternoon. It was a common practice to lock the shops at one o'clock and to open them after dinner at two. In 1783, people of fashion and of the middle rank dined at four or five o'clock. No business was done in the afternoon, dinner of itself having become a very serious business.

In 1763, wine was seldom seen, or in a small quantity, at the tables of the middle rank of people. In 1791, every tradesmen in decent circumstances presents wine after dinner, and many in plenty and variety.

In 1763, it was the fashion for gentlemen to attend the drawing-rooms of the ladies in the afternoon, to drink tea and to mix in the society and conversation of the women. In 1783, the drawing-rooms were totally deserted: invitations to tea in the afternoon were given up; and the only opportunity gentlemen had of being in ladies' company was when they happened to *mess* together at dinner and supper; and even then, an impatience was sometimes shown till the ladies retired. Card parties, after a long dinner, and also after a late supper, were frequent.

In 1791, immoderate drinking, or pushing the bottle, as it is called, was rather out of fashion among genteel people. Everyone was allowed to do as he pleased in filling or drinking his glass. The means of hospitality, and the frequency of showing it, had increased; and excess on such occasions had decreased.

Young Ladies

In 1763, in the best families in town, the education of daughters was fitted, not only to establish and improve their minds, but to accomplish them in the useful and necessary arts of domestic economy. The sewing-school, the pastry-school, were then essential branches of female education; nor was a young lady of the best family ashamed to go to market with her mother. In 1783, the daughters of many tradesmen consumed the mornings at the toilet, or in strolling from shop to shop, etc. Many of them would have blushed to be seen in the market. The cares of the family were devolved upon a housekeeper; and the young lady employed those heavy hours when she was disengaged from public or private amusements, in improving her mind from the precious stores of a circulating library; and all, whether they had a taste for it or not, were taught music at a great expense.

In 1763, young ladies (even by themselves) might have walked through the streets of the city in perfect security at any hour. No person would have interrupted, or spoken to them. In 1783, the mistresses of boarding-schools found it necessary to advertise, that their young ladies were not permitted to go abroad without proper attendance.

Servants

In 1763, the wages to maid-servants were generally from £3 to £4 a year. They dressed decently in red or blue cloaks, or in plaids, suitable to their station. In 1783, the wages are nearly the same; but their dress and appearance are greatly altered, the maid-servants dressing almost as fine as their mistresses did in 1763.

In 1763, few families had men-servants. The wages were from £6 to £10 per annum. In 1783, almost every genteel family had a man-servant, and the wages were from £10 to £20 a year.

Going to the Theatre

In 1763, the question concerning the morality of stage plays was much agitated. By those who attended the theatre, even without scruple, Saturday night was thought the most improper in the week for going to the play. Any clergyman who had been known to have gone to the playhouse would have incurred church censure.

In 1783, the morality of stage plays, or their effect on society, were not thought of. The most crowded houses were always on Saturday night. The boxes for the Saturday night's play were generally taken for the season, so that strangers often on that night could not get a place.

The custom of taking a box for the Saturday night through the season was much practised by boarding-school mistresses, so that there could be no choice of the play, but the young ladies could only take what was set before them by the manager.

Impudent buffoons took liberties with authors, and with the audience, in their acting, that would not have been suffered formerly. The galleries never failed to applaud what formerly they would have hissed, as improper in sentiment, or decorum.

Public Dances

In 1763, there was one dancing assembly-room, the profits of which went to the support of the charity-workhouse. Minuets were danced by each set previous to the country dances. Strict regularity with respect to dress and decorum, and great dignity of manners were observed. The company met at five o'clock in the afternoon, and the dancing began at six and ended at eleven, by public orders of the manager, which were never transgressed.

In 1783 they met at eight and nine o'clock, and the Lady Directress sometimes did not make her appearance till ten. The young masters and misses, who would have been mortified not to have seen out the ball, thus returned home at three and four in the morning, and yawned and gaped and complained of headache all the next day.

In 1786 there were three new elegant assembly-rooms at Edinburgh, besides one at Leith, but the charity-workhouse was unprovided for to the extent of its necessities. Minuets were given up and country dances only used, which had often a nearer resemblance to a game of romps than to elegant and graceful dancing. Dress, particularly by the men, was much neglected; and many of them reeled from the tavern, flustered with wine, to an assembly of as elegant and beautiful women as any in Europe.

Sunday Behaviour

In 1763, it was fashionable to go to church, and people were interested about religion. Sunday was strictly observed by all ranks as a day of devotion; and it was disgraceful to be seen upon the streets during the time of public worship. Families attended church, with their children and servants; and family worship was frequent. In 1783, attendance at church was neglected, particularly by the men, Sunday was by many made a day of relaxation; and young people were allowed to stroll about at all hours. Families thought it ungenteel to take their domestics to church with them. The streets were far from being void of people in the time of public worship; and, in the evenings, were frequently loose and riotous, particularly owing to bands of apprentice boys and young lads. Family worship was almost disused.

In 1763, the clergy visited, catechised, and instructed the families within their respective parishes in the principles of morality, Christianity, and the relative duties of life. In 1783, visiting and catechising were disused (except by very few), and since continue to be so. Nor, perhaps, would the clergy now be received with welcome on such an occasion. If people do not choose to go to church, they may remain as ignorant as Hottentots, and the Ten Commandments be as little known as obsolete acts of Parliament.

Women of the Town
In 1763, there were five or six brothels, or houses of bad fame, and a very few of the lowest and most ignorant order of female skulked about the streets at night. A person might have gone from the Castle to Holyroodhouse (the then length of the city) at any hour in the night, without being accosted by a single street-walker. In 1783, the number of brothels had increased twenty-fold, and the women of the town more than a hundred-fold. Every quarter of the city and suburbs was infested with multitudes of females abandoned to vice, and a great many at a very early period of life, before passion could mislead, or reason teach them right from wrong.

Crime and Punishment
In 1763, house-breaking and robbery were extremely rare. Many thought it unnecessary to lock their doors at night. In 1783, 1784, 1785, 1786, and 1787, house-breaking, theft, and robbery were astonishingly frequent; and many of these crimes were committed by boys, whose age prevented them from being made objects of capital punishment. The culprits were uniformly apprehended in houses of bad fame, in which they were protected and encouraged in their depredations on the public.

In 1763, and many years preceding and following, the execution of criminals was rare: three annually were reckoned the average for the whole kingdom of Scotland. There were three succeeding years (1774–6) in which there was not an execution in Edinburgh. In 1783 there were six criminals under sentence of death in Edinburgh jail, in one week; and upon the autumn circuit, no less than thirty-seven capital indictments were issued.

WILLIAM CREECH, *Fugitive Pieces* (1815), pp. 61–117.

4

Fishwives and other Women 'Carriers' to Edinburgh

Till of late that carts have been introduced, the whole produce of the gardens, together with salt, and sand for washing floors, and other articles, was carried in baskets or creels on the backs of women, to be sold in Edinburgh, where, after they had made their market, it was usual for them to return loaded with goods, and parcels of various sorts, for the inhabitants here, or with dirty linens to be washed in the pure waters of the Esk.

This employment of women, which has certainly prevailed ever since Edinburgh became a considerable city, when joined to that of the fish-wives in Fisherrow, has occasioned a reversal of the sexes in this parish, and has formed a character and manners in the female sex which seems peculiar to them, at least in this county.

The carriers of greens, salt, etc., are generally the wives of weavers, shoemakers, tailors, or sievemakers, who, being confined by their employments within doors, take charge of the children and family, while the females trudge to Edinburgh about their several branches of business, long before day in winter, and return by mid-day or later, according to the time spent in selling their commodities. Their usual daily profits may be computed at 8d or 1s 3d, which, besides the free, social, and disengaged life which they lead, is a greater addition to the income of the family than they could earn by any other branch of industry.

The women who carry sand to Edinburgh have the hardest labour and earn least. For they carry their burden, which is not less than 200 lb weight, every morning to Edinburgh, return at noon, and pass the afternoon and evening in the quarry, digging the stones and beating them into sand. By this labour, which is incessant for six days in the week, they gain only about 5d a day.

The Fish-wives, as they are all of one class and admitted into it from their infancy, are of a character and manners still more singular, and are particularly distinguished by the laborious lives they lead. They are the wives and daughters of fishermen, who generally marry in their own cast or tribe, as great part of their business, to which they must have been bred, is to gather bait for their husbands and bait the lines. Four days in the week they carry fish in creels [osier baskets] to Edinburgh; and when the boats come in late to the harbour in the forenoon, so as to leave them no more time to reach Edinburgh before dinner, it is not unusual for them to perform their journey of five miles by relays, three of them being employed in carrying one basket, and shifting it from one to another every hundred yards, by which means they have been known to arrive at the Fishmarket in less than three-fourths of an hour. The fishwives who carry to Edinburgh gain at least 1s a day, and frequently double and triple that sum.

From the kind of life these women lead, it may be naturally concluded that their manners are peculiar, as they certainly are. Having so great a share in the maintenance of the family, they have no small sway in it, as may be inferred from a saying not unusual among them. When speaking of a young woman reputed to be on the point of marriage, 'Hout!' say they, 'How can she keep a man, who can hardly maintain herself?'

As they do the work of men, their manners are masculine, and their strength and activity is equal to their work. On holidays they frequently play at *golf*; and on Shrove Tuesday there is a standing match at foot-ball between the married and the unmarried women, in which the former are always victors.

Their manner of life, and the business of making their markets, whet their faculties, and make them very dexterous at bargain-making. They have likewise a species of rude eloquence, an extreme facility in expressing their feelings by words or gestures, which is very imposing, and enables them to carry their point against the most wary. It is remarkable that though a considerable degree of licentiousness appears in their freedom of speech, it does not seem to have tainted their morals, there being no class of women, it is believed, who offend less against the seventh commandment, excepting in *words*, than they do.

There seems to be no employment that conduces more to health and good spirits than theirs. Some of them have been brought to bed, and have gone to Edinburgh on foot with their baskets within the week. It is perfectly well ascertained, that one was delivered on Wednesday morning, and went to town with her creel on the Saturday forenoon following.

The fisherwomen have a peculiar dress. On week days they never wear caps but handkerchiefs on their heads, tied under the chin. They always have yellow petticoats, which show off their complexion to advantage. Except on holidays, they seldom wear shoes or stockings. This is not from poverty but the nature of their employment, which obliges them to be frequently dabbling in water.

Statistical Account of Scotland (Parish of Inveresk, by Revd. Dr Alexander Carlyle, Minister) (1795), vol. 16, pp. 16-20.

INDEX

For Product Safety Concerns and Information please contact our EU
representative GPSR@taylorandfrancis.com
Taylor & Francis Verlag GmbH, Kaufingerstraße 24, 80331 München, Germany